A THEOLOGY OF THE
Christian Bible

A THEOLOGY OF THE
Christian Bible

Revelation ✝ Inspiration ✝ Canon

Denis Farkasfalvy, O.Cist.

THE CATHOLIC UNIVERSITY OF
AMERICA PRESS · Washington, D.C.

Image on page iii: Depiction of Noah's ark landing on the "mountains
of Ararat," circa 1278, North French Hebrew Miscellany, British Library
Add. MS 11639, fol. 521a, anonymous 13th century artist. Courtesy of
Wikimedia Commons.

Library of Congress Cataloging-in-Publication Data
Names: Farkasfalvy, Denis M., 1936– author.
Title: A theology of the Christian Bible : revelation—inspiration—canon
/ Denis Farkasfalvy.
Description: Washington, D.C. : The Catholic University of America
Press, 2018. | Includes bibliographical references and index.
Identifiers: LCCN 2018007863 | ISBN 9780813230290 (pbk. : alk. paper)
Subjects: LCSH: Bible—Inspiration. | Bible—Evidences, authority, etc. |
Bible—Canon. | Catholic Church—Doctrines.
Classification: LCC BS480 .F325 2018 | DDC 220.1—dc23
LC record available at https://lccn.loc.gov/2018007863

To the members of my Cistercian family,
old and young, past and present: fathers
and sons, brothers and friends in both
my communities, Zirc in Hungary and
Dallas in Texas

Contents

Preface

This book treats three topics in a sequence: revelation, inspiration, and the canon of the Christian Bible. Each topic contains disputed issues even within the confines of Catholic theology, to which my loyalties belong by both background and conviction. At the same time, as the book treats these topics, it acknowledges history as an important ecumenical equalizer. There are few other visible Christian cultural signposts that proved as solid and lasting as the Christian Bible, and all Christian denominations and churches find vital interest in the study of its provenance and canon.

The approach taken here is both historical and theological. We are dealing with seventy-some different literary works, published in large quantities in all languages and many formats in one single volume. Because they belong to a common sacred literary deposit (over 1,500 years, the bulk of these books belonged to common Christian history), all Christian denominations naturally take interest in investigating the unusual ties that hold these books in one collection as a common basis for theological exchange and worship in all Christian groups of the world. Throughout this book, I needed a basic point of view from which to explain how, in the self-understanding of the church, a theology of revelation and inspiration has been adopted early on for the church's beliefs and worship, both widely based on inspired scriptures. This fundamental point of view, which unifies this book, is faith in Jesus Christ as God's incarnate word, who creates all and reveals God's purpose of creation and providence through his salvific words and deeds to the human person.

The present work is, in some sense, a sequel to a previous one in which the church's traditional doctrine of inspiration and its hermeneutical implications were studied mostly from a historical but also from an apologetic perspective.[1] The previous book might give the impression, mainly by its title *Inspiration and Interpretation*, that here I am trying to publish its sequel or some sort of a second volume. However, the present book is of a more systematic nature, concentrating mostly on the modern history of Catholic teaching about inspiration, with links to recent theological thinking about revelation and recent research about the biblical canon. In a more specific way, however, I explore the teaching of the Dogmatic Constitution *Dei Verbum* of the Second Vatican Council, seeking to assess its historical and theological importance as well as its limitations in what it accomplished.

On these pages, as I attempted to redesign the outline of a theology of inspiration, I based my efforts on *Dei Verbum*, which I also tried to both interpret and complete. At times, I found myself in a bind or at least in an awkward position. For a long time I was involved in specialized studies of biblical inspiration and of the canon in the early church.[2] Later, as a member of the Pontifical Biblical Commission for almost twelve years (2002–13), I worked for the last six plenary sessions of that time (2008–13) with the other nineteen members of the commission to address questions linked with the reception and interpretation of *Dei Verbum*, specifically the concept of biblical inspiration and the truth of the Bible.[3] This experience helped me realize new perspectives that

---

1. Denis M. Farkasfalvy, *Inspiration and Interpretation: A Theological Introduction to the Bible* (Washington, D.C.: The Catholic University of America Press, 2010).

2. Denis M. Farkasfalvy, *L'inspiration de l'Écriture sainte dans la théologie de saint Bernard*, Studia Anselmiana 53 (Rome: Herder, 1964); Farkasfalvy, "Theology of Scripture in Saint Irenaeus," *Revue bénédictine* 78, nos. 3–4 (1968): 319–33; Farkasfalvy, "'Prophets and Apostles': The Conjunction of the Two Terms before Irenaeus," in *Texts and Testaments: Critical Essays on the Bible and the Early Church Fathers*, ed. W. E. March (San Antonio: Trinity University Press, 1980), 109–34; Farkasfalvy, "The Apostolic Gospels in the Early Church: The Concept of Canon and the Formation of the Four-Gospel Canon," in *Canon and Biblical Interpretation*, ed. Craig C. Bartholomew et al. (Grand Rapids: Zondervan, 2006), 7:111–22; Farkasfalvy, "Biblical Foundations for a Theology of Inspiration," *Nova Et Vetera* 4, no. 4 (2006): 719–46; Farkasfalvy, "The Dogmatic Constitution on Divine Revelation, *Dei Verbum*: Inspiration and Interpretation," in *Vatican II: Renewal within Tradition*, ed. Matthew Lamb and Matthew Levering (Oxford and New York: Oxford University Press, 2008), 77–100; Farkasfalvy, "Inspiration and Incarnation," in *"Verbum Domini" and the Complementarity of Exegesis and Theology*, ed. Scott Carl (Grand Rapids and Oxford: Eerdmans, 2014), 3–11; and William R. Farmer and Farkasfalvy, *The Formation of the New Testament Canon: An Ecumenical Approach* (New York: Paulist Press, 1983).

3. Pope Benedict assigned this task to the PBC after the Synod of Bishops in 2008, but the

my education and previous research could never have provided. At the PBC, I was one of the few members old enough to have had from my school years some background knowledge about the preconciliar teaching from having taken a traditional course about inspiration and canon in pre–Vatican II times. This experience was combined in my memory with a live recall of the Council's own history with the same topic—from the rejection of its first "schema," *De fontibus revelationis,* in 1962 to the following emergence of *Dei Verbum* in 1964—resulting in a critical gap of almost fifty years of discontinuity that occurred between Vatican II and the resumption of the topic under Pope Benedict's papacy. After the Council, due to the fast-changing Catholic theological climate and biblical scholarship after Vatican II, I gained a new perspective by watching the Biblical Commission's struggle with a task for which, frankly, the majority of the PBC felt inadequately prepared. Another point of view on this topic emerged from witnessing transformations and novelties in recent patristic studies, which, especially in the last two decades, began to pay special attention to the development of the New Testament canon. My own involvement in such studies was often distracted or sidetracked, but changing opportunities for participating in biblical and patristic scholarly work kept on coming my way. Today, I realize that the importance of studying inspiration and canon took an ecumenical dimension and that, consequently, this topic continues to attract the interest of theologians and common-rank faithful alike.

While preparing this book, an important publication, a collection of essays edited and introduced by Scott W. Hahn and sponsored by the St. Paul Center for Biblical Theology, appeared about the theology of inspiration.[4] The date of first impression on this volume is 2010, yet it explicitly quotes my book in inspiration several times,[5] leaving for me

---

work was finished only in 2013 under Pope Francis, after which it was reviewed by Fearghus O'Fearghail; Pontifical Biblical Commission, *The Inspiration and Truth of Sacred Scripture,* trans. Thomas Esposito, OCist, and Stephen Gregg, OCist (Collegeville, Minn.: Liturgical Press, 2014).

4. Scott W. Hahn, ed., *For the Sake of Our Salvation,* vol. 6, *Letter and Spirit* (Steubenville, Ohio: St. Paul Center for Biblical Theology, 2010).

5. Brant Pitre, "The Mystery of God's Word: Inspiration, Inerrancy and the Interpretation of Scripture," in Hahn, *For the Sake of Our Salvation,* 6:47–66. He quotes my book on pages 53–54 in notes 24, 25, 27, 30, and 37. Also, Michael Waldstein, "*Analogia Verbi:* The Truth of Scripture in Rudolph Bultmann and Raymond Brown," in Hahn, *For the Sake of Our Salvation,* 6:93–140, quotes my book several times in the same volume: see 6:97n14, 6:136nn110–11.

no doubt that, unbeknownst to me, the volume edited by Scott Hahn has also functioned as a "prequel" for this present work. In addition, this second prequel exhibits true cross-fertilization of ideas as, with explicit references, it outlines the content of some previous publications I had earlier made about inspiration. Rereading them in this summary stimulated me to further clarify and develop them.[6] These references may also document that Catholic biblical theology is returning to the topic of inspiration with renewed efforts to integrate the Dogmatic Constitution *Dei Verbum* of the Second Vatican Council into a pursuit of renewing modern biblical exegesis.

There have also been numerous initiatives among Protestant biblical scholars, especially those with an evangelical orientation,[7] to review the topics of inspiration and canon within their own denominational perspective as they reflect on the foundations and presuppositions of the theological studies conducted at a large variety of universities and seminaries and ever-growing publications of books, journals, and websites.

Finally, I add a comment of appreciation and thanks to one of my students at the University of Dallas, Jean-Paul Juge, who, with exceptional interest in the subject and skills for editing theological texts, has carefully read the manuscript and greatly helped with the book's final redaction.

---

6. I am referring to Matthew Levering, "The Inspiration of Scripture: A 'Status Quaestionis,'" the concluding article of Hahn, *For the Sake of Our Salvation*, 6:281–314, quoting Farkasfalvy, "How to Renew the Theology of Inspiration?," *Nova et Vetera* 4 (2006): 307–13 (notes 114–21; 123–26).

7. Under the subtitle "Evangelical Debate Today," Matthew Levering surveys these studies with a rich bibliography in his previously quoted article, "Inspiration of Scripture, A 'Status Questionis,'" 290–99.

A THEOLOGY OF THE
Christian Bible

INTRODUCTION

Among the major documents of Vatican II, *Dei Verbum* stands out as one of the most neglected and least understood. The reason is debatable, but certainly one of the primary reasons is that both concepts, "inspiration" and "inerrancy," which traditionally had been linked and studied back to back in seminary curricula and introductions to biblical studies textbooks, have in recent decades vanished from many programs. Some would say that their study was left in a state of chronic disrepair.

This suspicion cannot be further explored without an overview of the changing fortunes that Catholic biblical studies encountered in the twentieth century. In Catholic theology, for the first half of the century, the modernist crisis occupied center stage, a matter that was not satisfactorily settled before the end of the Second World War (1945) or even before the closure of the Second Vatican Council (1964). Yet the changes that occurred under the reign of Pius XII appeared at the time to be progress toward a theological renewal. Both the enthusiastic response to Pius XII's encyclical *Divino Afflante* in 1943 and a much less cordial reception of the encyclical *Humani Generis* issued by the same pope in 1950 have shown that these encyclicals signaled contrary movements of the proverbial pendulum in the workings of both the papal *Magisterium* and the unsettled *opinio communis* of the theologians. Shortly thereafter, in 1958, the year Pius XII died, the most important book of the century on biblical inspiration was published by Karl Rahner under the title *Über die Schriftinspiration*.[1] Insignificant in appearance and only eighty-

---

1. Karl Rahner, *Inspiration in the Bible*, trans. Charles H. Henkey (New York: Herder, 1961).

eight pages in length, it raised a list of questions that had accumulated in theology during the previous hundred years and that, in large part, remains unsettled to this day. Rahner's essay on the problems of modern *Inspirationstheologie* appeared as the first volume in a prestigious series of publications, Questiones Disputatae, launched by the publishing house Herder in Germany with high expectations but with only limited success. It was an exceptional book that passionately demanded a full reexamination of the concept of biblical inspiration.[2] It has, however, failed to achieve its goal due to an inadequate follow-up during turbulent decades in Catholic theology after the Council. Many of the problems the book dealt with—as well as some issues it did not envision—have never been reexamined or discussed in depth. Rahner raised the challenge of a complete reexamination—*Durchdenken*—of the concept of inspiration, but this has not been achieved; Rahner himself never again published anything significant on the subject. While the Council's document *Dei Verbum* was based on a new understanding of revelation and on rich documentation of patristic sources, its attempt also to include a new theology of inspiration was not as successful: it was not able to break loose from the traditional Thomistic model of "double-authorship"—that is, divine and human authors linked together by "instrumental causality."[3]

Immediately before the Council, Yves Congar published a patristic dossier about the theology of revelation—specifically, the concept of tradition.[4] This book provided the essential documentation of the patristic sources for renewing the theology of revelation. Unfortunately, similar patristic research examining Rahner's thesis on inspiration had not been conducted or, at most, had taken place only sporadically in isolated efforts.

It might appear pretentious to undertake now, almost sixty years after Rahner's challenge, a fresh reexamination (the *Durchdenken* he proposed) of the theology of inspiration in terms of those issues that Rahner had raised in 1958. Yet this task may not be as overwhelming as it might have looked at that time. Because of the passing of time and of our better

2. "Den Begriff der Inspiration neu durchzudenken"; Rahner, *Inspiration in the Bible*, 16.
3. It must be said right away that *Dei Verbum* abstained from an explicit use of philosophical concept; thus the term *causa instrumentalis* does not appear in it.
4. Yves Congar, *La Tradition et les traditions: Essaie historique* (Paris: Fayard, 1960).

understanding of the historical background of *Dei Verbum*, we can now single out three publications that might best reveal why Rahner's *Über die Schriftinspiration* received few and misguided responses and why this book, even at the Council, contributed only modestly to the theology of inspiration.

In 1943, concomitantly with the publication of *Divino Afflante,* the German Jesuit Augustinus Bea, who at the same time played an emmient role in relaxing antimodernist censures of the Holy See under Pius XII, published a short article in the Roman theological journal *Angelicum.*[5] There he thought to have proven unambiguously that in the majority of patristic texts, and in both the documents of the *Magisterium* and the writings of St. Thomas Aquinas, the formula *Deus Auctor Scripturae* meant God's *literary authorship* of the scriptures. Bea was aware that the meaning of the Latin word *auctor* must not be identified with that of the corresponding expressions in modern languages (*author, auteur, autore, Verfasser*), which usually designate a literary author. He was also aware that the Council of Trent and the First Vatican Council did not dogmatize God's literary authorship of the Bible; yet he insisted that, at least since the time of Gregory the Great's *Moralia in Job*, a unanimous Latin tradition was formed, understanding God's authorship of the Bible as literary. Thus he thought that the Council of Trent and Vatican I, followed by the papal encyclicals *Providentissimus Deus, Spiritus Paraclitus,* and *Divino Afflante,* passed down a unanimous teaching over the centuries, which made him conclude that this understanding (of literary authorship) of *Deus Auctor Scripturae* is taught by the church as *de fide* by the church's ordinary *Magisterium,* although it may not be found in conciliar or magisterial documents with the explicit specification that the expression must be understood in the sense of a *literary authorship.*

Bea also recognized that the oldest patristic texts speaking of God as the *auctor* of both testaments were originally directed first and foremost against the Manichaeans and (originally) against the Marcionites, since in the old texts emphasis is placed on *both* testaments and not on *auctor*;

5. Augustinus Bea, "*Deus Auctor Scripturae*: Herkunft und Bedeutung der Formel," *Angelicum* (1943): 16–31. This article is by now quite outdated but remained in bibliographies like those in both *The Jerome* and *The New Jerome Biblical Commentary*. It is generally regarded and quoted as valid; see Hahn, *For the Sake of Our Salvation*, 6:31n52, adding, "Vatican I describes God as the literary author of the books of Scripture."

yet, he thought that this emphasis of the ancient texts was of negligible importance or irrelevant (*belanglos*). All in all, in his judgment, God's literary authorship must be recognized as the primary meaning of the formula and must be treated as part of the deposit of the faith.

It is not clear whether Rahner ever raised doubts about Bea's interpretation of the theological tradition and its sources. In his book of 1958, he makes several references to Bea's views,[6] but rather than quoting this article of 1943, he always refers to one of Bea's older works, a textbook of 1935, in which, long before his research on the church fathers, Bea already stated, in textbook style as an established fact, that God was the literary author of the biblical texts.

Two years after Vatican II, a major work on inspiration was published by Luis Alonso Schökel containing the first modern attempt to reexamine in depth the traditional textbook theology of inspiration.[7] Unfortunately, at its first publication, this book, originally in Spanish, drew insufficient attention until its revision and translation into English. Its impact was even further diminished by the fact that, soon after Vatican II, interest in the theology of inspiration subsided, and for a while, at least in Catholic circles, little or no serious discussion followed. Nonetheless, Alonso Schökel was the first Catholic biblical scholar to reexamine the patristic heritage that Bea had hastily reviewed in 1943. To begin with, Alonso Schökel wanted to answer two important questions: (1) Was in fact *Deus Auctor Scripturae* the main paradigm used by tradition to express the divine origins of sacred scriptures? (2) Even if the response to the first question was in the affirmative, does this principle express an article of faith in the specific sense that, according to Catholic dogma, God must be considered the literary author of all biblical texts? Alonso Shökel carefully combed many important passages from the church fathers, as well as the magisterial documents, all referring to God as the "author" of holy scripture.[8] After presenting a list of authoritative texts, Alonso Schökel rightfully asks, "Is it, therefore, a *dogma* that God is the literary author

---

6. Rahner, *Über die Schriftinspiration* [Inspiration in the Bible] (Freiburg im Breisgau: Herder, 1958); see, for example, 22n7, 27n10, and 72n39.

7. Luis Alonso Schökel, *La Palabra Inspirada* (Barcelona: Herder, 1966), trans. Francis Martin, OCSO, as *The Inspired Word* (London and Rome: Burns and Oates and Herder: 1967).

8. The earliest patristic texts belong to the late second century. The most important authoritative texts stating the divine authorship of the scriptures are the profession of faith proposed by the

of the Scriptures?"[9] His inquiry brought about some surprising results. First, it became clear that in some sense the divine authorship of scriptures is explicitly and unanimously taught by tradition as an essential element of the Catholic faith. Unfortunately, however, the question about God's specifically literary authorship became murkier than before. Alonso Schökel saw clearly that, besides the ancient ambiguities of the word *auctor* (which can mean simply *creator*),[10] a further distinction had to be introduced, as Rahner had already proposed, when distinguishing between "originator" (in German: *Urheber*) and "writer" (in German: *Verfasser*). This was indispensable in deciding if God's authorship, indeed, was literary. At this point, however, Alonso Schökel surprises the reader on two accounts. First, he shows that God as "author" of the scriptures is not the chief (or a frequent) patristic paradigm as Bea had suggested, and thus Rahner's antithesis of *Urheber/Verfasser* (a bit obscure for most non-Germanic readers) must not be considered as a central isssue. Yet, at this point, Alonso Schökel declares that, once the distinction is made, it appears that patristic sources are more in favor of speaking about a divine *Verfasser*—that is, of God as a *literary author*—than of a mere originator or *Urheber* of the biblical texts. The latter would reduce and understate the special divine authorship that tradition teaches about the biblical texts. Thus, probably unwittingly, Alonso Schökel appears to obfuscate—maybe even eliminate—the speculative theological problems that Rahner's essay raised. But these cannot be pushed aside: there remains *the absurdity of assigning to the scriptures two literary authors as two causes of one reality on the same level.*[11] Therefore, on the one hand, by diffusing Rahner's distinction between *Urheber* and *Verfasser*, Alonso Schökel tried to marginalize the issue of God's literary authorship, but on the other hand, he showed a preference for Bea's position affirming God's literary authorship of the scriptures. In other words, Alonso

---

Roman Church to Michael Palaeologus (1274), followed by the Councils of Florence (1442), Trent (1546), and Vatican I (1870).

9. Alonso Schökel, *The Inspired Word*, 79.

10. See as an example a famous Christmas hymn by Sedulius: *Beatus auctor saeculi*. In medieval Latin texts most occurrences of the word *auctor* have this sense of "originator" or "creator." *Auctor mundi* is a divine title.

11. Rahner, *Inspiration in the Bible*, trans. Charles H. Henkey (New York: Herder, 1961), 24–26.

Schökel continued to speak about God as a *Verfasser* and left the weighty philosophical problems raised by Rahner hanging in the air.

A third work responded more timely to Rahner's book of 1958; it appeared in a brief article by Yves Congar in 1961.[12] This was not much more than a substantial book review criticizing Rahner for reproducing the patristic tradition on inspiration with insufficient depth. Yet, instead of questioning Rahner's philosophical remarks about divine authorship in terms of metaphysical causation, Congar focuses on the human authors. He points out that the patristic tradition, when speaking of the human originators of the Bible, talked less of the "nascent Church" than about the "prophets and the apostles," who were concrete and chosen people to whom, within the framework of the *historia sacra*, the authorship of the two testaments' writings was attributed. Thus, Congar argues, Rahner leaves out large portions of what tradition had to say about the specific and personal aspects of inspiration. In this remark, in which Rahner received a most important critical—and corrective—review for his book, Congar alone made the point that the theology of inspiration must be inserted into the context of a theology of revelation, as well as into enriched patristic research, and thus be liberated from a web of philosophical abstractions that the concept of a double literary authorship (*Deus Auctor* and the *hagographi*), coupled with the elusive concept of instrumental causality, later imposed on the treatment of inspiration.

It seems to me that it was to Congar's merit that *Dei Verbum* was able to assign *revelation* as the proper theological context for a renewal of the theology of inspiration. Yet, as we will see in this book, the problems Rahner raised—which presupposed Augustinus Bea's ideas about the patristic tradition—have never been sufficiently confronted. Thus *Dei Verbum* followed a path designated by Congar but did not—and possibly could not—respond to Rahner's challenge and thus did not result in a renewal (by an authentic and creative *Durchdenken*) of the theology of biblical inspiration.

---

12. Congar, "Inspiration des écritures canoniques et apostolicité de l'Église" [Inspiration of the Canonical Scriptures and the Apostolicity of the church], *Revue des sciences philosophiques et théologiques* 45 (1961): 32–42.

I ✛ THE CHRISTIAN NOTION
OF BIBLICAL INSPIRATION

———•❖•———

From Revelation to Scripture

Christian churches regard a set of ancient books that they use for worship, theology, and personal edification as holy depositories of their beliefs and teachings and as documents linking them to their historical origins. Most importantly, they consider them to be written under the influence or "inspiration" of the Holy Spirit.

Many of these books, composed in a Jewish milieu and a time period prior to Jesus, are customarily referred to by Christians as "the Old Testament," while the collection of books that originated after Jesus' time form the New Testament.[1] Yet in the Christian churches all biblical books are encompassed by the wider notion that they transmit "God's word" for all mankind; although time and again it is also said that this "word of God" had first addressed as divine revelation some particular human beings and was transmitted only through them to a wider public. At the same time, the literary authorship of all these texts is assigned to human agents through whom God, in the course of a history of salvation, entrusted his revelation in written form to a human community,

1. On the question of the theological usage of "Old Testament" vs. "Hebrew scriptures," I find very helpful the distinctions and connections pointed out by Roland E. Murphy, OCarm, "The Old Testament/*Tanah*: Canon and Interpretation," in *Hebrew Bible or Old Testament? Studying the Bible in Judaism and Christianity*, ed. Roger Brooks and John J. Collins (Notre Dame, Ind.: Notre Dame University Press, 1990), 1–8.

referred to as "God's people," or "Israel," or "sons of Abraham, Isaac, and Jacob," and, in the New Testament, as the church.

In both Christian tradition and Jewish sources, the use of the inspired scriptures was always linked to the assumption of a double provenance; scriptures were habitually quoted both as "the word of God" and as books by specific human writers. Expressions like "thus says the Lord" are routinely found in the Bible, but these same texts are also attributed to particular human authors who allegedly wrote them. A psalm would be typically referred to as authored by David, a quotation from the Pentateuch as coming from Moses, and prophetic texts from some individual, often identified by name, as the writer. A similar approach is applied to the writings of the New Testament. Most apostolic letters open with a reference to a particular figure of the earliest Christian generations, while four books, carrying the word "Gospel" in their title, report Jesus' deeds and words and link the book in its title to a person whose name, inserted with the preposition "according to" (κατά), contemporary readers were expected to identify with that of someone known to the earliest Christian communities.[2] Already in the gospels, the words of Jesus are quoted as statements made with divine authority,[3] but other texts receive their authority by reference to the Apostle Paul or to one of Jesus' lifetime disciples.[4] While in the early second century the expression "scriptures" normally also meant for Christians the holy writings of the Jews, around 150 A.D., "scriptures" signified also Jesus' words and deeds or texts by apostolic authors.[5]

2. As it may be well known to the reader, today's New Testament scholarship distinguishes itself by pointing out the anonymity of the canonical gospels; see Raymond E. Brown, *An Introduction to the New Testament* (New York: Doubleday, 1997), 123. However, studies by Martin Hengel about the gospel titles (*Evangelienüberschrifte*) have shown that the proliferation of the canonical gospels took place in early Christianity with an unambiguous and consistent designation of the literary author; see Hengel, "The Titles of the Gospels and the Gospel of Mark," in *Studies in the Gospel of Mark*, trans. John Bowden (London: SCM, 1985), 64–84.

3. See, for example, the expression "You have heard that it was said to your ancestors—but I say to you" surrounding Jesus' comments on the divine commandments (Mt 5:21–22, 5:27–28, 5:31–32, 5:33–34, 5:38–39, 5:43–44).

4. It is at times remarked that, of the New Testament, only Hebrews and possibly First John were disseminated with no explicit reference to an author. However, on the one hand, in view of the ending of Hebrews (12:22–25) and, on the other hand, because of deep-seated connections between First John and the Fourth Gospel, even this exception is doubtful.

5. Second Peter, commonly dated to about 125 A.D., may be the earliest document calling both Paul's letters and the Old Testament scriptures: "And regard the patience of our Lord as salvation,

In Judaism, references to the inspired books were organized either in a twofold or threefold manner.[6] At the time of Jesus, the sacred books of the Israelites were not solidified in a closed list. Yet there was a clear enough concept of what "scriptures" in general meant, either in terms of "the Law and the Prophets" or, less frequently, referenced as a triple collection of books consisting of the Law (Torah), the Prophets (Navi'im), and the Writings (Ketuvim), each containing written records of God's words addressing the people of Israel. "Torah" meant the Pentateuch (the five books of Moses), "Prophets" signified either the "early prophets," which refers to some historical books (Joshua, Judges, 1–2 Samuel, and 1–2 Kings) or, under the name of "Later Prophets," the prophetic books in the sense of our contemporary Christian usage (including four major prophets—Isaiah, Jeremiah, Ezekiel, and Daniel—and twelve "minor prophets"), while the "Writings" meant various kinds of other books (the Psalms, Job, Proverbs, Song of Songs, Ecclesiastes, Ruth, Daniel, 1–2 Chronicles), to which occasionally other miscellaneous groups of books were attached. In present-day Modern Hebrew, the word for "Bible" is the acronym TANAKH (Torah—Navi'im—Ketuvim), reflecting this same tripartite organization of Judaism's sacred books.

Traditionally, the sacred books of the church were also often referred to as various collections of writings transmitting divine revelation. This appears most frequently either in a two- or three-pronged (or even four-pronged) manner as "Prophets and Apostles," "Law, Prophets, and the Apostles," or a fourfold collection consisting of "the Law and Prophets," combined with "the Gospel(s) and the Apostles," this latter pair designating all books of the New Testament. We see here the fusion of two terminologies: a Jewish one ("the Law and the Prophets," often reduced in Christian parlance to "the Prophets")[7] and a Christian terminology

---

just as also our dear brother Paul wrote to you, according to the wisdom given to him, speaking of these things in all his letters. Some things in these letters are hard to understand, things the ignorant and unstable twist to their own destruction, as they also do to *the rest of the scriptures*"; 2 Pt 3:15–16. In Justin Martyr the meaning of the word "scriptures" include texts quoted from both testaments.

6. See Stephen G. Dempster, "Torah, Torah, Torah: The Emergence of the Tripartite Canon," in *Exploring the Origins of the Bible: Canon Formation in Historical, Literary, and Theological Perspective*, ed. Craig A. Evans and Emmanuel Tov (Grand Rapids, Mich.: Baker Academic, 2008), 87–128.

7. Ancient Christian exegesis routinely referred to David (the alleged author of all psalms) as a prophetic figure and, similarly, to Moses, the assumed author of the Pentateuch, a prophet, with a reference to Dt 18:18.

referring to "the Gospel(s) and the Apostles," or simply "the Apostles."[8]

As stated before, these traditional ways of speaking of the scriptures project the concept of a double origin: divine and human. Both terms "prophets" and "apostles" evoke divine election, office, and message by which some chosen human beings were selected to transmit God's word. At the same time, this traditional Christian parlance about scriptures also conveys Christological implications. It meant that in Christianity, all scriptures of both testaments were viewed with an essential reference to Christ. Such an outlook was consistent with the tendency of calling all scriptures of the Old Testament "prophetic" to imply that all Jewish scriptures anticipate the peak of salvation history in Christ. Ever since the time of Paul's letters (cf. Rom 15:4; 1 Cor 10:4–6), we find the idea expressed that the Hebrew scriptures were ultimately destined for the church, not only on account of their divine origin or inspiration, but because of their divinely intended meaning, which, in salvation history, reached its completion and brightest manifestation in Jesus Christ. In a similar way, according to a general Christian outlook, all scriptures of the New Testament are regarded as "apostolic" because they all come from Christ through his chosen disciples of the first community, gathered around the original twelve, whom Jesus had selected at the beginning of his ministry. These then, enlightened by the Spirit, gave witness to the world about Jesus' words and deeds and their meaning, with both their narrative and their message having their special focus on Christ's death and resurrection.

In the New Testament, the writing and the grouping of God's word did not come about as the result of a long process of sorting out a set of documents of the past, as if it were by a protracted and hesitant development that the early Christian documents coalesced into the Christian canon. In fact, the concepts we mentioned previously, such as "the Law and the Prophets," "Prophets and Apostles," and "the Law and the Lord and the Apostles," antedate the canon and implied the idea of a list of sacred books. The use of these expressions demonstrably preceded the existence, in a formal sense, of a canon of authoritative holy books in the

---

8. This was easily done ever since the four gospels began to be called "apostolic gospels" and were counter-distinguished by this terminology from a growing number of apocryphal gospels in the second century. See Irenaeus's main thoughts, which will be discussed in Chapter 11.

church. The terms describe various subgroups of sacred writings, which were used in conscious reflection and retrospective assessment of the normative roots of the church's beliefs; only later did they begin to be used in a more technical sense, when an explicit need arose to speak of an authentic documentation or written attestation of the church's apostolic roots. One may say that the expressions "Prophets and Apostles" appeared in Christian usage as soon as it was chronologically possible for the church to look back at its origins as past; at the same time, the need arose to define its identity in terms of a faith, described in concrete and stable terms.[9] In the last chapters of this book we will return to these questions about the origin of the canon and provide more specific details.

The Biblical Concept of Revelation

In this section I am both developing and summarizing the biblical theology of revelation on the basis of theological anthropology that is found in various presentations in most theological handbooks of the postconciliar renewal.[10]

God's Encounter with Man

In the way they present themselves as the word of God, all biblical books assert that God is their ultimate source, and therefore it is God who with authority addresses the reader through them. Yet by putting the divine word into human terms—as expressions of human happenings, emotions, thoughts, perceptions, and notions—the biblical books also evoke concrete relationships between God and human beings, from which these experiences and their verbal expressions flow. We are not only saying here that the *idea* of "God's word expressed in human words" *logically implies* some previous relationship between God and man. The biblical books concretely refer to encounters of specific human beings with God. These books ultimately derive their origin from acts of faith,

9. See Farkasfalvy, "'Prophets and Apostles,'" 109–34.
10. The most important source is René Latourelle, SJ, *Theology of Revelation* (Cork, Ireland: Mercier, 1968); see further bibliographical references on 131n135. There is really no space here for a more detailed treatment of modern personalistic philosophy, which laid foundation to the kind of theological anthropology that I am outlining in these pages.

elicited in response to such experiences, not through random individuals but through spokesmen and leaders divinely chosen for the sake of establishing communities of faith.

In the biblical texts there appears consistently an understanding that authentic relationships between God and man presuppose specific conditions. Without them the biblical concept of revelation assumed in the biblical texts cannot be understood. We formulate them in four points:

1. God Is Always the One Who Initiates

No matter how true it is that man seeks God, God seeks man first and addresses him; when deciding to disclose himself he invites man to listen; God is the one who both initiates and commands, while, from the beginning of human history, the human being appears to be endowed with a desire for God, which one may even call *natural*, though it is rooted not in man's physical nature but in a grace that elevates him. Most importantly, any actual and personal contact between God and man produced by a divine deed comes from unmerited grace.

2. The Encounter Is Personal

When God addresses man, he deals with him as a person—that is, as a relational being whose self-awareness is actualized only when he meets another and enters into a relationship of knowing and loving. This means that God addresses man in the way he created him, a social being for whom it is "not good to be alone" (Gn 2:18). The Yahwistic creation story of Adam giving names to the animals before receiving in Eve a mate from his flesh and bone because he must not be alone, delivers deep teaching about the essentially relational nature of the human being (Gn 2:18–25). Jesus refers to this passage not only to speak about the indissolubility of marriage, but to point out that to be social is something inherent to the human being from his first creation (Mt 19:4; Mk 10:6). Furthermore, in the Bible there appears a general awareness that in revelatory encounters, God approaches individual human beings not only for the sake of eliciting one individual's response, but also to employ the person addressed to be an intermediary who approaches, addressing them on God's behalf.

3. God Addressing the Human Being Creates Community

Thus, when addressing a human being, God solicits from man not a passive sort of listening, but a response. Man receives God's word as a command to act upon, not only to order his personal life according to divine mandates, but also to transmit God's message to communities of all sizes, both small and large, to form, reform, or transform them.

4. God Creates by His Word a People of His Own

In both the Old and the New Testaments, the word of God forms communities of faith and salvation. Throughout the Old Testament, God builds, forms, and guides Israel to turn them into his people; in the New Testament, God's word addresses Israel to transform and expand it, with both continuities and discontinuities, into a new people, the church, so that God's people would entail a worldwide convocation of all peoples of all times.

Covenants

The community God forms by addressing man by his word goes beyond mutual speech and listening, as it calls man to enter into successively expanding and eventually stable relationships with himself. These relationships between God and his people are bilateral, although not symmetric. When addressing man, God does not deal only with isolated individuals, but with persons who are relational and social—that is, persons for whom relating to the self and to others implies relating to *all others* with an implied intentionality to build a community encompassing all members of the human race. For the human being, the path to the self leads through "the other," a rule that is essential for all humans: awareness and concern for the self implies relatedness to every other human being. As a rule, man searches for his identity by exploring the identity of other human beings and promotes his own happiness through providing happiness for others. In this way his understanding of God refers not just to "my God," but "our God"; his reaching out to God brings him to transcend not only the self or a few additional "others," but all others—that is, all fellow human beings.

According to the Bible, it is connatural to the human being that, in his experience, God is the one who reaches out to him so that he may establish with God lasting communion. Among the usual formulas of the Old Testament, one typically finds expressions like "I will establish a covenant"[11] or "they will be my People and I will be their God."[12] In these examples, we perceive not only mutuality between God and man, but also the evidence of God's free, mysterious, and transcendental Being. After initiating contact, God proposes a lasting covenant and, at the same time, rather than diminishing, enhances man's freedom while demanding man's response of faith and fidelity.

With the advent of the New Testament, the covenantal relationship between God and Israel is neither terminated nor replaced; rather, the same relationship, which was experienced from old by Israel, comes to fulfillment in the unbreakable bond of the incarnation. In Jesus, God's people is reborn, and the covenant is sealed into a perpetual union by the incarnate Son's sacrificial blood and risen body, provided at the Eucharistic banquet that cements the community of the believers, into a body born from water and the Holy Spirit.

Revelation as a Historical Process

With the creation of the cosmos ("heaven and earth"), thus, *before* man is actually created, God's speech begins to address man. Thereafter, God creates the human being as man and woman, so that out of their union he may create the rest of mankind and address them both individually and in their mutual relationships (in their interrelatedness as husbands and wives, parents and children, ancestors and descendants). As Genesis 3 narrates, before the creation of new human beings began by sexual reproduction (Gn 4:1), man (Adam) and woman (Eve) fell into sin—not each in a separate way, but virtually at once and, in fact, by complicity. They rebel and disobey "together" not in a merely synchronized way, but in active cooperation, as if forming a united front of resistance against the Creator. Their sin involves elements of pride, envy, moral autonomy, and rivalry, and their falling into sin is followed by mutual blame that poisons their own rela-

---

11. See the references to all mankind in Gn 6:18, 9:9, 9:17, then to Abraham in Gn 19:7, 9:13. 9:19, and to Israel in Ex 6:4–5, 19:5, 34:10; and Dt 29:12, 29:14.

12. Jer 24:7, 31:33; 32:38; Ez 31:27; Zec 8:8.

tionship. While Genesis 3 carries all the ingredients of a first sin, one must not overlook that it is embedded in a wider theological narrative with a sequel of other paradigmatic "first sins" (chapters 2–11). These ten chapters demonstrate how the three fundamental alienations implied in sin (from God, from the self, and from other human beings) cumulatively belong to the nature of sin and bring about devastating consequences by perverting the meaning of procreation. Although the biblical texts contain, strictly speaking, little reflection about original sin as an abstract concept (*peccatum*, either *originans* or *originatum*), the primary characteristics of sin clearly appear in man's tragic loss of friendship (closeness, familiarity, intimacy) with God and all human beings' tragic alienation from each other, as well as from their place and role in the world. Although the first man and woman are presented to have been created as adults, after the first sin, when the program of sexual reproduction is announced (Gn 4:1), the creation of the human race is depicted to be a slow and painful process in which every single person of subsequent generations is born from male seed and out of female womb and reaches adulthood only gradually. In this process, each human being born "outside of Paradise" experiences physical need and suffering, constant struggles for survival by which one can only delay an unavoidable end: death. To use the sweeping statements of the Epistle to the Romans, through the transgression of one man's sin death entered the world where it began to reign (Rom 5:12) so that human life is little more than a hopeless struggle for survival. In this perspective, man is not the crown of creation, for each human being is born "lacking the glory of God" (Rom 3:23). Thus sin, suffering, and death begin to dominate all lives. Not only the first parents, but all human beings were banished "east of Eden" (Gn 4:16) with no self-redemption in sight.

In its philosophical meditation, the book of Wisdom quickly comes to the disappointing conclusion that in spite of his glorious beginnings at creation, the human being reveals discontinuity and lack of purpose: "God did not make Death and takes no pleasure in destroying the living, for uprightness is immortal" (Ws 1:13), yet "the godless call for Death with deed and word; counting him a friend, they wear themselves out for him; with him they make a pact, worthy as they are to belong to him" (Ws 1:16).[13]

One must stop here for a moment for special reflection about original

---

13. I quote here from the *New Jerusalem Bible*.

sin. In the course of the twentieth century, there appeared trends and countertrends in Western Christian thought disputing the roots of the theology of original sin. It is alleged that this traditional teaching has a much too narrow biblical base, while it owes many of its important elements to an Augustinian misconception of concupiscence, alien to a "healthier" Hebrew outlook on sexuality as we find it in Genesis or Proverbs. Augustine's understanding of original sin (*peccatum originale originans*[14]—that is, the sin of Adam) as an individual act of "eating a forbidden fruit" comes, many claim, from his reading of Genesis 2:4b–3:23 *ad litteram*, with no attention to its wider literary and theological context, which speaks of man's pride, his rivalry with God and with his fellow man, idolatry, fratricidal envy, and desecration of the work of creation. All these motives penetrate chapters 1–11 of Genesis and present cumulative evidence for what Augustine insistently affirms: all human beings are born in need of redemption.[15] In my opinion, it would be incorrect to relativize the traditional Christian reading of Genesis 1–3 with its focus on the sin of Adam and Eve, resulting in their eviction from the Garden of Eden; the story is certainly meant to narrate the first sinful human act *before any further human reproduction.* Man's original sinfulness is presented in Genesis 1–11 in the perspective of "primeval history" so that Genesis 2:4b–3:23 must be seen in the context of an anthology of primeval history ("variations on a theme"), producing their cumulative impact on human beginnings. These chapters constitute a set of selected stories, narrating from several points of view the transformation of God's original creation into a generalized picture of a miserable state of "sinful mankind," the cumulative effect of a process caused by successive acts of human self-emancipation. In these texts the loss of man's innocence is said to have been caused by his refusal to accept the order of creation in willful rebellion against God, resulting in further alienation from him, as well as from his own self and other human beings. Thus, we face in a sequence of narratives the first murder (shedding blood, envy leading to fratricide, desecration of the earth, establishment of man's passion for vengeance in Gn 3:24–4:16) and the story of the Flood (where

14. In post-Tridentine theological parlance, this means that the first sin by the first couple as committed by individuals causes mankind's state of sinfulness.

15. For a concise and well-balanced presentation of the connection between Gn 1–11 and the theological tradition about original sin, see Claus Westermann, *Genesis 1–11: A Continental Commentary*, trans. John J. Scullion (Minneapolis: Fortress, 1994), 275–78.

human perversity results in a universal devastation of God's creation in Gn 6:1–7:20), followed by divine attempts to rescue man by offering him reconciliation through covenants. The idea of restarting human history appears with Noah but quickly ends (Gn 9:9–29) and is followed by the paradigmatic story about the origin of human disunity when man again follows his pride and self-exaltation through organized rivalry against God; now he seeks full autonomy by means of building in a collective effort the Tower of Babel (Gn 11:1–9). These stories are about one central theological theme that fills all space between the statements "God has created man in his own image and likeness ... male and female he created them" (Gn 1:27) and the sad conclusion that all human offspring end up being born outside of the Garden ("east of Eden"; compare Gn 4:16) and banished from God's intimacy (Gn 3:22).[16] From the narrative of the Flood, where all humankind is shown to be at the verge of extinction but is saved by the rescue of Noah, a new, singular ancestor through whom the race continues, it is hard not to see one item underlined with insistence. Mankind spreading out the second time over all the earth needs an even more radical salvation plan: some sort of a remaking of creation. Once the human being is ejected from his privileged original state, it becomes clear that he is permanently in a state of sinfulness, which all humans share "not only by imitation but propagation."[17]

The sacred books dealing with man's falling into a sinful state anticipate that God was about to provide collective paths to redemption, because man does not sin in isolation but in unbreakable interdependence due to the genetic, cultural, and psychological linkage among human beings. Correspondingly, God's salvation plan must also be communitarian. Salvation history thus begins with the election of another man, Abraham (Gn 12:1), with his wife Sarah, from whom God intends to fashion a people of his own, and through whom eventually all mankind will be blessed

16. Of course, we recall this phrase due to the fascinating novel *East of Eden*, by John Steinbeck, but we must also attend to its critical interpretation: "It [East of Eden] is not a piece of geographical information but a reference to life 'outside,' in a state of alienation from God"; Westermann, *Genesis 1–11*, 314.

17. This traditional phrase was reaffirmed by the Council of Trent (Heinrich Denzinger and Adolf Schönmetzer, *Enchiridion Symbolorum* [*Freiburg: Herder, 1976*], no.789) but must not be transformed into an exegetical conclusion. I am trying to emphasize the revelatory character of Gn 1–11 to balance out what we often encounter: a naive historicization into a chain of point-wise conceived episodes of ancient history.

(Gn 12:3). The election of Abraham and the forming of a patriarchal clan aim at creating a large nation from Abraham's descendants. In Egypt, they become numerous but are also reduced to slavery. Then Moses is chosen to transmit God's word and, through an adventurous history of liberation, to mold Israel into God's people. The nation of Israel is formed by divine deeds: from the crossing of the Red Sea and wandering through the desert to legislation at Sinai, a story is presented detailing the experience of continued formation of a nation in which the revealed religion of YHWH, a strictly monotheistic faith with a moral code, is inculcated through many encounters with God, all mediated by Moses.

This process of education, filled with episodes of legislation, trials, betrayals, and punishments, is narrated as sacred history, accumulated in the memory of Israel as a process of revelatory experiences that then continue further in the Promised Land under other national and spiritual leaders (judges, kings, and prophets). On various levels of immediacy and faithfulness, God's words were expected to be transmitted to God's people. Prone as they were to fall into idolatry, they were, nevertheless, repeatedly rescued through faithful and salvific interventions by their merciful God. Israel's identity is built around a salvation history that was to become a universal paradigm for all human beings. God's people as a whole did, just like any individual, appear stubborn and seemingly hopeless with their apparently addictive urge to fall back into their original rebellion. Yet new opportunities for salvation emerge through new manifestations of God's ongoing faithfulness to his project. Israel's fluctuating history, played out in two rival kingdoms, Samaria in the north and Judah in the south, finally ends in full disaster by defeat and then exile, apparently putting an end to all national independence so that all religious institutions and even the religious heredity of the past perish in the invasions and deportations that follow. God's people undergo waves of destruction by a string of major powers of ancient history (Assyrians, Babylonians, Persians, Greeks and Romans). The Israelites are, however, constantly reminded that this history is ultimately governed by an all-powerful and faithful God, present amidst his wayward people through "his servants, the prophets," whose call is to interpret the signs of the times as God's messengers.[18] As a result,

18. See 2 Kings 2:9, 17:13. 23, 21:10, 24:2; Jer 7:25, 25:4, 26:16, 35:15, 44:4; Ez 38:17; Dn 9:6, 9:10; Am 3:7; Zec 1:6.

the nation's spiritual heritage does not fully perish but, time and again, is recovered in increasingly spiritualized ways so that as Israel's political power diminishes, it obtains a more and more important role in God's universal plan of salvation. God re-chooses Israel time and again so that it becomes his instrument of salvation for all mankind.

In a new epoch of gracious encounters with God in the person of Jesus of Nazareth, a conscious continuation of this same salvation history takes place. In reference to the people of God, which consisted of Twelve Tribes, Jesus chose twelve disciples (Mt 10:1–4; Mk 3:13–19; Lk 6:12–16; Jn 6:70–71) through whom the final phase of God's salvation plan is constituted. These twelve begin to function in the role of a new set of patriarchs: they signify a new beginning, as they were trained to learn Jesus' message and became chosen witnesses of his life, teaching, death, and resurrection. Through their faith in Jesus they are led into the relational core of the mystery of the One God; they learn that in the person of Jesus God, the Father has sent his Son as his eternal Word for the purpose of extending over mankind his inner life by granting them his Spirit and offering all human beings to participate in it. A new understanding of God as the source of all personhood is revealed: an eternal dialogue in a Trinity of Persons that constitutes the ultimate intimacy within the one God.

God's full self-disclosure takes place in Jesus: God's word made flesh, a fully human, carnal, and mortal being in personal distinction but natural identity with God the Father as his Son. The fullness and peak of God's self-manifestation is constituted in the sacrificial act of his Son, by which, out of love and obedience, Jesus accepts dying as a victim of human acts of violence. In response, the Father not only raises Jesus to life, but accepts his destroyed human existence as a sacrifice of atonement and turns his revived humanity into the prototype of a new human existence and a newly created human race. In his new state, Jesus is raised from death to new life as "the first-born of the dead" who can now launch a worldwide mission through his disciples to transform the rest of history.

Revelation Conceptualized

In Catholic theology, *divine revelation* is a specific, almost technical concept about God's self-manifestation to the world by means of words and deeds in salvation history.[19] This process constitutes a sequence of divine interventions in history for the sake of human salvation, soliciting the recipient of the divine word to respond by faith and understanding through acts of perception, belief, and reflection as well as deliberate free decisions of obedience and through announcing publicly God's message by human verbal expressions and activities.

God's self-disclosure in salvation history presupposes *natural revelation*, included in the divine act of creation, through which the physical universe comes to exist. Man, a rational and free being, belongs to the created world; by his natural faculties he is capable of understanding God's self-manifestation through his work of creation (see Rom 1:20). In addition, God's personal acts of self-disclosure by which he reaches out to draw man into a personal relationship with him constitute "supernatural revelation." Only by grace can man be elevated to respond to God by acts of faith and so be drawn into participation in God's inner life. As it happens with man's whole life, so also his participation in divine revelation takes place within history. According to the biblical account, when this specific history begins, God enters into a covenantal relationship with man. The offer of a covenant is narrated first in the history of Noah (Gn 6:8, 9:9–17), then in the story of Abraham (Gn 15:18), and in that of the rest of the patriarchs (17:2–21). The same covenant "of Abraham Isaac and Jacob" (see Ex 3:1) is finally offered through Moses and creates the people of Israel as a nation.

When witnessing God's salvific deeds, man comes to an understanding that all this history happens for mankind's sake. In other words, man discovers that in the process of revelation he is not a mere witness, but the subject for whose sake salvation history was established to begin with, and he is also the personal being whose happiness is here at stake. When learning about his own salvation, man's cognitive faculties are of first-ranking importance, including his subjectivity, which is involved to a far larger extent in the history of salvation than in the process by which man scientifically explores the physical universe. As it is known, even in

19. The Dogmatic Constitution *Dei Verbum* of the Second Vatican Council expresses essentially this same concept in its first chapter, nos. 1–6. *Dei Verbum* has the merit of including in its text, through explicit references, what previously the Council of Trent and the First Vatican Council implicitly said on this topic. However, *Dei Verbum* remains very short, almost abrupt, in two directions: (1) the communitarian dimension of revelation (revelation as constitutive of God's people) and (2) the linking of "natural" and "supernatural" revelation—that is, creation and revelation.

scientific thought we come to the realization that full objectivity is never obtained because, by the simple acts of observation, the physical reality we are trying to explore becomes modified. Also with respect to salvation history, one may observe something similar, but by proceeding one step even further: only when learning about God's salvific self-manifestation does man truly "come about" or "come to be created" as he discovers himself to be the object of divine benevolence and someone for whom "God gave his only Son, so that everyone who believes in him might not perish but might have eternal life" (Jn 3:16). In the act of encountering God man learns about himself—that is, comes to know who and what he is. It is in the act of faith that man becomes a partner in dialogue with God: speaking to him, God elevates him into an interlocutor by inviting him to a relationship that otherwise man would not be able to enter or sustain.

The concept of revelation in Christianity, therefore, involves God speaking to man, as well as man listening *and* responding by faith. At the same time, the person who becomes the recipient of revelation is sent to transmit the word of God he receives to other human beings. The hearer of God's word receives also the task of transmitting God's word. This task means ongoing listening to God, cultivating the remembrance of the divine word in continued relationship with both God and the human beings to whom he transmits God's word.

The Notion of Inspiration
God's Written Word in the Old Testament

The aforementioned considerations describe God speaking to man as he, by his word, gathers around himself a people of his own, so that he continues speaking through selected spokesmen as chosen intermediaries (Abraham, Moses, David, Elijah, Isaiah, Jeremiah) by using them for charismatic functions of teaching or leadership or both (Judges, Kings, Prophets). This historical process, in which God's people are gradually formed, does not take place in isolation from mankind's cultural history.[20] Rather, it is in interaction with other ethnic and religious groups

20. This thought needs to be further nuanced. In the Bible each constitutive event of Israel, such as the call of Abraham, the call of Moses, and the Exodus, is described as an event of segregation followed by a period of "education" under divine guidance in a new environment: the

amid challenges, confrontations, and conflicts with various social and national groups. God's special project, his people, is exposed to various formative influences coming from the rest of mankind, involving groups that did not have the privilege of having been chosen to be "God's people" in the same specific sense of this term. While constantly expected to retain its strict monotheism and exclusive loyalty to the God who chose it, Israel is, at the same time, repeatedly confronted with a whole range of animistic, polytheistic, atheistic, and agnostic influences on all levels of the human experience. For Israel, therefore, the historical process of revelation includes two antithetical aspects. On the one hand, it demands ongoing adjustments and responses to influences coming from other human groups; on the other hand, it requires faithfulness similar to that of God, who initiated this process and keeps on trying to form his people in an attitude of unfailing loyalty.

To persevere faithfully to its call, in spite of the challenges of history, God's people needed to retain the memory of God's revelatory acts and pass down this memory from generation to generation. As tools of faithful remembrance, memory aids had to be created to link subsequent generations. This process required not only an oral tradition but a transition from an oral to a written form of transmission, since writing was the main tool for a more permanent and longer-lasting preservation of collective memory, arching over generations and providing resistance to the destructive force of passing time.

Archaeological studies of ancient Egypt, Mesopotamia, and the regions between them have shown that when moving within these lands, Israel abundantly drew from the culture of the surrounding societies by learning the art and acquiring the tools of writing by which verbal tradition could be recorded in permanent and stable form. Although it is not known exactly how and when (but earlier than the first millennium B.C.), Israel made its revolutionary step of transition from an oral to a written culture and thus began to put its religious narratives and poetry into a written deposit of sacred traditions.[21]

---

wanderings of the patriarchs, Moses' flight, the people's journey of forty years in the desert. At the advent of the New Testament, Jesus' flight to Egypt, John's initial ministry in the Judean desert, and Jesus' forty days of fasting in the desert consciously recall this paradigm of preparatory separation.

21. One option would be to assume that when leaving Egypt, the Israelites in general (not only Moses) were already initiated into a written culture. But the evidence we have is more in favor of

Conceptually, "biblical inspiration" means a divinely guided process, accompanying and extending revelation into written expression for the people of God so that it may be easily preserved from generation to generation in fixed forms. In this process, God's word becomes stabilized by literary means, and God's people are enabled to reread and thus time and again recall in a fixed—that is, virtually unaltered—form what they had previously heard. It is reasonably assumed that the most ancient written traditions of Israel antedate the time of Solomon and even David, while the written forms of the prophetic traditions certainly reach back to the eighth century B.C.[22]

The return from the Babylonian exile and the restoration of the Temple in Jerusalem unfortunately did not result for Israel in a reestablishment of the Davidic kingdom or in a rebirth of a politically independent state. As a consequence, the importance of the scriptures greatly increased. When Israel's sacred written tradition took a definitive shape, the written form of the Law of Moses (the Torah) obtained central pace and, continued by the narratives of Joshua, Judges, and Kings, became introductory to a continuous historical narrative of the nation's pre-exilic history. This was later linked to a gradually growing collection of prophetic and sapiential writings.[23]

Post-exilic Israel had no other choice than to increasingly rely on its sacred books and its prophetic heritage. What is distinctly new in this era

---

the assumption that the beginnings of Hebrew literature come from Canaanite sources. However, since the discoveries of ancient northwestern Semitic cities in modern Turkey and Syria (like Ugarit), we are aware that these regions contained ancient written culture as early as the sixteenth to fifteenth centuries B.C.

22. These projections are very conservative. Raymond Brown, in an effort to summarize a consensus, assigns the most ancient literary compositions of the Old Testament to the twelfth century B.C.; see Brown, "The Canon of the Old Testament," in *The New Jerome Biblical Commentary*, ed. Raymond E. Brown, Joseph A. Fitzmyer, and Roland E. Murphy (Englewood Cliffs: Prentice Hall, 1990), 1037. The oldest physical textual remains of ancient Israelite literacy are probably inscriptions in the Sinai Peninsula from which scholars make various extrapolations about literacy in ancient Israel; see Susan Niditch, *Oral World and Written Word: Ancient Israelite Literature* (Westminster: John Knox Press, 1996).

23. My intention is not to narrate here the post-exilic formation of the Hebrew Bible. All I am pointing out here is that, after the exile, the scriptures become the only lasting institution through which the Jews are able to adhere to their religious traditions. The emergence of a canonical consciousness that binds together law, history, prayer (the Psalms), and wisdom traditions as written texts and their reedition are explained by the vacuum created by the long absence of temple worship and the termination of Israel as an independent nation.

is a growingly retrospective attitude toward both the oral tradition and its reappropriated written form. This chiefly happens by a systematic rereading, expanding, and reediting of the ancient prophetic texts (Isaiah I–III, Jeremiah, Ezekiel, and several of the minor prophets) by actualizing their content rather than pushing it into a distant and "frozen" historical past. Yet Israel never again becomes a sovereign nation. Instead, it falls victim to mutual rivalries and the changing fortunes of newly emerging, rising, and falling empires. To define its faith and religious practices, Israel kept on adhering to written documents containing its sacred traditions, while practically all its other religious institutions (state, kingdom, dynasty, temple, and priesthood) collapsed and remained in ruin for a long time. The word of God, as it is found in written sources, is now increasingly regarded as a direct gift from God, provided to Israel through Moses and through "God's servants the Prophets."[24] The traditions contained in sacred writings become, therefore, more and more manifestly a living source of God's word. In the prophetic texts the monotony of the formula "Thus says the LORD God," repeated at public readings verbatim hundreds of times, takes on the function of reminding readers and audiences that through these texts God actually summons and addresses his people with the immediacy of the spoken word.[25] The rebuilding of the Temple and reestablishment of the cult only enhances this process. In the worship of the Second Temple, sacred tradition is more closely linked to written sources than before and further encourages an even more stable and permanent possession of the sources in solidified written form.

Thus in the formation of the Hebrew scriptures, the concept of God's *spoken* word merges with the idea God's *written* word so that, in the Hebrew Bible, titles, introductory paragraphs, quotation formulas, and cross-references emphatically present the message of the book as "visions and words" and never merely as texts.[26] Nonetheless, when the texts are being copied, there emerges a growing demand for verbal precision so

24. The expression "God's servants the prophets" appears early in post-exilic books: 2 Kings 9:7, 17:23, 21:10, 24:2; Jer 7:25, 24:4, 26:5, 29:19, 35:15; 44:4; Ez 38:17; Am 3:7; Zec 1:6; Dn 9:6, 9:10.

25. The phrase "Thus says the Lord" occurs more than 370 times in the Bible, mostly in Isaiah, Jeremiah, and Ezekiel.

26. The assumption of an actual divine speaker behind the text is the ultimate truth of the divine authorship that in modern times led to an impasse in the debate about God as the Bible's literary author.

that, at the threshold of the Christian era, the idea of inspired scriptures becomes a hybrid concept, which may be summarized paradoxically as if meaning, "Thus *speaks* the Lord in his *written* word." In the Bible and both Jewish and Christian tradition, the concept of sacred writing retains the image of "God who speaks" but, at the same time, increasingly focuses on fixed written texts in which God's word is preserved.

At the end of the intertestamental period, Judaism began to regard its scriptures as fruits preserved from the past rather than fresh fruit still ripening and being produced and harvested. At this time the historic flow of prophetic activities was thought of as if ebbing away or, in some sense, belonging altogether to the past. A passage found in First Maccabees illustrates this mentality when, after the rededication of the Temple, a dilemma emerges regarding the desecrated altar.

They discussed what should be done about the altar of burnt offering which had been profaned, and very properly decided to pull it down, rather than later be embarrassed about it since it had been defiled by the gentiles. They therefore demolished it and deposited the stones in a suitable place on the hill of the Dwelling to *await the appearance of a prophet* who should give a ruling about them. (1Mac 4:44–46)

The foreword of the book of Sirach, written by its translator into Greek, a grandson of the book's author, expresses a similar historical perspective when referring to the Jewish scriptures as "the Law and the Prophets and the rest of the books" as a collection of written sources belonging to a historical past that must be cultivated with only few other minor writings attached.[27] The collection of "sacred books" was never declared by any authority as a closed list of canonical books. Yet "the Septuagint," sponsored around 200 B.C. by Hellenized Jews in Alexandria to translate the holy books of Israel into Greek, proves that by that time forces were effective at work to share the Jews' religious and cultural heritage with non-Jews in the form of major literary project. As a result, for the Greco-Roman world at large, a general access was opened to the "holy books" of Judaism.

This accessibility of the heritage of Judaism in the international language of the Roman Empire was certainly a providential fact for the na-

27. See Dempster, "Torah, Torah, Torah," 87–127.

scent church, but it was equally important for Christianity emerging from Judaism to have a Greek vocabulary and patterns of biblical thought in Greek in which they were able to express the newly received revelation of Jesus Christ.

Books Transmitting New Testament Revelation

The disciples of Jesus did not begin their movement by writing but by preaching "the gospel" (τὸ εὐαγγέλιον) which originally meant the message about Jesus' words and deeds. The first Christian missionaries presented this message not only as a sequel or continuation, but as the fulfillment of the scriptures of Judaism. The form and content of what the apostles of Jesus initially preached, the "apostolic kerygma," is known to us from fragmentary reports and references in the earliest literary products of the nascent church, constituting two main groups of literary sources.[28] An older group is formed by the letters of Paul addressing Hellenistic communities that he founded and with which he stayed in touch through correspondence between the years 48 and 50 A.D. until his death under Nero (around 65).[29] The other group is formed by the Synoptic Gospels, which contain accounts of Jesus' words and deeds in episodic form and end with disproportionately lengthy narratives of his death by crucifixion, to which as final episodes, the initial evidences of his resurrection are added.[30]

From these documents we can conclude that, in a short period of time after the resurrection—about two decades—faith in Jesus Christ began to spread vigorously among both Jews and non-Jews in Palestine and Syria and then beyond these areas. With the time of the Jewish war (66–73), resulting in the destruction of the Temple and of the whole Jewish establishment of Jerusalem, the contemporary *koine* Greek language became

28. The derivation of the word "apostle" (in Greek, ἀπόστολος), is not fully known. According to the evangelist Luke, Jesus not only chose his twelve special disciples, but named them apostles (Lk 6:13) probably using the Aramaic word *shaliach*, which means a fully authorized personal representative. This thesis, proposed by Karl Heinrich Rengstorf in 1955 [see Gerhard Kittel, ed., *Theological Dictionary of the New Testament* (Grand Rapids: Eerdmans, 1967), 1:398–446] was disputed; modifications were proposed, but his thesis was never disproved.

29. This concept needs to be somewhat expanded in view of Paul's Epistle to the Romans, in which he addresses a community he has never met before.

30. The last verses of the Gospel of Mark (16:9–16) constitute a special literary and critical problem that does not affect the question about the basic outline of the early gospels and/or their literary genre.

the most important tool for transmitting the message as well as the story of Jesus, although the use of Aramaic and ancient Syriac continued. Thus, from around the middle of the first century, the formation of the New Testament began, first in the composition of individual books in Greek and then in the process of gathering them rather rapidly into a collection of sacred books in a normative sense, so that around the years 100 to 125, practically all books that today form the New Testament were written, and by the end of the second century the New Testament obtained its shape.[31]

Therefore, in terms of simple historical facts, within about one century after its formative years, the Christian church, whether in dispute or in doubt, developed the custom of referring to two sets of books. The first set consisted of the Jewish scriptures, understood as "the Law and the Prophets" (in the sense used previously), while the second set was a newer and smaller collection of apostolic writings, preponderantly gospels and epistles attributed to Paul and to some of Jesus' original apostles. Of the first set, called later "the Old Testament," two editions existed: one in Hebrew (with a small part in Aramaic), the other in Greek, mostly translations from Hebrew, called the Septuagint, this latter having been created by and for Hellenistic Jews about two centuries before Jesus. The apostolic writings were all in Greek; consequently, their frequent references to the Jewish scriptures were made mostly from the Septuagint. Around the year 100 A.D., Christians began to look back at their own origin as historical past. While they saw themselves increasingly separated from Judaism, they kept using as scriptures the sacred writings of the Jews. They have, of course, also realized that they relied preponderantly, often exclusively, on the Greek texts, which they continued to regard as providing a translation and not the original works.

About a hundred years later, at the time of Irenaeus and Tertullian,[32] Christians routinely argued in all their discussions about their faith by quotation formulas and references to these two sets of scriptures. By the end of the second century, Christians habitually discussed doctrinal ques-

---

31. This chronological window is very generous; we will need to say more about in our last chapters. A large majority of scholars assume that the composition of the four canonical gospels preceded Papias (about 130 A.D.), and the collection of the Pauline epistles reached at least one editing before Marcion (well before 120).

32. Irenaeus's *Adversus Haereses* is usually dated to 185, while the last version of Tertullian's *Contra Marcionem* is dated to about 207.

tions with specific references to texts taken from "the scriptures" of the Septuagint and the teaching of the apostles, known mostly from four gospels and a collection of apostolic letters.[33] The four-gospel canon by this time was explicitly defined and known, and a Pauline corpus was stabilized in the process of several editions throughout the church,[34] so that further questions of details about the canon of either testament were discussed in reference to the linkage of these sources according to the Christian concept of revelation, most often in terms of *prophecy* or *apostolicity*.[35]

The church's separation from Judaism took place before either Judaism or Christianity had determined its canon of holy books. Yet, in either religion, the formation of a canon rapidly advanced in the first half of the second century. For Christians, the acceptance of the four gospels and the letters of Paul implied the acceptance of the Septuagint, but in no more narrow terms than by considering them as a channel through which the Law and Prophets became accessible to a worldwide hellenized cultural community. On the opposite side, after the Second Jewish War (135 A.D.), the surviving Jewish community saw no other choice left than to follow a narrower understanding in the Palestinian Pharisaic tradition of the Jewish scriptures and to insist that their scripture must be based on exclusively Hebrew texts. What is important here is to see that for the surviving Jewish communities the first major steps toward a closed canon had to take place in making moves in contradistinction from the Christian appropriation of the Septuagint. Ultimately, Jews and Christians parted not just in possession of two different canonical collections but, more importantly, with different outlooks about their sacred books.

33. This is well expressed in many texts by Irenaeus, but especially in the preface of his third book, *Adversus Haereses*, where he recapitulates the design of his work. Now, he says, after having described what the Gnostics teach, he will "adduce proofs from the Scriptures," proceeding "in defense of the only true and life-giving faith, which the Church has received from the apostles and imparted to her sons."

34. An essential update on this topic is found the following publications: Evans and Tov, *Exploring the Origins of the Bible*; E. Earle Ellis, *The Making of the New Testament Documents* (Atlanta: Society of Biblical Literature, 1999); John J. Clabeaux, *A Lost Edition of the Letters of Paul: A Reassessment of the Text of the Pauline Corpus Attested by Marcion* (Washington, D.C.: CBQ, 1989); David Trobisch, *Die Endredaktion des Neuen Testaments: Eine Untersuchung zur Entstehung der christlichen Bibel* [The Final Redaction of the New Testament: An Essay on the Formation of the Christian Bible] (Freiburg, Switzerland: Universitätsverlag; Göttingen: Vandenhoeck and Ruprecht, 1996); C. E. Hill, *Who Chose the Gospels? Probing the Great Gospel Conspiracy* (Oxford: Oxford University Press, 2010).

35. We will see more details about this in chapter 9.

2 ✣ INSPIRATION

THE MODEL OF DOUBLE AUTHORSHIP

From ancient times, in fact already in the pre-Christian era, believers and theologians assigned to the Bible some sort of a dual provenance—that is, both a divine and a human origin. In logical terms, such a view involved two steps. First, when some human *speech* was identified as transmitting God's word, a conclusion would be drawn that this word came from God through a human intermediary. A second thought follows that in its *textual form*, God's word had to be regarded as coming from a divine source. Yet only in the Scholastic treatises on inspiration was this second step clearly distinguished from the first. In the biblical texts the two phases do not appear fully distinguished, because biblical texts are either thought of as divine utterances or as what human authors wrote, quoted as God's word. The custom of quoting the Bible as speech remains in use in modern times. Only in recent centuries did theologians begin asking specifically how the biblical texts' dual provenance should be understood in literary terms. Such inquiry eventually led to the assumption of two *literary* authors, one divine and one human, and to thoughts about their *authorship* in basically identical analogous and univocal senses. Yet, until the present the biblical text continues to be quoted with traditional formulas as God's "spoken word," as if equivalent to the audible transmission of revelation by the preaching of prophets and apostles: *fides ex auditu*. In the last two centuries, Catholic teaching began to treat the Bible's origins clearly in terms of *literary* authorship, with Scholastic textbooks of the late nineteenth and early twentieth centuries tending to affirm that God is the author of the biblical texts *in a literary sense*. They use quotations using the term *auctor* indiscriminately to demonstrate their thesis as based on longstanding doctrinal tradition almost unanimously held by the church fathers.[1] But this claim is not so easily proved. Many who read of the acts of the Council of Trent and the First Vatican Council in translation can easily find statements about God as the "author" of all scriptures of both testaments.[2] However, the Latin term *auctor* has a much broader meaning than its modern equivalents (*author* in English, *auteur* in French, and *autore* in Italian with semantic equivalents in other languages).[3] As a rule, modern papal encyclicals and other recent magisterial pronouncements follow previous church documents. Consequently, neither in conciliar pronouncements nor other texts of the *Magisterium* must the word "author" and the concept of authorship be further specified to mean a literary author,[4] because, until most recent times, documents of the papal *Magisterium* were always published, including by Vatican II, in Latin. It is also generally admitted that early patristic sources, which the local church synods and ecumenical councils echoed or copied, had usually focused on the divine origin of *both* testaments with an explicit

1. In the older *Jerome Biblical Commentary*, ed. Raymond R. Brown, Roland E. Murphy, and Joseph Fitzmyer (New York, London, and Sidney: Prentice Hall, 1968), chapter 66, on "Inspiration and Inerrancy," by Richard F. Smith, the assumption is upheld that *Deus Auctor Scripturae* means, at least since the early Middle Ages, "literary authorship" and is dogmatized by Vatican I in the sense of declaring that the biblical books "have God as their author" (col. 500). In the *New Jerome Biblical Commentary*, by the same editors in 1990, we find this chapter newly written (no. 65) with the title "Inspiration," by Raymond F. Collins, who admits, in agreement with Luther and Calvin, Trent, Vatican I, and Vatican II equally, that the biblical books have God as their author, but now a cautious comment is added: "The 'author' formula indicates that God is the ultimate source of both but does not necessarily ascribe literary authorship to him"; Collins, "Inspiration," 1028.

2. "Omnes libros tam Veteris quam Novi Testamenti, cum utriusque unus Deus sit auctor" [Every book of both the Old and New Testament, since God is the author of both]; Session IV on April 8, 1546 : Dz 783. "Qui quidem libri integri ... Spiritu Sancto inspirante conscripti Deum habent auctorem" [These books, written in their entirety under the inspiration of the Holy Spirit, have God as their author]; Session III, April 24, 1870: Dz 1787.

3. See Bruce Vawter, *Biblical Inspiration* (Philadelphia: Westminster, 1972), 22–24. On these pages he is in essential agreement with my statements, except that he presents Justin Martyr and Augustine as embracing a "dictational" model of divine authorship, which would implicitly attribute to God a *literary* authorship of the biblical texts.

4. The matter becomes ever clearer if we realize that *auctoritas* meant in antiquity and in the Middle Ages (quite regularly in the texts of St. Thomas Aquinas) first and foremost "authority" and not "authorship."

anti-Marcionite and/or anti-Manichaean intention. Thus in a patristic context, these statements focus on *both* testaments as attributed to the one and same creative and authoritative source, *the one God who alone is Creator.* The earliest examples of such passages come from the late second century (the texts of Tertullian and of early African synods), where the argument was not about biblical inspiration but about the doctrine of the one God and the unity of the scriptures, as all coming from the same *auctor.* Moreover, as many early Latin texts testify, in patristic and medieval Latin, *auctor* appears regularly as synonymous with *creator* and does not specifically designate a literary author.[5]

The Divine Author: Deus Auctor Scripturae

Before *Dei Verbum*

In neo-Scholastic textbooks published between the two Vatican Councils, we frequently find the following assumptions:

1. The statement "God is the author of Holy Scripture" (*Deus est auctor Scripturae*) represents the unanimous conviction of the church fathers, and is generally embraced by all medieval authors, including Thomas Aquinas.

2. In ancient documents, going back to the second century, *auctor* means a "literary author" (*auctor litterarius*).

The previous two statements must be regarded as articles of the Catholic faith—that is, matter infallibly taught by the *Magisterium.*

All papal encyclicals of the last two centuries—most importantly *Providentissimus Deus,* by Leo XIII (1893), *Spiritus Paraclitus,* by Benedict XV (1920), and *Divino Afflante* (1943) and *Humani Generis* (1950), by Pius XII—use the vocabulary of a "double authorship" and point to God as *auctor* of the scriptures. However, none of them specifies that God is meant to be "a literary author," although they all allow or possibly favor such an interpretation.

---

5. This is most obvious in liturgical texts. See, for example, the Christmas hymn of Sedulius from the fifth century, still in use: "Beatus *auctor* saeculi servile corpus induit"; see Anselmo Lentini, *Te Decet Hymnus: L'Innario della Liturgia Horarum* (Vatican City: Typis Polyglottis Vaticanis, 1984), 81. The Latin noun equivalent to the modern English "author" is *scriptor.*

In fact, with the decline of the knowledge of classical Latin, *auctor* became for more and more readers equivalent to "author" in the modern sense, and God's literary authorship of the Bible was routinely stated to be an article of the faith. Only specialized scholars remained aware that the presence of the term in ancient texts does not warrant this theory. In the Vulgate the term [*auctor salutis* (Heb 2:10 and 12:2) or *auctor vitae* (Acts 3:15)] has nothing to do with literary authorship.[6] In the Greek Bible the word corresponding to *auctor* is ἀρχηγός, whose meaning, however, is not linked to composing texts. All in all, in Latin Christian usage *auctor* is synonymous to *creator*, and thus in neither ancient nor recent texts does it signify literary authorship.

Nonetheless, in 1943, the German Jesuit (later cardinal) Augustinus Bea, Pius XII's closest adviser in biblical matters, published an article on the meaning of the formula *Deus Auctor Scripturae*,[7] claiming to prove that not only in the documents of the *Magisterium* and the texts of St. Thomas Aquinas but in the majority of more ancient (Latin) sources, the formula is to be understood in the sense of a literary authorship. The encyclical *Divino Afflante* was published in the same year and was met with enthusiasm by the vast majority of Catholic biblical scholars. Bea was considered by many as its "ghost writer" so that his essay about the scripture's divine authorship raised no controversy; in fact, it is not known to have been even challenged. By then divine literary authorship was nothing new, for it became part of the Roman textbooks, including Bea's own textbook of 1935, to which (rather than to his essay of 1943) Rahner makes his references in 1958 when characterizing the position of what he called *Schultheologie*, the "theology of the schools," represented in Roman textbooks. Another widely used old textbook on inspiration by Heinrich Hoepfl, edited by Benno Gut, similarly states that in the tradition the term "author" was employed in reference to the divine authorship of the Bible "according to its [the term's] common use, meaning a writer."[8] Rahner never contested this interpretation of the patristic

---

6. There are a few other uses of the word *auctor* in a nonreligious sense as "originator" in Jdg 6:29; Acts 24:5; and 2 Mc 2:29 and 2:31.

7. Bea, "*Deus Auctor Scripturae*," 16–31. Although now outdated, this essay was still included in the bibliographies of both *The Jerome* and *The New Jerome Biblical Commentary*. Bea's conclusion was based on a mistaken methodology by not distinguishing the various meanings and uses of the word *auctor* in antiquity.

8. This book was probably the last textbook on inspiration in Latin, published in subsequent

and conciliar texts and, unfortunately, when suggesting a *Durchdenken* ("thoroughly thinking through") of the theology of inspiration did not propose a review of the patristic evidence. Only a thorough reexamination of the concept of divine literary authorship could have provided new insights about the scheme of the Bible's "dual authorship."

In the Text of *Dei Verbum*

The Dogmatic Constitution *Dei Verbum* uses the word *auctor* in a careful and calibrated way. Quoting the First Vatican Council verbatim, *Dei Verbum* continues saying that, according to traditional Catholic teaching, the biblical texts have God as their author. Right after, it calls the divine author an *inspirator et auctor*,[9] while naming the human authors as *veri auctores*. Thus the term *auctor* is applied to both the divine and the human authors, but with different specifications. Manifestly an imbalance is intentionally introduced into this description of the Bible's dual provenance. Only the human authors are called *veri auctores*; God is not said to be a *verus auctor*. It seems, therefore, that *verus auctor* signifies someone who is an author in the conventional (modern) sense of the term, meaning a literary author. This concept is applied in the document only to "the hagiographers," not to God. Rahner's personal presence in the special committe drafting *Dei Verbum* was probably behind the fact that God was called *inspirator et auctor*,[10] which, in fact means exactly what Karl Rahner had previously proposed by calling him an *Urheber* (originator by inspiration), while denying that the term *Verfasser* (equivalent to the Latin *verus auctor*), could be applied to God.[11]

---

editions by Heinrich Höpfl, Benno Gut, Adalbertus Metzinger, and Louis Leloir, Benedictine authors teaching at the Papal University Sant' Anselmo in Rome up to the days of Vatican II. The book stated, "Recto concluditur terminum 'auctoris' adhiberi secundum usum communem in sensu scriptoris" [Rightly one concludes that the term "author" is being employed according to its commun use in the sense of a writer]; Hoepfl et al., *Introductio Generalis in Sacram Scripturam* (Naples and Rome: Polyglottis Vaticanis, 1950), 24.

9. In *Dei Verbum* the term *auctor* is applied to God only twice. In no. 11, with a footnote citing Vatican I, the term "God" as "author" directly refers to the Holy Spirit as the agent of inspiration (*Spiritu Sancto inspirante conscripti Deum habent auctorem*). The insertion of the unusual term *inspirator* in no. 11 consistently specifies further to tell specifically in what sense God is author of the biblical texts, a sense that *is not being applied anywhere to human authors*, who cannot be called *auctores inspirantes*.

10. This is a *hendiadys*—that is, an expression with two terms, to signify one special concept of authorship.

11. This should not appear as a much-too-subtle exegesis of the conciliar text. By this formula-

Nonetheless, we must remain aware that the general context of *Dei Verbum* is that of revelation. God is dealt with in this document first and foremost as the *Revealer*, who communicates with man "in many and various ways" (Heb 1:1) as he posits *inner-worldly* acts of communication in mankind's course of history by acting, speaking, teaching to provide, most importantly, verbal and even written expression of all that he reveals. In the full context of the document, revelation is understood in terms of both words and deeds, while inspiration belongs to a subsequent phase of divine action, prompting and guiding human authors to express divine revelation in writing. As *Dei Verbum* repeatedly asserts,[12] in this process divine authorship must be understood as divine influence aimed at creating fixed literary expression so that, at the end, the written text, in which revelation is solidly deposited, may actively *continue to transmit* the word of God for the people of God—ultimately, the church.

The concept of divine authorship of scripture as explained in *Dei Verbum* goes beyond mere semantics. The expression *inspirator et auctor* not only avoids saying that "author" implies "God producing books in the way human authors do," but also indicates that God's revelation, which began in his words and deeds, continues when it is transmitted in the scriptures as their written expression. In no way do the human authors set limits to the divine author, the One who prompts and guides them. In spite of all their creative and technical skills, which the human authors invest to authentically express revelation, their receptivity and comprehension are time-bound and culturally conditioned so that what they write is limited by their human nature. But the action of the divine author, using the human author as his instrument, does not lose its transcendence and sovereignty when *causing* scripture. The human authors' actual mindset while writing (the *authorial intent*) is, therefore, not equivalent to the inspiring divine author's *intent*.

---

tion the new committee preparing *Dei Verbum* for the last session of the Council was able to avoid discussing Rahner's question about *Urheber* vs. *Verfasser*, which had been only inadequately treated in theological literature. At the same time, the term *auctor*, which was contextualized in the document by various modifiers, easily met the approval of the Council.

12. Paragraph no. 11 begins with the sentence "Divinitus revelata, quae in Sacra Scriptura litteris continentur et prostant, Spiritu Sancto afflante consignata sunt" [Those divinely revealed realities that are contained and presented in Sacred Scripture have been committed to writing under the inspiration of the Holy Spirit]. In this sentence *afflante* is synonymous with *inspirante*.

The transmission of revelation by inspired writers is not like an athletic "relay" where God and the human author(s) would be linearly linked on the same level to pass down thoughts and concepts of divine provenance until at the end, when these—the thought and concepts—finally reach the writer, God's thought would simply coincide with human thoughts and creativity and thus be put to writing, His thought would be reduced to the intent of the human writer. While God condescends to man's level of understanding and uses the human authors like tools to express his thought,[13] God's word is not locked into human words. If God were the literary author of the biblical text in the same sense as the hagiographer, then his word would fully coalesce with man's self-expression. Such a theory leads either to the naive concept of divine dictation or to an equally unacceptable concept of a divine appropriation of a human composition, as if a human author's utterance or literary compilation could fully, exactly, and adequately contain—no more and no less—what God and man comunicate in perfect concordance. As a result, the "authorial intent" of both man and God would coincide. The notion of "a divine literary production" would compress God's speech and man's writing into one single entity and deprive the scriptural word of its distinctive quality or pedigree—namely, its transcendental character and potential to convey the limitless power of the Holy Spirit.[14]

Most importantly, if God's authorship of scripture were understood as literary and therefore coextensive to the authorship of its human author, the unity of the scriptures rooted in the oneness of salvation history (in contemporary language: "the canonical context") would vanish, because the authorial intent of the human writer is necessarily restricted to a finite human life's horizon and, therefore, cannot encompass the fullness of salvation history. The unity of the scriptures comes from the divine author and not from the human authors. This is why, beginning from the second century, patristic texts as well as church synods and councils spoke of "the same Spirit" who inspired both testaments. The

---

13. For the patristic metaphors comparing the human authors with tools or musical instruments, see Alonso Schökel, *Inspired Word*, 58–66.

14. The Pauline passage reminds us, "For we know, brothers and sisters beloved by God, that he has chosen you, because *our message of the gospel came to you not in word only, but also in power and in the Holy Spirit* and with full conviction; just as you know what kind of persons we proved to be among you for your sake"; 1 Thes 1:4–5.

Holy Spirit alone can guarantee continuity in salvation history by linking all books of the Bible with Christ. Similarly, the fulfillment of the words of the scriptures or their plenitude in Christ (which one may call its *sensus plenior* or "spiritual meaning") cannot be regarded as a genuine meaning of the biblical text without assuming that the divine author's influence is of a higher order than literary authorship: God as *auctor scripturae* is supratemporal, exercising a transcendental authorship without the limitations of a literary author. *Dei Verbum* connects revelation with the unity of scripture in the same way:

This plan of revelation is realized by deeds and words having an inner unity: the deeds wrought by God in the history of salvation manifest and confirm the teaching and realities signified by the words, while the words proclaim the deeds and clarify the mystery contained in them. By this revelation then, the deepest truth about God and the salvation of man shines out for our sake in Christ, who is both the mediator and the fullness of all revelation. (*Dei Verbum*, no. 2)

These remarks apply most clearly to the Old Testament, where the process of inspiration has extended itself over several centuries. Only the Holy Spirit "in whom" or "by whom" the scriptures were written can endow these books with depth and height or, to be more specific, with "salvation historical" (Christological) relevance that transcends the limits of a human writer's historically conditioned knowledge and purpose. When stating that scripture must be interpreted in the same Spirit in whom it was written, *Dei Verbum* expresses the same idea, although and with clear emphasis on the fundamental differences between the ways God and a human author determine the meaning of the text:

The interpreter must investigate *what meaning the sacred writer intended* to express and actually expressed in particular circumstances by using contemporary literary forms in accordance with the situation of his own time and culture.... But, since Holy Scripture must be read and interpreted *in the same Spirit* in which it was written,[15] no less serious attention must be given to *the content and unity of the whole of Scripture* if *the meaning of the sacred texts* is to be correctly worked out.[16]

15. A footnote makes reference to a sentence in St. Jerome's Commentary to Galatians: Quicumque igitur aliter Scripturam intelligit, quam sensus Spiritus sancti flagitat, quo conscripta est: licet de Ecclesia non recesserit, tamen haereticus appellari potest [Whoever, therefore, understands scripture differently from the meaning demanded by the Holy Spirit *in whom it was written* may be called a heretic]; Patrologia Latina 26, 417.

16. *Dei Verbum*, no. 12, italics by me. The official English text as it appears on the Vatican web-

In the modern theology of inspiration the tendency grew to focus on the inspired author's subjectivity and identify the meaning of the biblical text with the hagiographer's authorial intent. One might dispute if, indeed, the neo-Scholastic theology of inspiration was aware of the reductionist implications of this tendency. Yet, when historical-critical exegesis limited itself to the reconstruction of the "authorial intent" and declared that it alone could determine the authentic meaning of the text, it set a priori limits for the exegete to indicate what a text could or could not mean. At the same time, this method, compromising the unity of the two testaments and the theological basis for canonical unity among the books, promoted the fragmentation of the Bible into its individual components. With the arrival of source criticism, the effect of fragmentation went beyond single books, breaking down individual books into their literary sources. This approach was one of the fundamental reasons rendering theological interpretation increasingly problematic and seemingly incompatible with the use of the historical-critical method.[17]

Portraying "the divine author" like an author employing a ghost writer—that is, as a literary author standing "behind" another literary author (the hagiographer)—constitutes a false lead. Although both the *Magisterium* and ancient tradition state that "everything asserted by the inspired authors or sacred writers must be held to be asserted by the Holy Spirit (no. 11 of *Dei Verbum*)," the converse is not true: not everything that the Holy Spirit asserts is also asserted (as consciously understood and fully appropriated thought) by the human writers. God alone knows the full meaning of the text. The inspired text, however, exercises its revelatory role in a similarly *historical fashion*—namely, in the course of God's salvation plan by both enlightening past words and deeds and anticipating what God intends to reveal more fully in the future. Briefly, divine authorship of the scriptures neither means God and man coauthoring a text nor God becoming a writer in the human sense. Instead, it is a must for a theology of inspiration to explore in what sense God can be *the author of a literary work without being its literary author*.

---

site had a disastrous typo: "in the sacred spirit" instead of "in the same Spirit." Fortunately, more recent editions of the *New American Bible* contain a correction.

17. See a collection of essays on these issues: Craig G. Bartholomew and Heath A. Thomas, eds., *A Manifesto for Theological Interpretation* (Grand Rapids: Baker, 2016): especially, Michael W. Gohee and Michael D. Williams, "Doctrine of Scripture and Theological Interpretation," 48–71.

On the practical level, speaking of the "divine authorship" of the Bible as equivalent to literary authorship risks obscuring the transcendental character of divine authorship by placing God and man upon a common playfield where two authors, human and divine, would appear not only to cooperate, but be in fact rivals, limiting each other's freedom. Such a model of dual authorship would also raise the problem of how much the human author really understands in depth of what he is writing. For he certainly does not know "the end of the story," which is eschatological. Only by unduly narrowing the model of the dual authorship (and instrumental causality) could one allow the divine author to be involved in literary authorship while avoiding admitting that he is permanently handicapped by the innate deficiencies of his human instruments.

We must recall how the neo-Thomistic model of the inspired author came to a startling conclusion: under God's actual influence men are speaking God's word as their own, *even if* they remain—more often than not—*unaware* that their words are ultimately not their own literary product. We must come back to Rahner's argument: a literary work cannot have two different literary authors, because that would mean that the same effect was produced under the same aspect by two causes of the same kind. In other words, a *dual literary authorship* for the Bible is ontologically untenable.

Nonetheless, by the middle of the twentieth century this dual literary authorship of the biblical texts became *doctrina communis* in most textbooks. It was neatly tied to the doctrine of instrumental causality transplanted from St. Thomas's *Summa*, who, indeed, dealt with this topic in four sections about prophecy (II-II, q. 171–74), but in a significantly different context. The neo-Thomists severed this theory from its original context and applied it not only to prophets but to all scriptural authors or "hagiographers." Since Thomas's *Summa* does not treat the theology of scriptural inspiration, the transfer of Thomas's teaching into this new context appeared throughout the twentierh century as if it needed to be defended for this "valid extension" of the Thomistic doctrine on prophecy.[18] Is it, indeed, legitimate to extend Aquinas's concept

---

18. In von Balthasar's words, "Die Frage nach dem 'Wie' der Bibelinspiration hat Thomas wie seine Vorgänger und Zeitgenossen wenig beschäftigt; sie ist erst im Gefolge der modernen Bibelkritik

of prophecy to a general concept of biblical inspiration? Doubts were newly raised when biblical research proceeded to transform the concept of prophecy and restrict it, even within the Old Testament, to explicitly anticipatory visions (that is, predictions) of future events.[19]

The committee drafting *Dei Verbum* was certainly aware of the problematic presuppositions of the neo-Scholastic synthesis. Due to the fiasco of the original schema *De Fontibus Revelationis*, this new committee distanced itself from neo-Scholastic theology. Consequently, *Dei Verbum* omits all references to the language *of instrumental causality* and avoids speaking of God's "literary authorship."[20]

God as Author of Scripture after *Dei Verbum*

Many have hoped that *Dei Verbum* would become a fresh start with only tenuous connections to previous textbook theology. Others might have been surprised at the sharp turn it has taken away from previous scholarship. Certainly, venerable textbooks, some reedited right before the Council, had to be quickly retired.[21]

What *Dei Verbum* presents about revelation met, to my knowledge, with no significant dissent. This new theological understanding of revelation was launched in the new theological climate of both France and Germany, as it quickly developed after the Second World War, and was enthusiastically embraced in both dogmatic and fundamental theology.

---

augetaucht" [The question about the "how" of biblical inspiration has little preoccupied Thomas or his predecessors and contemporaries; it has come up only as a sequel to modern biblical criticism]; Hans Urs von Balthasar, *Thomas von Aquin: Besondere Gnadengaben und die zwei Wege des menschlichen Lebens; Kommentar zur Summa Theologica II–II, 171–82* [Thomas Aquinas: Special Charisms and the Two Ways of Human Life; Commentary on the *Summa Theologica*, II, 171–82], vol. 23, *Die Deutsche Thomas-Ausgabe* [The German Thomas Edition], ed. H. M. Christmann (Vienna: Pustet, 1958), 359.

19. Von Balthasar is clearly aware of the difficulties of such a procedure as he writes, "Man darf nicht alles auf die Bibelinspiration anwenden [One is not supposed to apply everything (in Thomas's teaching about prophecy) to biblical inspiration]; ibid., 360, quoting Synave and Benoit from their French Commentary of the *Summa*.

20. This first schema, rejected in its entirety at its first introduction, was presented by Fr. Sebastian Tromp, SJ, as its relator. He was also the author of a widely adopted Roman textbook, *De Sacrae Scripturae inspiratione* (Rome: Pontifical Gregorian University, 1932), which strictly followed the neo-Scholastic "synthesis" as an application of the *Summa*.

21. The last one we quoted, by Höpfl, Gut, Metzinger, and Leloir, was published during the first year of the Council, but was quickly phased out as a textbook.

With regard to inspiration, however, there was less unanimity. *Dei Verbum* retained the general scheme of dual authorship without offering any support to the notion of God's literary authorship. A first reading of the document might create the impression that, in *Dei Verbum*, the Council intended to do little more than "to recapitulate the traditional teaching on inspiration."[22] Outside of Catholic biblical scholarship it seemed that already before Vatican II, the doctrine of inspiration was in decline. Raymond Collins writes of "liberal Protestants, effectively denying [the] inspiration [of the Bible] by silence." The same author adds (in the New Jerome Biblical Commentary of 1990) that "recent Catholic writings" about inspiration are characterized by "realism," meaning that they focus on speaking about "the word of God" as "human words" without much further elaboration.[23] It seems that such a focus on the human word was disturbingly close to neglecting, even denying, inspiration as an issue irrelevant for biblical theologians. In the post-Conciliar years, as Catholic exegesis plunged into wholesale experimentation with the historical-critical method, suddenly the theology of inspiration in its entirety began to appear as a sterile and speculative exercise. If we consider the development of Catholic thinking on this matter in larger time periods (like thirty to forty years), it appears that, after the Council, the reception of *Dei Verbum* became problematic mostly because its teaching on biblical inspiration and the truth of the Bible (*inerrancy*) was not perceived as important for the new trends in exegesis. At the same time, the subject suffered neglect in the theological curricula of seminaries and universities.[24] However, as a well-informed and precise German work on contemporary transformations of the understanding of biblical inspiration explains, the "problem of irrelevance" is already detectable in *Dei Verbum*. For already in the first chapters of the conciliar document, as soon as it begins treating the transmission of rev-

22. Collins, "Inspiration," 1024.
23. Ibid., 1031.
24. This matter is complicated. In the second half of the twentieth century, the theology of inspiration began to be taught not by specialists of biblical studies (now calling themselves "exegetes" and obtaining no advanced degrees in theology) but rather by systematic theologians specializing in the relatively new discipline of Fundamental Theology. (This was the course that, as young professors, Karl Rahner, Henri de Lubac, and Joseph Ratzinger began teaching.) By the 1980s, in most Catholic institutions, due to shifts of curricula and further specializations, biblical exegesis was taught by professors who, in their biblical studies, have never taken any course on inspiration, inerrancy, or canon.

elation, its initially broad "salvation-historical" outlook becomes "short-circuited" and fades into a more timid line of thought, which replaces "deeds and words" with *revealed truth* communicated to individuals and guaranteed by the Holy Spirit, who influences the minds of hagiographers in their work producing the inspired texts.[25] Since *Dei Verbum* was a text on revelation, it remained legitimately sketchy on elaborating everything else (including inspiration, canon, and hermeneutics), and its brevity may not have to be regarded as a deficiency. Yet here may be the ultimate root of the problem: on the one hand, the Council fathers realized that they had to cover the topic of inspiration, but, on the other hand, they and their theological advisers realized that they were unprepared to treat the subject of inspiration more thoroughly.

What caused this unpreparedness is not easy to determine. It appears that the immediate cause was a lack of serious effort in the preconciliar years to respond to the objections that Karl Rahner's book raised in challenge to the neo-Scholastic synthesis reigning in Catholic universities and seminaries. But more distantly, there was unpreparedness in a more specific sense: Rahner's call for an "overhaul" (new *Durchdenken*) of this topic produced only sporadic responses in terms of essays or monographic studies about the church fathers' theology of inspiration. Augustinus Bea's position about *Deus Auctor* remained unchallenged, because no one checked his patristic dossier. With some exaggeration, one might say that some theologians just did not do their homework. At the Council, Bea himself went through a metamorphosis of his personal profile, changing from an antiquated theologian, ready to retire, into a leading churchman closing ranks with the progressive wing, an icon of renewal in theology and ecumenism. This was made easy by his alleged role in authoring *Divino Afflante*, which gave him the image of a forerunner of the Council and a reformer preparing for the postconciliar transformation of Catholic biblical studies. No wonder that, in this perspective, his purported finding that the church fathers unanimously taught God's literary authorship of the Bible sounded just right and that

---

25. Helmut Gabel, *Inspirationsverständnis im Wandel: Theologische Neuorientierung im Umfeld des Zweiten Vaikanischen Konzils* [Understanding the Changing Concept of Inspiration: New Theological Orientation in the Field Surrounding the Second Vatican Council] (Mainz: Matthias Grünewald Verlag, 1991), 122–23.

this issue remained dormant until and beyond the Council. Only by exception do we find today someone like Scott Hahn, who, in the name of orthodoxy, insists on God's literary authorship while quoting Bea. It seems that no publication has previously confronted Bea's thesis to show its lack of compelling evidence. This is why now, more than seventy years later, Hahn could quote this essay as a text witnessing to a longstanding patristic tradition, safely possessed by preconciliar scholarship.[26]

Furthermore, for almost a century before Vatican II, theologians kept on insisting on a neat conceptual and real *distinction* between revelation and inspiration. The concept of revelation introduced into *Dei Verbum* demanded quite an opposite view. As it happened, revelation was transmitted at first through oral and only later through written channels in a process that kept tradition and scripture interconnected in mutual penetration. Yet, the Second Vatican Council found itself in a quandary about this issue. Both progressives and conservatives wanted to close an incessant interconfessional debate that began—and at times raged—between Catholics and Protestants about the relationship on "Scripture and Tradition."[27] In the last decade before the Council, this topic became extremely sensitive. An ultraconservative resolution of the debate was included by the Council's Preparatory Commission in the document *De Fontibus Revelationis*. Only on the last session of the Council was a new document, the first version of *Dei Verbum*, introduced.[28] The drafters of this document (an entirely new committee)

26. Cf. Scott W. Hahn, ed., *For the Sake of Our Salvation*, 6:31. In the same volume's introductory essay Hahn writes, "Inspiration is thus defined as a mystery of divine authorship in the literary sense of the term." In note 52, Hahn quotes Bea's essay published in German in 1943.

27. The problem goes back to the Council of Trent. Shortly before the Second Vatican Council, Joseph Geiselman published a new interpretation of the Tridentine doctrine about scripture and tradition, showing that Trent made no decision about this question and therefore has not really defined what later the common Catholic position became: each of the two, scripture and tradition, contains only parts (*partim ... partim*) of all revealed truths; see Geiselman, *Schrift und Tradition* (Freiburg im Bresgau: Herder, 1959).

28. The full story is not at all so smooth, for it required a papal intervention by John XXIII, who on November 1962 took the topic from the agenda. It was two years before, on the last session on March 7, 1964, the topic was reintroduced to the Council. Another papal intervention by Pope Paul VI occurred at about paragraph 12 of the same *Dei Verbum* in November 1964, during the last session of the Council; see Joseph Ratzinger, "Origin and Background," in his commentary of *Dei Verbum*, in *Commentary on the Documents of Vatican II*, ed. H. Vorgrimler (New York: Herder and Herder, 1969), 2:155; René Laurentin, *Enjeu du Concile: Bilan de la Première Session* (Paris: Seuil, 1963) 27–45.

must have tacitly recognized that they were unable to present a theology of inspiration in any way commensurate to what they said about revelation. During the entire history of Vatican II, only the birth pangs of *Dei Verbum* required papal intervention, at first for blocking the whole first draft and then on the last session for resolving the tough resistance of a minority about biblical inerrancy. From the need of a papal interventions alone, an altogether rare occurrence at an Ecumenical Council, especially Vatican II, we might see why, for about forty years, *Dei Verbum* was exposed to mixed reactions. Contrary to what the document's subtitle suggests, most of the controversies that followed were not about revelation but about biblical inspiration and inerrancy. While other documents of the Council, like the Apostolic Constitutions on the Liturgy (*Sacrosanctum Concilium*) and the Church (*Lumen Gentium*) received high grades and enthusiastic reception, *Dei Verbum* was dragged through unresolved disputes.[29]

During his papacy Pope Benedict XVI made major efforts to promote the reception of *Dei Verbum*. In 2009 one of the important themes of his Post-Synodal Apostolic Exhortation *Verbum Domini* aimed at the promotion of biblical studies by advocating a more theological exegesis for the Bible. It is noteworthy how in this document the pope reached back to the theme of the Bible's divine authorship. While making an explicit comparison between inspiration and the incarnation, an important topic for *Dei Verbum*, Benedict brought up the theme of the scripture's dual authorship but with some variance in the wording:

A key concept for understanding the sacred text as the word of God in human words is certainly that of *inspiration*. Here too we can suggest an analogy: as the word of God became flesh by the power of the Holy Spirit in the womb of the Virgin Mary, so sacred scripture is born from the womb of the church by the power of the same Spirit. Sacred scripture is "the word of God set down in writing under the inspiration of the Holy Spirit" (*Dei Verbum*, no. 22). In this way one recognizes the full importance of the human author who wrote the inspired

---

29. Gabel's book shows that the transformations (*Wandel* in the German title), which occurred in modern theology of inspiration, took place in response to Rahner's book of 1958, yet all with a delay and only after the Council, at a time interest in the topic began to fade. While Gabel criticizes Rahner's methodology (*Inspirationsverständnis im Wandel*, 138–40), he fails to point out that a serious reconsideration of the patristic evidence has never taken place, so that Bea's assertions about it were left unchallenged.

texts and, at the same time, *God himself as the true author* (*verus auctor*; italics in the text are mine).

It appears curious that at the end of the passage we find some sort of a reversal of the terminology of *Dei Verbum* where only the human author was called *verus auctor*. It is most unlikely that the term here is the outcome of an oversight, although most probably it was personally written by the pope. It is much less likely that the aging Joseph Ratzinger, one of the youngest of those who had drafted *Dei Verbum*, used the opportunity to settle a score with Karl Rahner, whose thinking and terminology are reflected in the text by calling only the human authors *veri auctores*. Quite probably the pope simply restored a vocabulary previously used in papal encyclicals, which freely employed the concept of a dual authorship before Rahner's book challenged it. *Verbum Domini* tried to rescue the terminology of this dual authorship from an academic discussion on German semantics (*Urheber* vs. *Verfasser*), which—one must admit—most non-German-speaking theologians were hardly able to follow, certainly not without a dictionary.[30]

In *Verbum Domini*, God is called *verus auctor* simply to mean that he is the ultimate *auctor* (originator, creator, source of provenance) of the Bible. It seems that the English version of the text correctly expresses this: God is *the* true author, not *a* true author, although this cannot be said so precisely in Latin where there are no definite articles. Essentially, Pope Benedict reclaims the expression *Deus Auctor Scripturae* to be used in the sense of divine authorship of scripture as a literary work without claiming God to be a (or the) literary author. The traditional expression is saved with no link to a specific theory of inspiration.

---

30. In addition, by commenting on the analogy between inspiration and Incarnation, Pope Benedict might have thought that naming God "true author" would complete *Dei Verbum*, for, in the context of the incarnation, God can *also* be called a "true author" in the same sense in which God is to be called "verus homo"—truly a man—just as God the Father is the true Creator (*auctor*) of Jesus' humanity. Thus Benedict readmits the use of *verus auctor* for God without reintroducing the idea of a divine writer, for, in the narrowest sense, the specific Latin term for the German *Verfasser* would be *scriptor*, a term nobody wanted to apply to God. Nor did the pope in *Verbum Domini* make any allusion to the neo-Thomistic theory of instrumental causality.

The Human Author or Hagiographer

In ancient Christian tradition the attribution of each biblical book to one single human author is frequent but allows some exceptions. In most books of the New Testament, a reference to a human author can be found in the title or the opening lines of the book. In most existing manuscripts, the titles of the books of the New Testament are consistently linked to either a single evangelist or one single apostle (Paul, Peter, John, James, or Jude).[31] It is, however, noteworthy that in seven Pauline letters at least one additional sender is mentioned (Sosthenes in First Corinthians, Timothy in Second Corinthians, Philippians, and Colossians, and Philemon Silvanus and Timothy in both First and Second Thessalonians); yet, arguably, Paul speaks in all of them in his own name, and the canonical titles rightly consider Paul to be their sole author. The letters of Peter, James, and Jude are sent in the name of only one apostle. The three Johannine "letters" form a special case, and so does the Letter to Hebrews; neither case can be fully discussed here. Yet, to be brief, First John is certainly not a letter, nor is Hebrews, although its last paragraphs show that its reception into the canon took place in connection with an assumed Pauline authorship. As a rule, the formation of the New Testament canon shows that, in general, tradition assumed for each book a single human author, or at least a single authority standing behind the document.

For the Old Testament the matter of an alleged authorship cannot be so simply generalized. Both the texts and the traditional attributions in titles indicate more diversity, further tensions, and consciously broad generalizations. Both Jews and Christians had the custom of attributing all psalms collectively to David as their author, and, indeed, many of the psalms' subtitles say the same. Several subtitles of the psalms, however, explicitly refer to other authors.[32] Generally in ancient tradition, the author of a wisdom book would be typically Solomon (see Prv 1:1; Cant 1:1; Eccl 1:1); similarly, the whole Pentateuch is attributed to Moses in spite

---

31. We will further examine in what sense this link is made with the Greek preposition *kata*, meaning "according to."

32. "Psalm of Solomon," for Ps 72:1 and 12:1; "Psalm of the Sons of Korah," for Ps 46:1, 47:1, and 48:1; and "Psalm of the Sons of Asaph," for Ps 49:1, 73:1.

of the fact that the last chapters of Deuteronomy narrate his death. This kind of referencing of a book to a single author is not the expression of some naiveté or ignorance, nor is it due to a lack of interest in historically verifiable authorship, but rather is a device for theological contextualization, which is artificially applied to some biblical books by attributing them summarily to one or another outstanding personality in salvation history. Many examples show an awareness that often the titles are to be taken in a strict authorial sense, but often, to the contrary, in an ahistorical sense, as is the case with the prophetic books in their final edition. The appearance of Cyrus's name in the book of Isaiah (44:28, 45:1, and 13) is just one of many examples showing that editors and copyists did not hesitate to unify historically distant compositions under a common title.[33] All sixty-six chapters of the book are subsumed under one title as if coming from the same prophet, who lived in the time of King Hezekiah, though, evidently, long portions of the text claim a postexilic origin. A much shorter but equally patent and famous example is Psalm 51. The subtitle specifically ascribes it to David and links it to his infamous adultery with Bathsheba, followed by the death of her husband, Uriah, caused by David, yet the psalm ends with references to the Temple that was built a generation later (under the reign of Solomon), and even the Temple's destruction, which took place several centuries later.

In ancient Judaism and Christianity, references to the authors of the biblical books have a wide range of meaning, either by suggesting actual composition by an individual leader of Israel or by pointing in a summary fashion to a person as fountainhead of a flow of tradition to which a particular book belongs. A name might be also a code-like indicator of the literary genre, as is the case when a wisdom book is attributed to Solomon. In some cases the titles refer to fictitious persons (Job, Jonah, Esther, or Judith), who are no indicators of an author but the name of the main character of the narrative. Of these an especially striking example is the book of Jonah, who was not only and simply a fictitious prophet, but rather the caricature or stereotype of a prophet in a stylized context of Babylonian history.[34] However, the titles of most prophetic

---

33. Cyrus the Great (about 600–530 B.C.) lived about two centuries after the historical Isaiah, usually dated to the eighth-century B.C.

34. The fact that in two gospels we read about Jesus speaking of Jonah (Mt 12:39–41, 16:4;

books refer to a real personality whose authentic preaching or writings are found in the book named after him, even if there is enough evidence suggesting later hands of disciples or editors.[35] A book may show vestiges of several layers of an extended editorial process, which literary and critical examination can detect to various degrees of probability when discovering gaps between textual units. Large sections of the Old Testament—including all historical books (Joshua, Judges, 1–2 Samuel, 1–2 Kings)—obtained their canonical status not because their author was claimed to be known, but rather because they contain long-held traditions about the history of the people of God between entering the land of Israel and their return from the Babylonian exile.

The term "hagiographer" (*hagiographus*), used in textbooks and magisterial documents, goes back to St. Jerome's Commentary on 1–2 Samuel,[36] which explains it with a reference to the Septuagint by distinguishing between prophets, who received revelation in form of visions, and hagiographers, whose intellect was enlightened without such visionary experiences. In neo-Scholastic textbooks, which keep a rigorous conceptual distinction between revelation and inspiration, the term "hagiographer" became technically to mean the human author of a biblical text regardless if he was a recipient of revelation.[37] The corresponding Latin expression *hagiographus* (or *auctor sacer*) appears in the original text of *Dei Verbum*,[38] where it means a recipient of *inspiration* or a human author of a biblical book. Obviously, if we continue a strict distinction between revelation and inspiration, while admitting a plurality of human authors, the term "hagiographer" may even stand for any person in

---

Lk 11:29–32) according to general Jewish beliefs, which listed him as a historic figure among the prophets of Israel, should not affect this conclusion. The literary genre of the book of Jonah intentionally depicts an unreal person whose fictive life story, however, implies important conclusions about the history of the Jews and their relationship to the Gentiles.

35. This is implied in the book of Jeremiah by its description of the role of Baruch and in the book of Isaiah by its references to postexilic events like the edict of Cyrus (Is 44:28, 45:1).

36. PL 28, 552A, 553A, 554A.

37. We are dealing here with transformations that St. Thomas's concept of inspiration underwent in the neo-Scholastic approach. In the latter inspiration and revelation were fully distinguished to the extent that a hagiographer could have been a biblical author who had no understanding of the revelatory content of his composition. Some authors writing about the Song of Songs meant exactly this: the book was originally a secular chain of wedding songs edited to become part of the Jewish scriptures.

38. Five times in *Dei Verbum*, once in no. 11 and four times in no. 12.

a chain of tradition. In this way, however, we might inadvertently reintroduce the neo-Scholastic idea of revelation to mean first and foremost conceptual knowledge and obscure the concept of revelation as *words and deeds*—that is, revelatory events. Such a tendency would again lead to the notion of inspiration as an artificial mental construct, built for the sake of a theological system, not characterizing truthfully the biblical word as we encounter it. In such a context, inspiration would begin to appear as an elusive concept, describing a mysterious divine action influencing a generic human author to write down some revealed material, regardless of what this material is all about. Inspiration would be easily called a "theologoumenon," or a mere product of theological abstraction, made up for the sake of describing how revealed truth became framed in human notions and propositional statements, regarded all along as a set of utterances by the divine author. The resulting view of inspiration would be false, not because of what it says but because of what it omits—namely, the soteriological context of revelation that gives it life and relevance.[39] If the notion of revelation loses the historical dimension of human existence, then it also becomes isolated from its biblical context and from the similarly historical nature of the incarnation— that is, from the process in which God, when becoming flesh, begins to speak and entrusts his speech to written medium. Since St. Jerome, the category of the hagiographer has been reshaped many times and has become largely unfit to describe the various activities of all human beings who contributed to put revelation into writing. If we want to liberate the theology of inspiration from superimposed concepts borrowed from antiquated elements of the discourse about prophecy, the best option might be to eliminate the term "hagiographer" altogether.

The expression *verus auctor* as it appears in *Dei Verbum* presupposes the modern concept of a writer—that is, a conscious and purposeful author who composes his text with awareness and independence. This understanding is what we usually project when dealing with literary works, past and present. The literary authors of the biblical books may remain anonymous, but they still take on an important and holy role when transmitting the word of God into written compositions. For

39. See the excellent analysis of the neo-Scholastic treatises about biblical inspiration in Gabel, *Inspirationsverständniss im Wandel*, 70–79.

most books of the Old Testament, modern biblical studies assume an extended period of incubation during which the tradition of God's people is shaped through some chosen persons' experiences, both individual and collective. Revelation received is transmitted in the form of oral traditions or preliminary compositions until the biblical books obtain their final form. "Inspiration" means the continued divine action that accompanies revelation by choosing, prompting, and guiding human beings to transmit, pronounce, and help preserve God's word in multifarious and repeated ways (see Heb 1:1), until it becomes a final text in fixed and consolidated documents.

God and the Human Authors Linked

A General Concept of Instrumentality

Prior to the neo-Scholastic systematization of the theology of inspiration, a variety of metaphors were used for illustrating the link between God and the human authors. These metaphors rarely expressed philosophical intent. Their purpose was usually rhetorical, aiming at visualizing the double provenance of the biblical books in opening paragraphs of treatises, sermons, or commentaries. In these texts, a bishop, an abbot, or a preacher tried to explain a text's divine provenance while analyzing its human—mainly literary—characteristics but, as a rule, without engaging in philosophical reflections about the way divine inspiration and human authorship are linked. Often by using antithetical terms about divine excellence and human imperfection, commentators or preachers simply projected a linear chain of causes and effects:

GOD → THE HUMAN AUTHOR → BIBLICAL TEXT

This model also appears, or is at least implied, in biblical texts when referring to some passages of the Bible. Here we quote a few examples:

"I spoke to you through Moses" (Jo 20:2).

"But neither he nor his servants nor the people of the land listened to the words of the LORD which he spoke through Jeremiah the prophet" (Jer 37:2).

When the LORD first spoke through Hosea, the LORD said to Hosea," (Hos 1:2)

"I spoke to the prophets; it was I who multiplied visions, and through the prophets gave parables" (Hos 12:10).

"No prophecy ever came by the impulse of man, but men moved by the Holy Spirit spoke from God" (2 Pt 1:21).

"Brethren, the scripture had to be fulfilled, which the Holy Spirit spoke beforehand by the mouth of David" (Acts 1:16).

"That he may send the Christ appointed for you, Jesus, whom heaven must receive until the time for establishing all that God spoke by the mouth of his holy prophets from of old" (Acts 3:20–21).

In this language the human author (often shown as a speaker) usually means one specific person whom God (also described as "speaking") employs so that the final (assumedly *written*) outcome would qualify as a word *spoken* by God. This *general concept* of the Bible as "God's word through human words" represents the unanimous teaching of the church fathers as it asserts its double provenance; the application of the philosophical concept of instrumental causality appears only later in the classical Thomistic tractates about prophecy with no references to the general category of biblical inspiration. In any case, the great Scholastic authors of the Middle Ages did not speak of the books of the New Testament (for example, of the gospels) as resulting from prophecy.

As a rule, ancient and medieval tradition was satisfied with illustrating the connection between divine and human authors in the form of metaphors (flute and flutist; writer and pen; scribe and dictation), of which none is either equivalent to a twofold literary authorship or implies the philosophical idea of instrumental causality. Modern authors recognize that the medieval Scholastic terminology about prophecy, when explaining the connection between God as the principal cause and the human author as a secondary (or instrumental) cause, offers a model in need of some "serious modifications."[40]

We must here repeat: Rahner's succinct critique of the neo-Thomistic concept of dual authorship is philosophically correct.[41] However, he does

---

40. See von Balthasar, *Thomas von Aquin*, 23:360–62. Although von Balthasar was inclined to agree with Pierre Benoit's neo-Thomistic treatises on inspiration, he warns against using this model without modifications (*starke Anpassungen*); ibid., 359–60.

41. "Under the same respect, an effect may come forth only from one cause" [Dasselbe Werk kann unter derselben Rücksicht nur einer Ursache entstammen]; Rahner, *Über die Schriftinspira-*

not clarify that layer of the theological tradition his criticism addresses. It may not apply so obviously to St. Thomas's texts, which refer to the ancient prophets mentioned in 2 Peter 2:21 as men *speaking* under the influence of the Spirit in an instrumental role. But in the neo-Scholastic theory of inspiration, this model is applied to *writers* (*scriptores sacri, auctores sacri*, or *hagiographi*) functioning as divinely employed instruments while retaining their normal mental faculties and freedom of will. In this way, the neo-Scholastic textbooks express an important and valid concern in one respect: they follow in the footsteps of Thomas by denying that biblical inspiration would have anything to do with the Hellenistic model of "mantic" inspiration. The latter was a theory about inspired speech widely accepted in antiquity, used to explain how at ancient pagan shrines gods and goddesses spoke through their priests and priestesses in response to questions posed by the pilgrims. According to this concept of Hellenistic prophecy, the spokespersons of the gods were thought of as taking a fully passive role, transmitting their message as if in some mystical rapture or drunken frenzy. In other words, the speaker, serving as an inspired instrument, has not necessarily appropriated the divine message. For ancient Christian writers, it was an apologetic concern to insist that the Christian Bible was not produced according to the model of mantic inspiration, an accusation that was revived in modern history of religions by the so-called *religionsgeschichtliche Schule* in its general effort to derive early Christian doctrines (the divinity of Jesus, the sacraments of initiation, the Eucharistic Banquet, "religious experience" as a definition of revelation) from Hellenistic sources. Due to such apologetic concerns, adherence to St. Thomas's theory of prophetic inspiration, and even its application (albeit in the context of an antiquated psychology) to describing the human

---

tion (Freiburg im Breisgau: Herder, 1958), 25; my translation. Rahner restates this argument on the same page and tries to formulate the issue in a very careful, ontologically argued formulation that becomes esoteric: "We do not say that the same work cannot have two literary authors (*zwei Verfasser*), a divine and a human; but we say: it is not possible that the origination (*Urheberschaft*) of these two causalities could establish the same literary authorship (*Verfasserschaft*) as its *a priori* goal from the same point of view and in the same dimension." He seems to remain, however, unsure if tradition indeed posits a double *literary* authorship in the sense of *Verfasserschaft* for scripture; he only excludes that this could mean "two causes for the same effect." On the previous page, he correctly explained that divine authorship in the sense of "transcendental causality" is not a satisfactory solution, either, because the authorship of the Bible must mean categorical causality within the framework of salvation history.

author's role, was well intended and correct in what it had denied. Yet, by the middle of the twentieth century the neo-Scholastic model of inspiration became alien to modern epistemology and psychology, concentrated all attention on the instrumentality of the human authors, and deflected attention from the objective side of inspiration—that is, the inspired text.

By the time of Vatican II, the textbook theology of inspiration became unusable mainly for the following five reasons: (1) its antiquated concept of revelation; (2) its full investment into a single-author model incompatible with modern biblical research; (3) its adherence to an outdated Aristotelian psychology and epistemology; (4) its neglect to deal adequately with the inspired text; and (5) a single-minded preoccupation with inerrancy as the *main consequence* of inspiration.

Nonetheless, it seems to me that the most important reason for this theology of inspiration to lose relevance and hit a dead-end was its insistence on a two-author model in the sense of two literary authors. In such framework it was inevitable to posit the two causes as being in rivalry with each other: God and man working simultaneously on the written expression of divine revelation, seen as comprehensive and all-encompassing "Sacred History," yet limited through the lenses of individual human authors, one author at a time, each trapped in his historically restricted authorial intent. Modern biblical studies could not deal with the tensions implied in this doctrine. Most importantly, this model became incompatible with a new vision of revelation according to which, under God's transcendental action, from the very beginning of history a universal salvation plan was unfolding. We must not forget that, at the same time, the historical-critical method came also to the conclusion that most biblical books took their origin with the participation of many authors and in combination with extended oral tradition and multiple redactions.

An overemphasis on God's role as a literary author, in combination with the seemingly liberating insight of the fundamental role of the literary genre and of the original author's intent, resulted in an unsolvable theological conundrum. God's authorial intent—the transcendental meaning of the scriptural text—either fell out of sight or became chained to a human author's authorial intent, within the confines of a single human being's consciousness. Due to its enthusiastic reception and liberating effect of *Divino Afflante*, as it promulgated a new era of Catholic exegesis, harvesting the importance of the literary genres, this problem growing out of an exclusive cultivation of the literal meaning was not even perceived. Yet, the encyclical has aggravated the problem when emphasizing both the priority of the literal meaning of the text and linking this meaning to the literary genre, determined by the human writer in his original text.[42] In this context, any encouragement to seek the true meaning of the text as one that transcends human limitations and comes from the Holy Spirit appeared as of little value. Searching both for the human author's intent and for a meaning that transcends human limitation appeared to be pursuing mutually contradictory goals.[43]

The traditional neo-Scholastic doctrine also lacked room for collective authorship. It was unable to integrate the activities of the inspired author or authors into the flow of an oral tradition involving a chain of several human preachers, writers, and editors. To those who understood the biblical texts as coming from such activities and authors, the neo-Scholastic theory of inspiration appeared to be an improbable construct. Exegetes could not apply it to the reality of the biblical text they were working with. By the second half of the twentieth century,

---

42. "In *Divino Afflante Spiritu* Pope Pius XII affirmed clearly the primacy of the literal sense 'The foremost and greatest endeavor of the interpreters should be to discern and define that sense of the biblical words which is called literal ... so that the minds of the author may be made abundantly clear'"; Raymond E. Brown, *The Critical Meaning of the Bible* (New York and Ramsay, N.J.: Paulist Press, 1981), 24.

43. The following quotation form *Divino Afflante* illustrates (after its first "but") an anxious minimalism about any spiritual sense of scripture, which modern Catholic theology began to explore as early as the 1950s: "Let Catholic exegetes then disclose and expound this spiritual significance, intended and ordained by God, with that care which the dignity of the divine word demands; *but* let them scrupulously refrain from proposing as the genuine meaning of Sacred Scripture other figurative senses. It may indeed be useful, especially in preaching, to illustrate, and present the matters of faith and morals by a broader use of the Sacred Text in the figurative sense, provided this be done *with moderation and restraint; it should, however, never be forgotten that this use of the Sacred Scripture is, as it were, extrinsic to it and accidental, and that, especially in these days, it is not free from danger*, since the faithful, in particular those who are well-informed in the sciences sacred and profane, wish to know what God has told us in the Sacred Letters rather than what *an ingenious orator or writer may suggest by a clever use* of the words of Scripture. Nor does 'the word of God' ... need artificial devices and human adaptation to move and impress souls; for the Sacred Pages, written under the inspiration of the Spirit of God, are of themselves rich *in original meaning* [all italics by me]; endowed with a divine power, they have their own value; adorned with heavenly beauty, they radiate of themselves light and splendor, provided they are so fully and accurately explained by the interpreter, that all the treasures of wisdom and prudence, therein contained are brought to light"; nos. 26–27.

the neo-Thomistic theory of inspiration appeared as a naive theological exercise with mistaken premises, oscillating between the absurd and the ethereal. Due to its abstract character it did not seem to offer insight into how the biblical text may be regarded as "the word of God, living and effective" (Heb 4:12). Such frustrations often led to harsh words rejecting the topic of inspiration altogether as a meaningless pursuit.[44]

In contemporary biblical studies one usually assumes that a single-author concept of inspiration is not applicable to any other biblical books than the authentic Pauline letters, of which, indeed, most exegetes assume to have been written by the apostle himself by hand or dictation (see Rom 16:22). In the precritical phase of biblical studies, many of the books of the Old Testament, especially those with a known literary author like Isaiah, Jeremiah, and Ezekiel, were believed to have come about in the same way. By now, however, the results of literary and critical studies are commonly admitted: most of the books of the Old Testament, including the books of the prophets previously mentioned, obtained their final shape through a longer process of development.

The linkage between divine and human provenance of the biblical books must be conceived in a way analogous to the mystery of the incarnation. Holy Scripture has God as its author, but not in mere reference to the *divine nature*. God is the divine author in personal terms—that is, in reference to the Holy Spirit. This means that in biblical inspiration the personal subject of the divine action is the Third Person of the Trinity, the same Person through whom the Word took flesh from the Virgin Mary, and who, according to the Nicene Creed, "spoke through the prophets." He has descended upon Jesus to anoint him as Messiah and moved him to begin his ministry (Mt 4:1; Mk 1:12). This same Spirit Jesus sent from the Father to enable the apostles to carry out their worldwide mission and to remain in the church as divine force of life and sanctification. The divine author of the scriptures is, therefore, not just *Deus Auctor*, but the Holy Spirit: the inspiration of the scriptures is specifically attributed to him.

Finally, a theory of biblical inspiration is satisfactory only if it builds a bridge from God as *Inspirator et Auctor* (no. 16 of *Dei Verbum*) to the

44. Gabel, *Inspirationsverständnis im Wandel*, with a summary about the insufficiencies of the neo-Scholastic theology of inspiration, on 56–85.

inspired texts. By this bridge inspiration not only touches *inspired human authors* but affects the final outcome of their activities: the *inspired texts*. These are no mere literary monuments to a tradition but the word of the living God resounding in the church with commanding authority and urgency. In its exclusive preoccupation with the linkage of the divine author and individual human authors, the neo-Scholastic theory applied a sophisticated but outdated Aristotelian-Thomistic psychology to show how inspiration affects the faculties of the hagiographer and results in the creation of a text that is fully divine and fully human and thus endowed with inerrancy. Yet this theory missed the target when it failed to provide a plausible explanation for the origin of the inspired texts through which the Spirit continues to *speak* to the churches. These texts stand in the center of the daily life and liturgy of Christians, enabling them "to hear what the Spirit says to the churches."[45] This is an aspect we need to further explore by widening the field of our inquiry.

Inspired Authors and Books

In addition to the concerns that have already been expressed by Rahner, Congar, Alonso Schökel and others and have, to a degree, influenced the text of *Dei Verbum*, the contemporary discussion about inspiration is still preoccupied with the double-authorship model: it tries to redefine inspiration as a particular kind of divine action that brings about written verbal expressions (speech, texts, and books) so that the resulting texts owe authorship equally to God and to certain human beings. This orientation has been weakened but not abandoned.[46]

When we began to speak about biblical inspiration by the Holy Spirit

---

45. Rev 2:7, 2:11, 2:17, 2:29, 3:6, 3:13, 3:22. This formula repeated in each of the seven letters is not an "anomaly" proper to the book of Revelation. Instead, since the letters are literary products rather than pieces of actual correspondence between an apostolic missionary and a group of local churches, they retrospectively explain the purpose and role of the inspired writings in the church as a continued speech of the incarnate and risen Christ; see Ugo Vanni, *Lectura del Apocalipsis: Hermeneutica, exegesis, teologia* (Estella: Verbo Divino, 2005), 156–60.

46. See Vawter, *Biblical Inspiration*. This well-researched and thoroughly post–Vatican II work by a fine biblical scholar shows in its last chapter ("Toward a Synthesis") how a contemporary author cannot help switching back and forth between the double-author model and the understanding of inspiration as a charism of a community. In my view the thesis of "God as literary author," in the sense of a strict analogy between God and a literary human author, creates an unsurpassable obstacle to building an acceptable synthesis of biblical inspiration.

received from the Father through the incarnate Son, we meant to show that the inspired human author is a participant of the trinitarian mystery from which all authentic speech about God and his deeds for man's salvation originates.[47] This kind of speech (and consequently writing) done in the Spirit is to be understood, although analogously, as God's word, yet quite differently from the way it used to be explained in the neo-Thomistic tractates. Properly and perfectly, the word of God—Λόγος τοῦ Θεοῦ— is Christ, who alone can claim the "fullness of the Spirit" as the fountain of his revelatory speech and salvific deeds. He alone, whom the Father has sent by anointing him with the fullness of the Spirit at the incarnation is, therefore, the *primum analogatum* and the prototype of all inspired messengers.[48] Yet even he, while fully divine from the first moment in the womb, gradually developed and grew in "wisdom and age and grace before God and man" (Lk 2:52). Similarly, all inspired verbal manifestations of God constitute an interrelated history that participates in the historical work of revelation of God's Logos through Christ, the God-Man. The manifestations of the Logos are linked in various ways and to different degrees through the historical stages of revelation. Thus the books documenting them appear in a historically linked chain of written expressions of the one single incarnation of God through his Son in the Spirit.

Ultimately, the dual (or double) authorship needs to be seen as analogous to the incarnation, the peak Christological event that was initiated by the Holy Spirit forming the humanity of Jesus from his Virgin Mother. The essential insight here is that speaking of God merely as author and a divine causality in an ontological sense may not point out with sufficient clarity that the inspiration of the scripures belongs to God's inner-worldly operation within salvation history, through which he became man and redeems the human race by uniting it to himself. In this salvific operation the incarnation is the central, constitutive event that makes God's advent into the world happen by creating for him a permanent abode among humankind (see Jn 1:14). The incarnate Word speaks

---

47. I am exploring inspiration from the same perspective that Matthew Levering proposed in his book *Participatory Exegesis: A Theology of Biblical Interpretation* (Notre Dame, Ind.: University of Notre Dame Press, 2008).

48. "The Spirit of the Lord is upon me, because he has anointed me to bring glad tidings to the poor. He has sent me to proclaim liberty to captives and recovery of sight to the blind, to let the oppressed go free, and to proclaim a year acceptable to the Lord"; Lk 4:18–19.

what he hears from the Father (Jn 8:26); the apostolic church teaches what it has heard from Jesus, while the Law and the Prophets provide an anticipatory and preparatory speech of the same Logos speaking within history: "Moses wrote of me" (Jn 5:46) and "before Abraham came to be I am" (Jn 8:58). The Fourth Gospel's theological vision does not only refer to revelation in general but specifically to the written depositories of divine speech; therefore it speaks not only of Moses and Abraham as individuals but of the Torah. In the synthesis of John's Gospel the ultimate Revealer is God the Father, the subject (content) of revelation is the Son, and the agent who enables the patriarchs, Moses, and the prophets to speak God's word is the Spirit—the same Spirit whom the risen Jesus breathes upon the eleven on the evening of the resurrection (Jn 20:22). Revelation flows through these channels to become speech and writing and eventually accumulates in a permanent dwelling place on earth: the canon of the holy scriptures, which owe their authority to the prophets and the apostles.

It is at this point that a renewed concept of the dual authorship must be inserted into the theology of inspiration and needs some initial reflection. After the First Vatican Council this concept had been explored in multiple ways; since, however, monographic research targeting individual church fathers' theology of inspiration was only sporadic and rarely put into a theological context, the riches of tradition were only superficially scanned, never explored in depth.[49] Nonetheless, even in the

---

49. Most of such research is antiquated and mostly of an apologetic nature, trying to justify the neo-Thomistic approach to inspiration. On the well-informed *New Advent* website, the following bibliography appears in the following format. It strikes the reader as a true exhibit of dinosaurs:

CATHOLIC WORKS.—FRANZELIN, Tractatus de divina traditione et scriptura (2nd ed., Rome, 1875), 321–405; SCHMID, De inspirationis bibliorum vi et ratione (Louvain, 1886); ZANECCHIA, Divina inspiratio Sacrae Scripturae (Rome, 1898); Scriptor Sacer (Rome, 1903); BILLOT, De inspiratione Sacrae Scripturae (Rome, 1903); CH. PESCH, De inspiratione Sacrae Scripturae (Freiburg im Br., 1906); LAGRANGE in Revue Biblique (Paris, 1895); HUMMELAUER, Exegetisches zur Inspirationsfrage (Freiburg im Br., 1904); FONCK, Der Kampf um die Warheit der heil. Schrift seit 25 Jahren (Innsburck, 1905); DAUSCH, Die Schriftinspiration (Freiburg im Br., 1891); HOLZHEY, Die Inspiration de heil: Schrift in der Anschauung des Mittelaters (Munich, 1895); CH. PESCH, Zur neuesten Geschichte der Katholischen Inspirationslehre (Freiburg im Br., 1902).

PROTESTANT WORKS.—GUSSEN, Theopneustic (2nd ed., Paris, 1842), tr. Plenary Inspiration of Holy Scripture; LEE, Inspiration of Holy Scripture (Dublin, 1854); ROHNERT, Die Inspiration, der heil. Schrift und ihre Bestreiter (Leipzig, 1889); SANDAY, The oracles of

neo-Scholastic textbooks, the discussions about God's authorship of the
Bible, the human authors' true and fully authentic role as authors, and
the various explanations of the connections between God's authorship
and the human authors have always been accompanied with references
to the patristic tradition to show in episodic illustrations how both God
and men, through a particular kind of connectedness, made scripture
become what it is believed to be in the church: God's word in human
words.

Traditional textbooks treated biblical inspiration as *charisma*—that
is, special grace (*gratia gratis data*) offered to individuals chosen to be authors of biblical documents, prompting them to write as free agents (*veri
auctores*, in *Dei Verbum*, no. 11) for transmitting what they had received.
The neo-Scholastic textbooks of the late nineteenth and twentieth centuries concentrated on the subjective side of inspiration that reached an
individual human as a personal grace granted to benefit others. Through
this approach the objective aspects of inspiration were only selectively
covered with obvious preoccupation about inerrancy as inspiration's
chief effect. It was hard to prevent this perspective of biblical inspiration
from collapsing into a "truth-telling mechanism" in service of recording
without error the content of revelation. Unfortunately, *Dei Verbum* has
not fully succeeded in leaving behind this outlook, only adding a stronger soteriological emphasis when speaking about the truth of the text as
revelation put into writing "for the purpose of salvation" in the framework of the divine economy. But the conciliar document was not able
to fully explore the church's theological tradition about the riches of the
inspired text.

To further engage in this issue, we need to introduce here the explicit conceptual distinction between "subjective" and "objective" inspiration—that is, between the inspiration of the authors and that of the

---

God (London, 1891); FARRAR, The Bible, Its meaning and Supremacy (London, 1897); His-
tory of Interpretation (London 1886); A Clerical Symposium on Inspiration (London, 1884);
RABAUD, Histoire de la doctrine de l'inspiration dans les pays de langue francaise depuis la
Réforme jusqu'à nos jours (Paris, 1883).

The importance attributed to our topic in the nineteenth century is remarkable, as is the
sweeping scope of the individual books, which, however, never focused on one particular church
father for exploring one person's thinking on this matter in the context of his general theological
thought.

texts. An important reason for proposing this distinction comes from the evidence that church fathers spoke much more frequently about inspired scriptures than about inspired authors. Although this distinction casts no doubt that divine inspiration reaches the text through the human authors, it may be helpful to see how focusing on objective inspiration—that is, the sacred character of the texts—will provide a useful reminder of what the result of the charism of of inspiration achieves: through the inspired text, the church obtains permanent direct access to God's ongoing speech.

It is worth noticing that the only passage of the New Testament that in English translation cannot avoid using the verb "inspire" is 2 Tm 3:16. That verse, however, speaks of inspired texts and not of inspired authors:

All scripture is *inspired* by God (πᾶσα γραφὴ θεόπνευτος) and is useful for teaching, for refutation, for correction, and for training in righteousness, so that one who belongs to God may be competent, equipped for every good work. (2 Tm 3:16–17)

Much ink has been wasted on analyzing the meaning of the Greek participle θεόπνευτος by various grammatical comments and parallels. Today, an almost unanimous opinion translates it as a passive participle, indicating God (the divine Spirit) as the *subject* of the action and not the direct object. The passage refers to all scriptures (of the Old Testament) as "divinely inspired" or "breathed by divine [Spirit]" (rather than "breathing God,") although the great Origen and others rightly suggested that scriptures transmit a "divine breath" or, with an active verb, they "breathe God."[50] Yet the effort of expanding the field of inquiry is helpful as we reflect on the exegetical history of 2 Tm 3:16. For, regardless of how θεόπνευτος was understood, this verse speaks of all *scriptural texts* and not their authors. The larger scriptural context is then the following: all texts (of the Old Testament) take their origin from God's life-giving breath, the same kind of divine action by which he created the world (Gn 1:2) and the first human being (see Gn 2:7), raised Jesus from the dead (see Rom 1:4, 8:11), shares with all believers the gifts of redemption, and pours on them forgiveness and sanctification that will lead man to the resurrection of the body on the last day.

---

50. See G. W. H. Lampe, *A Greek Patristic Lexicon* (Oxford: Clarendon, 1961), 1:630.

Linking Revelation and Canon

The passage 2 Tm 3:16, referring to texts inspired by the Spirit, confirms that biblical inspiration is a process that does not stop at the human authors. God wants his word to be put in writing so that the written text γραφή may become available to those for whose sake he had set the process of revelation into motion. Therefore, just as inspiration belongs to the context of revelation, it opens the process of *canonization*, by which the scriptural texts obtain recognition by the church as divinely inspired. The process of inspiration necessarily continues through the formation of the canon. The inspired books become permanently enshrined in the church, the *locus* where the Word can become and can function (also) as scripture, when it is transmitted in conscious and secure ways for building up and nourishing God's people. In the same way in which revelation and inspiration are part of a salvation-historical continuum, inspiration and canonization are also inseparably united. Historically, they may not even be fully distinguishable. We can speak of them separately and examine them as two phases brought about in different developments, but only because we see them in hindsight as successive yet interconnected stages, through which God's gifts are granted and passed on to benefit his people.

The aforementioned considerations reveal their importance when we begin to deal with specific biblical texts. In many passages communicating God's words we find repetitious introductory phrases like "Thus says the Lord ...," or "And Jesus said in reply ...," which are revelatory prequels continued by inspirational sequels. In these scriptural texts a third process is also anticipated. When words and deeds of divine provenance are recognized as such, they are shown to be endowed with divine *auctoritas* (meaning both *authority* and *authorship*). As we have emphasized, in revealing himself God both acts and speaks. Therefore, his self-expression in the speech of Jesus or the Prophets and the Apostles constitutes an ongoing verbal commentary on sacred history. The outline offered here does not intend to alter, but rather to extend and consistently apply the vision of *Dei Verbum* about revelation, inspiration, and the formation of the canon as a finite but unbroken continuum. When pointing out these three steps, revelation/inspiration/canon, we intend to complete the synthesis of *Dei Verbum* by showing how to make a definite break with the neo-Thomistic system that *Dei Verbum* mostly ignored by silence but hesitated to reject. By following this outline, we may even make a few additional steps ahead in the direction of integrating the theology of the canon into a combined theology of revelation and biblical inspiration.

In our perspective, God will be shown as an *auctor* but as unlike any human literary author who wrote or redacted biblical texts. By now, all human authors of the Bible are dead; even if they were admired and talked about while on earth, they do not stand in the focus of the believers who read their writings. No matter how much I am interested in what Jeremiah, Isaiah, or Moses had in mind, I listen incomparably more to the *divine author* of the scriptures who is neither dead nor silent. To apply some phrases by Jesus, when scripture is being read we must listen to someone greater than Solomon; we read about something greater than the Temple (Mt 12:6) and somebody greater than Jonah (Mt 12:41–42 = Lk 11:31–32)—namely, the One "about whom Moses wrote in the Law" (Jn 1:45) and was promised to be sent after him as one like him (see Dt 18:18), but also revealed to be infinitely greater than Moses to address us anew so that we might hear with guaranteed authenticity, "Thus says the Lord." Reflecting on the inspired text in this way makes the theology of inspiration reveal a dimension that the notion of God as (literary) author of scripture is unable to penetrate. For we read:

Indeed, the word of God is *living and active*, sharper than any two-edged sword, piercing until it divides soul from spirit, joints from marrow; it is able to judge the thoughts and intentions of the heart. (Heb 4:12)

When the inspired word is delivered by its canonical reading in the church and is received with faith or in search of faith by the listeners, and then is being interpreted in *the same Spirit* whose inspiration once prompted the human authors to write, the living God addresses human beings who hear him. He does not write, *he speaks*. Such readings entail encounters with God, Speaker, and Revealer transcending time and thus providing the written text its actuality. We understand here the profound wisdom of the ancient interpretation of Psalm 61:12 in the Vulgate, echoed succinctly in a sermon by St. Bernard of Clairvaux:

Semel locutus est Deus. Semel utique quia semper. Una enim et non interpolata sed continua et perpetua locutio est.

[God spoke once, only once because always: for He is one single, uninterrupted, and eternal speech.][51]

51. St. Bernard of Clairvaux, *Sermones de diversis* 5.2; Jean Leclercq and Henri Rochais, eds., *Sancti Bernardi Opera Omnia* VI.1 (Rome: Editiones Cistercienses, 1970), 99. Bernard's text depends on St. Augustine [*Enarr. in Ps* 44 (Patrologia Latina 36, 497)] who, in his peculiar style, adds, "*Dicere Dei aeternum est*" [God's speech is eternal].

3 ✝ INSPIRATION AND INCARNATION

The Analogy Affirmed

Both *Dei Verbum* and Pope Benedict XVI's Postsynodal Exhortation *Verbum Domini* contain some weighty reflections connecting biblical inspiration with the mystery of the incarnation. In *Dei Verbum* we read:

In Sacred Scripture, therefore, while the truth and holiness of God always remains intact, the marvelous "condescension" of eternal wisdom is clearly shown, "that we may learn the gentle kindness of God, which words cannot express, and how far He has gone in adapting His language with thoughtful concern for our weak human nature."[1] For the words of God, expressed in human language, have been made like human discourse, just as the Word of the eternal Father, when He took to Himself the flesh of human weakness, was in every way made like men. (no. 13)

Central here is the reference to divine condescension, pointing out what makes the inspiration of the scriptures resemble the incarnation. As in the incarnation, God assumes a human nature so that he might be seen, heard, touched, listened to (that is, he might become an object of human experience), so in the inspiration of the scriptures, God accommodates himself to man in terms of human language. With a similar

---

1. In a footnote, the document refers to a text of St. John Chrysostom, *In Gen* 3:8, Sermon 17.1 (Patrologia Graeca 53, 134). This reference to divine condescension was already mentioned in *Divino Afflante* (no. 37, fn. 32), but four different passages of John Chrysostom are cited there.

intent, Pope Benedict XVI makes a direct comparison between inspiration and the incarnation:

The word of God is thus expressed in human words thanks to the working of the Holy Spirit. The missions of the Son and the Holy Spirit are inseparable and constitute a single economy of salvation. The same Spirit who acts in the incarnation of the Word in the womb of the Virgin Mary is the Spirit who guides Jesus throughout his mission and is promised to the disciples. The same Spirit who spoke through the prophets sustains and inspires the Church in her task of proclaiming the word of God and in the preaching of the Apostles; finally, it is this Spirit who inspires the authors of sacred Scripture.

At first sight what links inspiration and the incarnation is the sameness of the Spirit who brings about both; but at a deeper level we discover the reference to "a single economy of salvation" that the Holy Spirit holds together in its unity. The incarnation is the center of the work of salvation from which all means of redemption and sanctification obtain their meaning and efficacy.

Both *Dei Verbum* and *Verbum Domini* are modern applications of an ancient patristic theology of scripture, still awaiting full resuscitation. Several major figures of the preconciliar, patristic renewal were aware that the church fathers viewed the scriptures and their origin (revelation and inspiration) with this Christological parallel in mind. Hugo Rahner was probably the first to coin the German term *Schriftwerdung* to express the origin of the scriptures, in imitation of the German word *Menschwerdung* (incarnation as "becoming man").[2] By this Hugo Rahner suggests that, just as the Nicene Creed states that "the Word became man," we may say that "God became Scripture." This German term was taken over, although with some caution, by others, including Hans Urs von Balthasar. Other Catholic theologians like de Lubac, following in the footsteps of Origen, used a more nuanced term as he spoke of the various "enfleshments" (in French: *incorporations*) of the (Divine) Word. A prominent place among these "enfleshments" is assigned to scripture, in which the human and divine components (the letter and the Spirit)

---

2. Hugo Rahner, "Das Menschenbild des Origenes," *Eranos Jahrbuch* 15, no 47 (1947): 197–248. In the works of Hans Urs von Balthasar, Martin Hengel, Joseph Ratzinger, and others, it became a theological *terminus technicus*.

reflect the human and divine natures of Christ.[3] Such use of an incarnational language remained frequent in the Middle Ages.[4] In *Verbum Domini*, Pope Benedict XVI quotes St. Bernard's analogy between holy scripture and God's word incarnate in order to demonstrate that Christianity is not a "religion of the book" but is based on God's word, accessible in scriptures as living and personal:

All this helps us to see that, while in the church we greatly venerate the sacred scriptures, the Christian faith is not a religion of the book: Christianity is the "religion of the word of God," not of "a written and mute word, but of the incarnate and living Word."[5] Consequently the scripture is to be proclaimed, heard, read, received, and experienced as the word of God, in the stream of the apostolic tradition from which it is inseparable.[6]

This thought and language, although abundantly present in patristics and medieval theology (including the great Scholastic doctors Thomas and Bonaventure),[7] has faded from Catholic theology in more recent times. In the postwar renewal of patristic exegesis, a rehabilitation of Origen's biblical thought took place, with especially abundant participation by de Lubac.[8] Unfortunately, this movement did not gain lasting approval among many biblical exegetes who could not bridge the epistemolog-

3. With sensitivity for linguistic nuances and for the sake of emphasizing that there is but one incarnation, Henri de Lubac wrote a chapter under the title "Les incorporations du Logos" about Origen's doctrine of the analogies of the incarnation in the divine economy: de Lubac, *Histoire et Esprit: L'intelligence de l'écriture d'après Origène* (Paris: Aubier, 1950), 336.

4. See chap. 4, sect. 2, "L'analogie entre la parole biblique et le Verbe Incarné," in Farkasfalvy, *L'inspiration de l'Écriture Sainte dans la théologie de de saint Bernard*, 100–105.

5. This is a quotation from St. Bernard's *In laudibus Virginis Matris* (*Homiliae super "Missus est"*) IV.2, in Leclercq and Rochais, *Sancti Bernardi Opera Omnia*, IV.57.

6. *Dei Verbum*, no. 10.

7. Finding in St. Bonaventure's *Incendium* a similar concept, Mario Masini coins the term "inverbation" (of the Logos), distinguishing this from the *incarnation*; see *Lectio Divina: An Ancient Prayer That Is Ever New*, trans. Edmund C. Lane (New York: Alba House, 1998), 7. I obtained this reference from an unpublished lecture of Nathan Lefler.

8. With a compact survey of the last sixty years of Origenian literature, Peter W. Martens, in his *Origen and Scripture: The Contours of the Exegetical Life* (Oxford: Oxford University Press, 2012), reconstructs his portrait as a biblical exegete and narrates Origen's career with many references and a rich bibliography that illustrates the diverse reception of his legacy for ancient and modern students of the Bible. I speak here of a "rehabilitation" of Origen in the sense Henri de Lubac attempted it, mostly in his *Histoire et esprit*, vindicating him as a churchman and an authentic witness to the apostolic tradition, whose thought has in fact impacted all branches of patristic and medieval exegesis.

ical gap between their historical-critical standards and the spiritual exegesis advocated by the great church father of Alexandria. The exegetes suspected him of Platonism and of an alleged dependency on Philo; but, in truth, they found his thought irreconcilable with that of historical positivism, which held—and still holds—large domains of biblical research under its spell.[9]

Although Vatican II was followed among Catholic authors by diminishing interest in the theology of inspiration,[10] the analogy between scripture and the incarnate Word remained in use and continued to be seen as an important heuristic tool.[11] However, for a meaningful use of this tool, we first need to express in precise terms the doctrine of the incarnation, based on correct philosophical premises in reference to man's entire religious history. Orthodox Christology must view the whole of salvation history as an extension of Christ's salvific work, beginning with the creation of the first Adam, including the resurrection of Christ, and continuing all the way up to man's eschatological rebirth, to be achieved in the resurrection of our bodies on the last day.

The Christological Context

The precise understanding of the term "incarnation" is extremely important. In the strictest sense, it refers to a point-wise defined, historical event: the virginal conception of Jesus in the womb of Mary at the moment the individual human life of Jesus begins, with his ontological mode of exis-

---

9. In my essay "The Pontifical Biblical Commission's Document on Jews and Christians and Their Scriptures: Attempt of an Evaluation," *Communio* 29 (2002): 716–37, I pointed out how, in a collective document, distinguished Catholic biblical scholars remained inflexible in expressing a wholesale rejection of Origen's spiritual exegesis, as if the patristic renewal and its early alliance with the biblical renewal had never existed.

10. This diminishment of interest was no direct result of the Council but signaled a questionable sense of freedom with which Catholic exegesis embraced previously popularized non-Catholic trends. These are well characterized by a pair of brothers, both Protestant exegetes, writing, "The ancient theory of the inspiration and inerrancy of the Bible not only is impossible for intelligent people today, but represents a deviation in Christian doctrine, whatever salutary uses may have been made of it in the past by the Holy Spirit, who often turns human errors to good ends"; Anthony Hanson and Richard Hanson, *A Reasonable Belief: A Survey of the Christian Faith* (Oxford: Oxford University Press, 1980), 42, quoted by Collins, "Inspiration," 1033.

11. See the evaluation of Alonso Schökel's work in context of the postconciliar literature on inspiration in Gabel, *Inspirationsverständnis im Wandel*, 173–81.

tence being subsistence in the divine nature of the Son of God. This beginning is both ultimately and immediately caused by God alone through the creative force of the Holy Spirit. Christian faith regards this event at once in continuity and discontinuity with the human history that precedes it. Its continuity with the history of the human race is guaranteed by Mary, a member of the human race and a child of two parents by physical descent. However, her sinlessness and virginal conception constitute discontinuity. The virginal conception points with sharp precision to the locus of a direct divine intervention in human history. The beginning of a temporal existence for Jesus' individual human nature begins at a given moment of time and space; it apparently fits so seamlessly into history that at first nobody, for a while not even Joseph, notices it. Nevertheless, this is the very moment in which God's fundamental intervention into history in terms of his *personal advent* takes place in the most radical sense of the word.

For a human being, beginning always implies a clear-cut first moment of existence, followed by growth and development. Thus, the individual humanity of Jesus was inserted into the world abruptly; not in its fully developed form, yet as though it were clear ontological novelty (a sudden "new creation"). Nonetheless, like any other human being, Jesus' human nature developed gradually; both body and soul underwent a continued process of *becoming* by unfolding their faculties and establishing their relationships to the rest of the world according to the dynamics of human existence. While this individual human nature as a physical being was subject to development as was any other "fruit of a mother's womb," Jesus ontologically subsisted from his first moment of existence in the divine *esse*.

But in this sense of "growth and development," the incarnation of the Word is a process that has a temporal dimension from a prenatal phase to birth, to childhood, then adolescence, and finally full human maturity. Such a process must be seen as fully immersed in the created world's physical and social texture. The incarnation is, therefore, more than one single event of God's arrival into the world because the first moment of conception was followed by interactions with the world in various circumstances.[12] For Jesus himself, conception and birth were

---

12. Those Marcionite and Gnostic tendencies that, in the second century, eliminated the infancy narratives of both Matthew and Luke tried to picture the arrival of the Logos to the world as

the beginning of a chain of human experiences in interaction with a fallen world in its postlapsarian condition of mortality. Thus, as a process, the incarnation is, in the true sense of the word, *Menschwerdung*, a "becoming," in the way it is described by Paul in Philippians 2:7–11: a journey from birth to death, not just to any kind of death but death by crucifixion, and then further, a journey continued beyond death.

The incarnation's ultimate goal and meaning are revealed at Jesus' resurrection, which is again an instantaneous change, at which his human nature reaches fully new status. At this point, Jesus enters onto a superhuman stage where the Son begins to fully experience his divine personhood and consubstantiality (identity in nature) with God the Father *in his human nature*. The incarnation as a journey leads to this arrival in the kingdom at which the incarnate Son is finally constituted in fullness, so that his human condition is fully elevated to divine glory by the Holy Spirit (see Rom 1:4). This is not just the last occurrence in a long sequence of events, but an instantaneous becoming; it constitutes the summary and glorification of his entire human becoming. Jesus' whole humanity reaches a state of perfection at this arrival to God. Now the totality of Jesus' created human nature experiences the Son's consubstantiality with the Father and the Holy Spirit. Jesus' whole humanity is transferred, with all its parts, into this experience, by which his finite, historically fragmented human life is summarized and in this final state crowns the created cosmos in an anticipation of the eschatological endpoint. This is the true τέλος both as goal and final fulfillment, a total and comprehensive introduction of Jesus' human existence into eternity, which was first laid out in a successive temporal sequence on earth but is now, in the resurrection, introduced at once, in terms of eternal actuality, into the Father's glory. The same view is implied by Jesus' last word in John's Gospel: τετέλεσται, "it has been consummated" (Jn 19:30).

Therefore, in the full sense of the word, "incarnation" means Christ in his incarnate and risen state, achieved when his human nature, with body and soul, reaches perfection and is elevated into permanent discontinuity with the web of inner-worldly causes and effects that previously held him captive (*iam non moritur, mors illi non ultra dominabi-*

---

a sudden descent. Marcion's Gospel began with the sentence "Jesus then went down to Capernaum, a town of Galilee"; compare Lk 4:31.

tur).[13] At the same time, he is established into a new set of relationships of transcendental causality with the world he had redeemed. Having left behind a mortal and postlapsarian condition, Jesus channels and distributes all divine graces from the Father through the Holy Spirit and thereby effectively causes the redemption and sanctification of all people throughout all times. This means that by his humanity, the incarnate and risen Christ becomes also present, always and everywhere, in human history, to all persons who, through acts of faith, respond to God's manifestations in the world. This is the full meaning of John's Prologue about the Logos:

All things came to be through him, and without him nothing came to be. What came to be through him was life, and this life was the light of the human race; the light shines in the darkness, and the darkness has not overcome it. (Jn 1:3–5)

Inspiration, as a charism provided for those who contributed to creating the scriptures, is linked to the incarnate and risen Christ in several ways. First, as a God-given gift, this charism is effectively mediated by Christ. Moreover, in the Old Testament this charism allows "Moses and the Prophets" (compare Lk 16:29–31; Acts 28:23) to anticipate the event of the incarnation, as they, endowed with this charism by the Holy Spirit, post signs in the scriptures about the Lord's approaching advent into the world. God begins, in fact, the process of his coming through events and words, which are included in biblical texts and books to recall, memorialize, and explain the events of salvation history. Similar is the process that brings about written testimonies for the proclamation of God's word in the New Testament: in the community constituted through the incarnate Son's first disciples, revelation followed by inspiration channels the memory of the incarnation into the post-resurrection era of the church, in which word and sacrament obtain full meaning and efficacy through the presence and efficacy of the risen Christ. Thus, inspiration as a divine action in the Old Testament prepares and anticipates the incarnation, while, in the New Testament, God's culminating acts of salvation in Christ also become verbally deposited, memorialized, and enshrined in written documents.

13. I quote the shining translation of the Latin Vulgate. In the New American Bible: "Christ, raised from the dead, dies no more; death no longer has power over him" (Rom 6:9).

Scripture, produced by divine inspiration (inspired texts written by inspired writers) has a structure that the church fathers handled as realities reflecting the divine/human structure of the incarnate Word. As a literary product, scripture is fully human, but with respect to its meaning it both contains and manifests (veils and reveals) divine mysteries. To understand the analogy between the incarnate Christ and the scriptural text, one needs to operate with an orthodox Christology that equally avoids Nestorianism and Monophysitism.[14] Following the tendency of either of these heretical Christologies would bring the danger of collapsing scriptures into a one-layer reality: either by identifying it with the literal meaning, identified with the human authors' historically verifiable intent (the Nestorian option) or with the spiritual meaning that transmits divine meaning without true human (incarnate) mediation (the Monophysite approach). These Nestorian and Monophysite interpretations are not only antithetical, but, curiously, they also both resemble and project simplistic schemes of inspiration in which the human and divine components stand in mutual rivalry and tend to reduce or eliminate each other. Biblical Nestorianism and Monophysitism are frequently practiced. Biblical Nestorianism considers the human surface of the Bible as if its full meaning had been *adequately expressed* in historically and culturally conditioned terms. Nestorian interpretation erects stumbling blocks from self-contradictory concepts and philosophically incomplete or anthropomorphic paradigms. It reduces God's word to a time-bound human message. In such perspective, Jesus' critical words addressing the Pharisees are verified: "You search the scriptures because you think that in them you have eternal life; and it is they that testify on my behalf, but you refuse to come to me to have life" (Jn 5:39–40). Biblical Monophysitism, on the other hand, would result in bypassing the critical method and embracing every hint to the miraculous while explaining away any feature that, in a divine utterance, reflects human limitation. Monophysite exegesis leads to the denial of the principle of gradual growth and development in revelation, exactly because of eliminating the presence of human imperfection in both the events and the texts.

Christological orthodoxy guides the church to abstain from meth-

14. See Louis Bouyer, "Où en est le mouvement biblique?," *Bible et vie chrétienne* 13 (1956): 7–21.

odologies that dissolve the texts into their grammatical, historical, and literary components. Such methodologies frustrate exegesis by eliminating purpose and meaning that keep together the textual units in each book and the scriptural books in one canon. The incarnational model affirms that the Bible's ultimate meaning is the mystery of Christ, the Logos, as the single speech-act of God coming into the world to inhabit it in the course of salvation history. An integral Christian theology of inspiration, therefore, presupposes belief in the Word become man in Jesus, as the one "born of a woman at the fullness of time" (Gal 4:4), truly raised to life so that death no longer has power over him but makes him live for God (see Rom 6:9–10), and all who are "in Christ" may also receive that life which the Word incarnate mediates, by empowering the believers to become God's children (see Jn 1:12).

The incarnational model of biblical inspiration does not exclude other complementary (linguistic, historical, and critical) approaches. More importantly, this model provides three additional links to other theological disciplines.

First, we mention the link to trinitarian theology: God's revelation through his Son is expressed in written words through the Spirit. Second, the whole economy of salvation belongs to one single process; thus, the Bible includes Old and New Testaments, the "Prophets and the Apostles," on account of the same Spirit who "spoke through the Prophets" (*qui locutus est per Prophetas*) and descended upon the apostles on Pentecost. Third, this model of inspiration presupposes the canonical unity of the Bible.

Furthermore, the unity of the two testaments—that is, the oneness of the Christian canon fundamentally affects the reading and interpretation of the Bible in two ways. First, the revelatory context of inspiration demands that the Bible be read within the canon, the outcome of the process that consolidated the church as God's last eschatological convocation, establishing his people of the end times.

Second, the canonical scriptures are an integral part of the church's sacramental manifestations—that is, in visible/audible/tangible signs, which in the Eucharist nourish the faithful through Christ's ongoing presence. Liturgy also consists of words and deeds, transmitting the words and deeds of salvation history. In the way the Spirit extends the presence of the gloriously exalted Christ in the sacraments, so also does the inspired text transmit its revelatory content to the believing reader who can access through it—privately or in community—God's word in the Spirit. By church law no sacrament or sacramental sign is administered in the church without reading the scriptures, and, in general, the prayer life of the church is imbued by an abundant use of scriptural texts both in private and in community.

4 ✝ PURSUING THE ANALOGY

Revelation's Written Transmission and the Analogies of Inspiration

God does not take up a pen or pencil to write, nor does he choose a language or an alphabet to bring his thoughts and precepts to verbal expression. God inspires human beings to speak and write. In the nineteenth century two rival schools of thought surfaced: one for *Inspiratio Realis*, the other for *Inspiratio Verbalis*.[1] The former promoted the idea that divine authorship determined the content, while the latter attributed to God the verbal formulation of the texts. The *Magisterium* did not intervene, but a majority of twentieth-century Catholic theologians held that there was no valid way of exempting the texts themselves (as distinguished from their meaning) from being the product of divine inspiration.[2] *Dei Verbum* gives no room for a theory of inspiration that would not regard the biblical text as also inspired. Therefore, if biblical inspiration means *revelation continued by becoming expressed in writing*,

1. The dispute about verbal vs. real inspiration goes back to theological controversies between Thomists and Molinists, who represented the Dominican schools of theology vs. those of the Jesuits, respectively. The thesis of verbal inspiration claimed that God determined not only the content but also the verbal expression of revealed truth in the Bible, while real inspiration maintained that the words of the Bible were merely the products of the human authors. With neo-Thomism obtaining official approval from Leo XIII, the thesis of real inspiration lost supporters and ground. The last forceful supporter of real inspiration was the Jesuit Franzelin, the chief theologian of Vatican I under Pius IX.

2. The interpretation we gave to 2 Tm 3:16 also confirms the concept of inspired texts: "All scripture is inspired by God and is useful for teaching, for reproof, for correction, and for training in righteousness."

and if revelation means both events and speech, then the process that extends revelation into a verbal and written medium is a complex reality that does not stop at a mere internal enlightenment of the mind and the prompting of the will of the human author but impacts texts and books they produce, so that these become pregnant with divine meaning. The process by which inspired books come about is not univocally the same in all instances, but only analogously. In other words, the concept of biblical inspiration includes a certain diversity of internal and external human processes. They are denoted by the same concepts and words but understood analogously.

First, biblical inspiration applies analogously to the Old and the New Testaments, which are different expressions of God's one divine economy. In the Old Testament we are dealing with a history of salvation that developed around the patriarchs and Moses, followed by kings and prophets, who then led the people of Israel down a path that was destined to carry out God's still hidden salvific will on behalf of all humankind. In their limited perspective, centering first and foremost on Israel's salvation, the writers of the Old Testament are always postulating a further future fulfillment of God's concern about the salvation of all. Since the explicit context is almost always exclusively the salvation of Israel, essential aspects remain shrouded in mystery. The one who speaks to (and through) Abraham or Moses and the prophets is truly the one and only God; his word is a firm foundation on which faith can rely: "Yes, I have spoken, I will accomplish it; I have planned it, and I will do it" (Is 46:11). Nonetheless, the word of God means here both action to take place in the future and a written testimony guaranteeing or even testifying that divine action has already begun, for it is "a work in course." The last book of the Christian canon, the book of Revelation, speaks of God as "the one who is and who was and who is to come" (Rv 1:4–8, 4:8), indicating in this way an eschatological destination that is to happen in radical newness beyond Jesus' birth, crucifixion, and resurrection, although the "Christ event" has already happened at the fullness of time (Gal 4:4; Eph 1:10; Col 1:19, 2:9). Christ's coming points to a further fullness to be revealed in a dynamic sense "from grace to grace" (Jn 1:16; compare Eph 3:19). This radical difference between the two testaments indicates for the concept of inspiration a further diversification of the ways in which God provides written records of his speech to his people already through diverse literary forms (narratives, poems, reflections, prayers).

Inspiration as the process through which God speaks in human words cannot be adequately defined by a psychological reconstruction of interactions and links between the divine and human authors. Speaking of divine-human interaction, we refer here to a valid but per se much too wide and broad concept. Specifically, the process that leads to the production of biblical books includes also the omnipresent, divine providence watching over salvation history through its subsequent phases, in which both Israel and the nascent church undergo both inculturation and alienation by external, even fully foreign, influences, including various countercultural movements. Biblical studies have shown that biblical texts come about after oral phases: once traditions have been formed they are further shaped when transmitted; they coexist until they are ready to merge by being redacted into fixed texts.[3] The process by which revelation becomes incorporated into books seems to be riddled with mysteries of divine interventions as well as unexplored turns of human history that may not be mysteries per se, yet remain inaccessible due to the very nature of man's historical existence and epistemological limits.[4]

The contemporary concept of inspiration that *Dei Verbum* supports did not end the theology of inspiration, as Oswald Loretz had anticipated after Vatican II.[5] Admittedly, the rebirth of interest in the theology of biblical inspiration after the Council was slow. In the first two decades after Vatican II, a vacuum of interest appeared to be a silent vote in approval of Loretz's thesis that *Inspirationstheologie* was indeed dead. Yet a realization came about that this vacuum can be filled, but only through a slow process of critiquing, evaluating, and eventually completing *Dei Verbum*. The importance of Joseph Ratzinger's influence, first as theolo-

3. See, for example, the evidence that biblical scholarship uncovers vestiges of parallel traditions in the Pentateuch or in the synoptic and Johannine material. Such understanding of the biblical books' genesis is quite compatible with the concept of inspiration presented here.

4. The history of criminal justice has many examples showing that, even with plenty of available eyewitnesses, the reconstruction of events, no matter how much recent, is beyond human limitations.

5. Oswald Loretz, *Das Ende der Inspirationstheologie: Chancen eines Neubeginns*, vols. 1 and 2 (Stuttgart: Katholisches Bibelwerk, 1974–76).

gian, then as bishop and cardinal under John Paul II and finally as pope, cannot be exaggerated. Besides his numerous publications on *Dei Verbum*,[6] his Apostolic Exhortation *Verbum Domini* represents his greatest effort to promote the reception of *Dei Verbum* in both doctrine and pastoral practice.

As mentioned previously, biblical inspiration should be studied in two complementary ways. First, one explores (both historically and theologically) the human consciousness of the recipients and transmitters of revelation *in whom and through whom* as authors God's word eventually obtains written expression. Second, one approaches the inspired books within the history of God's people (Israel and the church) as they are formed to become signs of communication with God, posted with divine authority to provide written documentation of what God had revealed. The first explores subjective processes, while the second focuses on their objective outcome: the inspired books. Here again, the concept of inspiration is understood as analogous and not univocal.

The concept and language of inspiration, which we examined in the previous chapters, have largely been formulated and transmitted through a long chain of patristic and medieval writers. In subsequent centuries, under the pressure of the rationalists' biblical criticism, Christian theologians developed a long-lasting and mostly defensive war, with the eventual result that they distanced themselves from a number of traditional ideas. It may be enough to list a few: the Mosaic authorship of the Pentateuch, the concept of prophecy as precisely foretelling historical events (and thus the confused concept of the Old Testament's prophetic nature), and the apostolic authorship of the New Testament by individuals who were chosen by Jesus and who then played specific roles in composing its books.[7] A tone of defensiveness began to surround an often revisionist conversation about Christian exegesis in which, in the name of modernity, scholars began to blame or excuse the church

---

6. See Levering, *Engaging the Doctrine of Revelation: The Meditation of the Gospel through Church and Scripture* (Grand Rapids: Baker, 2014), 4–8.

7. Both tradition and the *Magisterium* left a number of questions open concerning the literary authorship of many books. Often historically proven authorship and canonicity must be treated separately. The clearest example is the Pauline authorship of the Epistle to the Hebrews, which, in spite of the liturgical custom of attributing it to St. Paul, never was authoritatively defined. I will return to such questions when treating the apostolic authorship of the New Testament.

fathers for historically dubious assumptions, portraying them as either naive or lacking historical consciousness. It seems, however, that behind the clashes between rationalists and faith-based interpreters, a frightening gap developed because of both sides' impoverished doctrines of revelation, inspiration, and the provenance of the Bible in general. In the post-enlightenment era, theologians tried to deduce traditional views about biblical inerrancy from theories of inspiration that would guarantee the truthfulness of all doctrinal statements supported by a list of verbal quotations from the Bible. Meanwhile, for regulating biblical studies, the post-Tridentine church turned to the tools of Scholastic theology for using them in its antirationalist and later antimodernist battles. When biblical exegesis further distanced itself from its patristic and medieval roots and focused exclusively on the literal sense of the Bible, its continued apologetic orientation pressured theologians to construe new theories of inspiration in defense of the Bible's inerrancy. Interestingly, in antirationalist debates, it was the Bible's infallible truth that needed new arguments to prove its divine provenance in terms of subjective inspiration, while in denominational controversies, clashes about the relationship of scripture and tradition led to renewed debates about the nature of the inspired text (objective inspiration) and the way its truth could be appropriated by the church and the faithful. In Catholic theology, both kinds of debates ended up in constructing a neo-Thomistic bastion for the theory of inspiration that was expected to give account for both the infallible truth of the biblical text and the problems of its many imperfections. The theory of dual authorship developed by neo-Thomism was supposed to become a fortress in which many Catholic theologians were expected to find refuge. Meanwhile the encyclical *Divino Afflante*, with its theory of the literary genres, was thought to have made another step ahead when it claimed to present an all-purpose methodology defending the truth of the Bible's literary meaning against both rationalists and fundamentalists, so that, in fact, many exegetes found a reasonable sense of comfort in its new papal guidelines.

The neo-Thomistic theory of inspiration was reactionary in the etymological sense of the word, because it was developed chiefly in a defensive reaction to rationalist and non-Catholic denominational positions. In a markedly different way, the theological renewal, which found its expression at Vatican II in *Dei Verbum*,[8] was the product of a theological renewal called *la nouvelle théologie* by its French promoters. As a program aiming a return to the sources (*ressourcement*), this theology was strongly supported by a patristic and liturgical renewal. But in the cased of *Dei Verbum* one cannot speak about completely ripened fruits of a new theological approach, for the document carries signs of incompleteness. Nonetheless, the document provided a new orientation, characterized by discontinuity with the immediate past, but also by being in profound continuity with long and consistent previous epochs of patristic and medieval sources.[9] The efforts of developing a truly new concept of inspiration in analogy with the incarnation of the divine Word and placing this analogy as the source of further analogies into its focus were perhaps the most significant development initiated by this conciliar document.[10]

The Incarnational View of Biblical Inspiration

The understanding of revelation in *Dei Verbum* was developed mostly in the decade following the Second World War; in a fully developed form it was already published by René Latourelle before the Council.[11] This concept was well received and supported by a new generation of theologians, many of whom were advisors for the leading members of the

8. It seems that the chief drafter of *Dei Verbum* was Yves Congar, whose book *La tradition et les traditions: Essai historique* (1960; Paris: Cerf, 1963) was published on the eve of the Council, with rich patristic documentation on revelation and inspiration.

9. In the case of *Dei Verbum*, Pope Benedict's distinction, applied to the interpretation of various conciliar documents, between a hermeneutics of "continuity and discontinuity" is helpful to recall but without indulging in oversimplifications. *Dei Verbum* broke with a *theological* tradition of not more than a hundred years, which was sterile and incapable of handling the topic of revelation and biblical inspiration, while it was in discontinuity with a tradition that had reigned earlier for more than thousand years.

10. There is no way to give an extensive bibliography of these developments beyond mentioning a few recent books, each referring to more comprehensive bibliographies: Francis Martin, *Sacred Scripture: The Disclosure of the Word* (Naples, Fla.: Sapientia Press of Ave Maria University, 2006); Levering, *Participatory Biblical Exegesis*; Levering, *Engaging the Doctrine of Revelation*; Bartholomew and Heath, *Manifesto for Theological Interpretation*.

11. Latourelle, *La théologie de la révélation* (Paris: Desclée de Bouwer, 1963). In English: *Theology of Revelation*. Another very helpful summary of the concept of revelation from the 1960s is found with a bibliography in Karl Rahner, Cornelius Ernst, and Kevin Smyth, eds., *Sacramentum Mundi* (New York: Herder, 1969) 5:342–59.

Council. This new theology of revelation provided a secure framework for the contextualization of biblical inspiration.

The approach to inspiration championed in *Dei Verbum* does not begin with a discourse about God as an author—someone who occasionally writes books—but as the Revealer whose self-disclosure to mankind through his chosen people not only gives voice to God's word, but also provides revelation with a subsequent verbal expression in writing so that God's word may resound through the rest of salvation history in a canon of scriptures. Briefly: God not only sets in motion an economy of salvation but effectively sees to it that his words and deeds become recorded in a fixed form for his people.

This way of looking at inspiration may reveal two things. On the one hand, instead of *Deus Auctor*, one would need to use more personal terms by speaking about *the Holy Spirit* linking the work of creation and redemption into a purposefully progressing historical process in which the human authors would include a wide variety of participants, engaged in various roles of human salvation history. Instead of a rigid class of individuals, known as the hagiographers, and a univocal concept of inspiration, one is led to deal with an analogous concept covering *a variety of ways* in which the final emergence of literary records and testimonies are seen bringing divine revelation to human verbalization by literary works.

In this perspective there appears, indeed, a sense in which the inspired authors can represent Moses, Isaiah, David, and Peter and Paul as speaking in the Holy Spirit insofar as these persons acted as human mediators transmitting God's self-disclosure through salvific acts and words. It is in this perspective that Jesus Christ, God's word become flesh, obtains in an intelligible way his role at "the fullness of time" (see Gal 4:4), as the central Actor of the drama of salvation, with the Holy Spirit as the main Narrator and Communicator of God's word. For the Christian theologian of revelation, it should be no wonder that, in the eyes of secular historians, the arrival of Jesus in history appears to be located in the backwaters of history, so much off-stage and off-center that mankind may be seen as if caught by surprise. Even Israel's expectations were overwritten and corrected in a fully unexpected way by the Word becoming flesh in the womb of a Virgin. As Prototype, or the *primum analogatum*—that is, the first and foremost of all analogies for God's inspired word appearing in salvation history—Jesus is God's full self-expression in the world in the event of his incarnation, even if for the secular eye his advent happened in obscurity.

The pursuit of this line of thought may be facilitated if we turn to a couple of ancient Christian texts that either directly or indirectly nourished the church for centuries. It may prove helpful to read them in a reversed chronological order: the first by Bernard of Clairvaux (1090–1153) and the second by Origen (185–254).

Two Ancient Texts: Bernard and Origen

Bernard of Clairvaux, from "In the Praise of the Virgin Mother" (Fourth *Sermon*, "Super Missus est")

This passage is famous for its mariological content and for its exceptional poetic qualities. It is usually read as a commentary on Mary's fiat to the Annunciation (Lk 1:38) and, in this context, summarizes a longstanding tradition about the parallelism between inspiration and incarnation:

Let it be, she said, according to your Word. Let the Word which was at the beginning with God (Jn 1:1), become flesh from my flesh according to your word (Lk 1:38). Let it be to me, I beg, not a Word pronounced that passes (Jb 7:5), but a word conceived so that it may remain, surrounded by flesh not by air.

Let it be to me not only audible by ear but visible by eye, touched by hand (Lk 23:9), and carried on shoulders. Let it be not a mere word written and mute, but incarnate and live that is not inscribed upon dead leather in voiceless symbols, but a living imprint in human form into my pure womb, not depicted by a lifeless pen but so obtained by the operation of the Holy Spirit. Let it be to me as it never happened to anyone before me and will not happen again after me.

For at sundry times and various ways God had spoken in former times to the Fathers through the Prophets (Heb 1:1): to some into their ears, to others through their mouths, to others even in their hand the word of God is reported to have come about (see 1 Sm 28:15). To me, I pray that it may be done in my womb according to your word.

I do not want it to be proclaimed by announcement, or signified through symbols or dreamed by dreams, but let it *be silently inspired, personally enfleshed, bodily implanted.* Therefore, may the Word that in itself could not have nor needed to have become, graciously deign, in me and to me, to become according to your word.[12]

This text is rarely quoted in reference to biblical inspiration.[13] However, the way it uses the verb *fieri* (to become) provides a link between Luke 1:38 and John 1:14, two central texts about the incarnation, and calls attention to the importance of becoming in both incarnation and inspiration. In Bernard's text, the Word's becoming flesh and scripture constitute both parallelism and gradual progression as if Mary had said, "Let the word *not only become scripture*, as it has in the Old Testament, *but also* let it now *become flesh in me.*" Bernard pairs off the word "fiat" in Mary's reply to the angel (Lk 1:38), a jussive form of *fieri*, with the Johannine prologue's *factum est* (Jn 1:14), the passive perfect of the same verb, meaning "has become."[14] In this way, Bernard's passage reveals itself as a forerunner to Hugo Rahner and Hans Urs von Baltasar, who verbally linked *Menschwerdung* (becoming man) with *Schriftwerdung* (becoming scripture), anticipating them by more than eight hundred years. Bernard then presents a list of contrasts between the pale and arid literary real-

12. "Fiat, inquiens, secundum Verbum tuum. Verbum, quod erat in principio apud Deum, fiat caro de carne mea secundum verbum tuum. Fiat, obsecro, mihi Verbum, non prolatum quod transeat, sed conceptum ut maneat, carne videlicet indutum, non aere.

"Fiat mihi non tantum audibile auribus sed et visibile oculis, palpabile manibus, gestabile humeris. Nec fiat mihi verbum scriptum et mutum, sed incarnatum et vivum, hoc est non mutis figuris mortuis in pellibus exaratum, sed in forma humana meis castis visceribus vivaciter impressum, et hoc non mortui calami depictione sed Spiritus Sancti operatione. Eo videlicet modo fiat mihi quo nemini ante me factum est, nemini post me faciendum.

"Porro multifariam multisque modis olim Deus locutus est Patribus in Prophetis: et aliisque in aure, aliis in ore, aliis etiam in manu factum esse verbum Domini memoratur; mihi autem oro, ut et in utero fiat iuxta verbum tuum.

"Nolo ut fiat mihi declaratorie praedicatum, aut figuraliter significatum, aut imaginatorie somniatum, sed silenter inspiratum, personaliter incarnatum, coporaliter invisceratum. Verbum igitur quod in se nec poterat fieri, nec indigebat, dignetur in me, dignetur et mihi fieri secundum verbum tuum"; Bernard of Clairvaux, *In laudibus Virginis Matris* IV.11, in Sancti Bernardi Opera Omnia, ed. Leclercq and Rochais (Rome: Editiones Cistercienses, 1966), 57. This text is partially quoted in *Dei Verbum*, no. 11.

13. In *Verbum Domini*, Pope Benedict XVI cites of Bernard's text only a short excerpt (no. 7).

14. The unfortunate mistranslation of Jn 1:14 as "word *was made* flesh" in many English liturgical texts (like the Christmas responsories and antiphons of the Breviary) show our contemporary misunderstanding of the "factum est" in the Latin text of John's Prologue as if it were a form of *facere* (to make), although it comes from *fieri* (to become). It refers to the incarnation as a "becoming" (in Greek ἐγένετο from γίνομαι) of God's Word, not his "being made." The Latin "factum est" in the Vulgate is not a passive form of *facere* ("is made") but a form of the deponent verb *fieri* ("to become") in perfect tense.

ity of the biblical word in its paper-and-ink appearance and the flesh-and-blood result of the incarnation in Mary's womb, where the Word is *Verbum vivum, invisceratum,* and *vivaciter impressum*—a word become alive, internalized, and vividly imprinted.

To fully understand this text we must realize that, contrary to what is often assumed, the twelfth-century Cistercian milieu was neither culturally isolated nor lacking in intellectual dimension. St. Bernard's text needs to be read, as it was written, in a vibrant social context. His four homilies *In the Praise of the Virgin Mother* follow a literary convention, as they appear to be sermons delivered to monks by their abbot, but in the twelfth century the monastic sermon was a well-defined literary genre. These four sermons are soaked in traditional Lukan exegesis and themes of medieval Marian devotion; they are also carefully chiseled into rhythmic prose.[15] Perhaps they were originally preached in some form, but as we have them, they were literary compositions, offered for being read and copied in monastic circles.[16] In fact, they constituted Bernard's exegetical debut and made his name widely known. As the preamble shows, the appearance of four separate sermons pronounced in the chapter room is only a literary disguise.[17] The last fifteen lines of the Fourth Sermon, forming an epilogue, suggest a defensive concern in response to critical readers: "I am quite aware that this will not please everybody." Bernard anticipates that some may not like his text's traditionalist bent, shown in a multitude of patristic references and allusions. He admits, "I said what I have received from the Fathers," but then declares his freedom to do what pleases his spiritual taste: "Those who might suggest

15. See Christine Mohrmann, "Observations sur la langue et le style de saint Bernard," in *Opera Omnia* II, ed. J. Leclercq, C. H. Talbot, and H. M. Rochais (Rome: Editiones Cistercienses, 1958), ix–xxiii.

16. In his research on Bernard's *Sermons on the Song of Songs,* Jean Leclercq made it clear that his monastic sermons follow a literary genre and thus, even if they might represent some form of actual preaching, the texts have been edited for the sake of circulation and reading: Leclerq, "Les sermon sur les Cantiques ont-ils été prononcés?," in *Recueil d'études sur saint Bernard et ses écrits* (Rome: Edizioni Storia e Letteratura, 1962), 193–212. The four homilies on the Annunciation belong to Bernard's earliest compositions (see "introduction" of the critical text quoted in n. 109). This might have been preceded only by the treatise *On the Steps of Humility,* which Bernard mentions in an early letter [Eph 18:5 (Opera Omnia VII.69)], but otherwise they antedate every other of his works.

17. Bernard's Homilies open with a "Praefatio" with the first words (*scribere me aliquid*) testifying that the author's original intention was to *write something* rather than to preach.

that my exegesis was superfluous and not needed, should realize (*noverint*) that I did not intend so much to present an exposition of the Gospel as to use the opportunity to speak about what delights me." It may not be an exaggeration to see in these bold lines a move to take possession of a genre of biblical commentaries that Bernard considers the rightful heritage of monastic theology.

However, this last short passage quoted here may be read also as a short manifesto placing a spiritual encounter with Christ into the focus. For Christ is the One whom the patriarchs and the prophets anticipated: he is God's word, not only "proclaimed" and "heard" but the Word who became incarnate and, therefore, even after his resurrection, remains within the reach of human understanding because, demonstrably, in his post-resurrection appearances he was visible and tangible. One of the first modern attempts to study Bernard as a theologian assessed this use of the Bible as the pursuit of a biblical experience, seen here as a medieval anticipation of the modern search for a Christian experience in the scriptures.[18]

The First Pages of Origen's *Commentary on John*

Origen was an important source for Bernard's way of reading the scriptures.[19] The passage that follows is found in Origen's *Commentary on John*[20] as a long and, for the contemporary reader possibly curious, meditation on the title: "*Euaggelion* (Gospel) according to John." Although Origen does not use the word "analogous," he sets up a broad system of analogous applications of the word *euaggelion* in successive steps. When compared to other canonical gospels, he says, the Gospel of John can be

18. See C. Bodard, "La Bible: L'expression d'une expérience religieuse chez S. Bernard," in *Saint Bernard théologien, Analecta S. Ordinis Cisterciensis* 9, no. 1 (1954): 24–45; J. Mouroux, "Sur les critères de l'expérience spirituelle d'après les sermons sur le Cantique des Cantiques," *Analecta S. Ordinis Cisterciensis* 9, no. 1 (1954): 253–67.

19. There is ample evidence that Bernard read whatever Latin translations of Origen he was able to access; see de Lubac, "Bernard, Grégoire, Origène," in *Exégèse médiévale*, vol. 1, part 2 (Paris: Aubier, 1962), 586–99.

20. Origen, *Commentary on John*. For studying the Greek text, I used the bilingual edition by Cécile Blanc, with introduction and commentary, Sources chrétiennes 120 (Paris: Cerf, 1966). I take the English translation from *The Early Chrstian Writings*, by Alexander Roberts and James Donaldson, accessible on the Internet: http://www.earlychristianwritings.com/text/origen-john1 .html.

called "gospel" in the strictest and most eminent sense of the word, yet, in a wider sense, all other apostolic writings and even the scriptures of the Old Testament with the whole economy of salvation and its final eschatological fulfillment may be called "gospel." It seems to me that in this text we encounter the first formulation of the Christian concept of biblical revelation in a flexible but well-organized system built around *euaggelion* as the key word. For Origen this may concretely and specifically mean Jesus Christ as the incarnate Word. Yet, in a broad sense, the totality of scriptures, including both testaments and the whole economy of salvation and even all of God's deeds and words accompanying man's journey on earth, are implied by the word "gospel." Quoting below a complete passage of book I (I.8) may be the best way to show how this system works.

Now an objection might be raised to our first definition, because it would embrace books which are not entitled Gospels. For the Law and the Prophets also are to our eyes books containing the promise of things which, from the benefit they will confer on him, naturally rejoice the hearer as soon as he takes in the message.

To this it may be said that before the sojourn of Christ, the Law and the Prophets, since He had not come who interpreted the mysteries they contained, did not convey such a promise as belongs to our definition of the Gospel; but the Savior, *when He sojourned with men and caused the Gospel to appear in bodily form, by the Gospel caused all things to appear as Gospel.* For when he had taken away the veil which was present in the law and the prophets, and by His divinity had proved the sons of men that the Godhead was at work, He opened the way for all those who desired it to be disciples of His wisdom, and to understand what things were true and real in the law of Moses, of which things those of old worshipped the type and the shadow, and what things were real of the things narrated in the histories which happened to them in the way of type but these things were written for our sakes, upon whom the ends of the ages have come (1 Cor 10:11). With whomsoever, then, Christ has sojourned, he worships God neither at Jerusalem nor on the mountain of the Samaritans; he knows that God is a spirit, and worships Him spiritually, in spirit and in truth; no longer by type does he worship the Father and Maker of all.

Before that Gospel, therefore, which came into being by the sojourning of Christ, none of the older works was a Gospel. But the Gospel, which is the new covenant, having delivered us from the oldness of the letter, lights up for us, by the light of knowledge, the newness of the spirit, a thing which never grows old, which has its home in the New Testament, but is also present in all the Scriptures. It was fitting, therefore, that that Gospel, which enables us to find the Gospel present, even in the Old Testament, should itself receive, in a special sense, the name of Gospel.

This idea is more fully developed in section I.11, where the concept of gospel includes in effect all human deeds, good and evil.

It ought not to be forgotten that in such a Gospel as this there is embraced every good deed which was done to Jesus; as, for example, the story of the woman who had been a sinner and had repented, and who, having experienced a genuine recovery from her evil state, had grace to pour her ointment over Jesus so that everyone in the house smelt the sweet odor. Hence, too, the words, "Wherever this Gospel shall be preached among all the nations, there also this that she has done shall be spoken of, for a memorial of her" (Mt 26:13). And it is clear that whatever is done to the disciples of Jesus is done to Him. Pointing to those of them who met with kind treatment, He says to those who were kind to them: "What ye did to these, you did to me" (Mt 25:40). So that every good deed we do to our neighbors is entered in the Gospel, that Gospel which is written on the heavenly tablets and read by all who are worthy of the knowledge of the whole of things. But on the other side, too, there is a part of the Gospel which is for the condemnation of the doers of the ill deeds which have been done to Jesus. The treachery of Judas and the shouts of the wicked crowd when it said, "Away with such a one from the earth," (Jn 19:6) and "Crucify Him, crucify Him" (Jn 19:15) of those who crowned Him with thorns, and everything of that kind, is included in the Gospels. And as a consequence of this we see that everyone who betrays the disciples of Jesus is reckoned as betraying Jesus Himself. To Saul, when still a persecutor it is said, "Saul, Saul, why do you persecute me?" and, "I am Jesus whom you persecute" (Acts 9:4-5).

In its vocabulary and in the manner it progresses, Origen's text appears, indeed, archaic, because, from the beginning of Christianity, the word *euaggelion* had this broad and comprehensive meaning. In Paul's authentic letters it means the message of and about Christ and not a text. In Mark 1:1 and at some other instances in Matthew (24:14, 26:13) and Mark (13:10, 14:9) the term seems to signify also, at least by connotation, the oral and possibly written narratives about Jesus. Yet, after Justin Martyr and especially Irenaeus, there is no doubt that *euaggelion* means a literary work: a book about Jesus' words and deeds. At Origen's time the plural of this noun is widely used, yet the gospel titles retain an archaic meaning of the word, which before the middle of the second century was always used in the singular; it meant Jesus' one and only message that is so indivisible that Irenaeus could call the four gospels one single *tetramorphous* or "quadriform" gospel—that is, a one entity in fourfold appearance.

This ecclesial usage of the word *euaggelion*, surviving in the gospel titles up to our day, made it possible for Origen to write the long passage quoted here about gospel as both one and yet multiform, the totality of the *Word become flesh and made accessible in the scriptures.*[21]

21. If I understood it correctly, this is the meaning of the word "participatory" in the title of a book by Levering, *Participatory Biblical Exegesis.*

5 ✦ THE IMPLICATIONS
OF INSPIRATION

⸺•◆•⸺

Inerrancy in the Neo-Thomistic Textbooks

Neo-Thomistic textbooks treat inspiration according to the following outline. First they prove its existence: *De existentia inspirationis*; then follows a chapter about its "essence," meaning its definition: *De essentia inspirationis*. This definition is then applied to every part of the Bible under some title like "the extension of inspiration." Finally, the *effects* or *consequences* of inspiration are treated, the most important of which is said to be the Bible's inerrancy (errorless truth): *De inerrantia scripturae*.

This outline is impeccably logical, and, indeed, if revelation consisted of conveying propositional truths and if inspiration were to be understood as guaranteeing God's literary authorship for every statement of the biblical text, then the most important feature of inspiration must be that it guarantees the truth of the text. But if revelation is viewed as a concrete historical process, consisting of events ("words and deeds") that bring into the world God's incarnate word, then inspiration must be seen as part of the same incarnational process that solidifies revelation into a permanent written form of God's enduring speech in the church.

The claim that inspiration results in an accumulation of sacred literature containing divinely guaranteed propositional truths, extractable by objective and unbiased exegesis with the tools of grammar and literary analysis, does not correspond well to the way Christian tradition regards the Bible. What the Spirit tells the church in the Bible is not equivalent to or reducible to what can be sorted out by a literal interpretation of the texts, so that the intent or mindset of the human authors may be historically reconstructed. An exegesis of this sort might be helpful and fascinating, but it disregards important and essential characteristics of the Bible as the depository of revelation. Not even salvation history can be legitimately identified as a narration of individual salvific events.

Revelation is granted in a context of salvation that implies redemption (rescue), reconciliation (forgiveness and conversion), and sanctification (entering the Body of Christ and the trinitarian community) for the human being as a person. Even if we disregard the fact that salvation history begins with creation and assume that it starts with chapter 12 of Genesis, the history of human encounters with God, from Abraham until the death of the last apostle(s), it cannot be reduced to the literal meaning of the records that scriptures offer, because "God meeting man" aims to achieve encounter and dialogue, not a mere transmission of ideas.

The Truth of the Bible in *Dei Verbum*

Limits and Insufficiencies

The renewed theology of revelation, which *Dei Verbum* presents, is not followed up by a correspondingly renewed concept of inspiration. To fully analyze the tension between the document's concepts of revelation and inspiration, one would need to go through a more minute analysis of the text and its history, a task that may not fully fit the purpose of this book. Yet, some reasons can be assessed. At the time of the Council, the work of fully disassembling the neo-Thomistic theology of inspiration was humanly impossible. A majority of the Council fathers and their theological advisors were educated in the neo-Thomistic tradition. Many excelled by promoting the neo-Thomistic synthesis in Catholic theology and were on their way to a higher status in their careers. One example is Augustinus Bea, SJ (later cardinal and the first president of the postconciliar Pontifical Council for Christian Unity), who was engaged in a lifetime of teaching this brand of inspiration theology.[1] Another author of a leading textbook on

---

1. Bea's textbook *De Scripturae Sacrae inspiratione* (Rome: Pontificio Istituto Biblico, 1935) is the only one that Rahner's *Über die Schriftinspiration* cited as representative of the *Schultheologie*, whose work Rahner sought to replace with his own.

inspiration was Sebastian Tromp, SJ, who had been author and presenter of the failed draft *De Fontibus Revelationis*, which *Dei Verbum* eventually replaced. When the Council opened, Tromp's textbook on inspiration was the only textbook still in use at the Gregorian University. A third person, a rising star, Pierre Benoit, OP, rector of the École Biblique in Jerusalem, was working on a new Thomistic synthesis; at the time of the Council many members considered him to be the most up-to-date expert on the topic.[2] A fourth luminary, equally present among the experts of the Council, Hans Urs von Balthasar, a major figure of the patristic renewal and the revival of the Origenian tradition, was also a renowned author of volume 23 of the German commentary of the *Summa Theologica* whose defense of the neo-Thomistic application of St. Thomas's theology on prophecy was quoted previously.[3] In the presence of these personalities, the time was certainly neither ripe nor opportune for disassembling the neo-Thomistic system into which these persons had been so heavily invested.

There were also new voices that began to emerge, demanding new research and a reevaluation of the patristic and medieval heritage. After Karl Rahner's *Inspiration in the Bible* in 1958, the second most significant attempt at renewing this topic was made by a young Jesuit, Luis Alonso Schökel. However, his *La Palabra Inspirada*, published in Spanish in 1964, remained virtually unknown until 1967, when an English translation appeared.[4] The large amount of material collected in Henri de Lubac's *Medieval Exegesis*, up to now the largest repertoire of ancient authors and texts on ancient exegesis, began to appear volume by volume immediately before and during the Council,[5] but its English translation lagged behind until 1998.

2. The dissemination of Benoit's writings on inspiration in English was slow; it had just begun during the Council. He had believed that he was moving beyond neo-Thomism, but his critics thought differently; see Pierre Benoit, *Aspects of Biblical Inspiration*, trans. Jerome Murphy-O'Connor and S. K. Ashe (Chicago: Priory, 1965); Benoit, *Inspiration and the Bible*, trans. J. Murphy-O'Connor and M. Keverne (London and New York: Sheed and Ward, 1965). During the years the PBC was working on its document on inspiration, the current rector of École Biblique, who was a member of the commission, did not quote these works or mention Benoit's name.

3. Von Balthasar, *Thomas von Aquin*, in *Deutsche Thomas Ausgabe*, vol. 23; see also *Origenes, Geist und Feuer: Ein Aufbau aus seinen Schriften* (Salzburg and Leipzig: O. Müller, 1938).

4. The translator, Francis Martin, then a young Trappist, later published significant work on inspiration and hermeneutics; see Martin, "Literary Theory, Philosophy of History and Exegesis," *Thomist* 52 (1988): 575–604.

5. De Lubac, *Exégèse médiévale* (Paris: Aubier, 1959–64).

One might state with some confidence that at the time *Dei Verbum* was being drafted, no Catholic theologian would have been able to extend the new theology of revelation into a theology of inspiration in any comprehensive manner. Consequently, *Dei Verbum* was not able to present a coherent vision and was bypassed for a time with a certain measure of indifference.

Merits of the Document and Its Limited Success

Dei Verbum succeeded in contextualizing the topic of inspiration into a renewed understanding of divine revelation. That was obvious to all who seriously examined the document.

Nonetheless, *Dei Verbum*, born amidst dramatic confrontations, remained a sign of contradiction until now. As the heated debates of the first session of the Council (causing in 1962 the demise of the Preparatory Commission's *De Fontibus Revelationis*) reemerged in the last session of 1964, the commission dealt almost exclusively with passages about inspiration and inerrancy. At the end, the new document was patched up for its controversial paragraphs and accepted with near unanimity. But its post-Conciliar reception was problematic with regard to its concept of inspiration and lack of clarity on inerrancy or—as its new language demanded—on the truth of the Bible.

The historical facts about the conciliar disputes have been described many times,[6] yet a calm and objective overview of the Council's proceedings is still difficult to reconstruct. Most of the issues brought up about biblical inerrancy go back to more than a hundred years ago and filled the whole timespan between Vatican I and II. Contrary to what many progressive Catholic biblical experts had wanted to believe, the appeasement brought about by *Divino Afflante* was unstable and short-lived. The exchanges at the Council have shown that inerrancy was widely seen as a monolithic concept that was to be rescued and maintained at any price by many, but was seen as linked to a burdensome legacy and, at least in its traditional sense, was untenable. In fact, traditional statements of inerrancy were felt to be in serious conflict with the outlook of most

---

6. See Martin, "The Transmission of Revelation," in Lamb and Levering, *Vatican II: Renewal within Tradition*, 55–76; Farkasfalvy, "The Dogmatic Constitution on Revelation: Inspiration and Interpretation," in ibid., 77–100.

exegetes, especially with regard to the historicity of most biblical narratives. Shortly before the opening of the Council, high-ranking officials of the *Holy Office* (predecessor of the present Congregation for the Doctrine of Faith) carried out a witch hunt, today usually referred to as the "Msgr. Romeo affair," which resulted in the censoring and suspension of highly esteemed Catholic professors at the Pontifical Biblical Institute, including Fr. Stanislas Lyonnais and Fr. Maximilian Zerwick.[7] During the years of the Council, in Roman academic circles, this was still a story of recent memory. It might be argued that the intervention by Cardinal König of Vienna, demanding the admission of errors in the Bible, was *at that time* an understandable, some dared to suggest calculated, but in any case unfortunately excessive move—an "overkill"—intending only to shock the audience but not to cause international uproar. The cardinal demanded, in the name of modern scientific historiography, the admission that some biblical texts were "deficient in truth" (*a veritate deficere*). The intervention created confused reactions. Some remained convinced that the preparatory committee's document *De Fontibus Revelationis* had to be revoked, but conservative forces probably felt that they had to reunite and not allow further attacks against biblical inerrancy. Consequently, a curious situation evolved, while both sides probably expected a different outcome. Because the question about what to do with *De Fontibus Revelationis* was curiously worded in such a way that "yes" meant the rejection and "no" meant the retention of the prepared text, a two-thirds majority of the votes was needed to obtain rejection. In any case, on November 20, 1963, the voting resulted in 1,368 *yes* vs. 822 *no* votes, so that a two-thirds majority (required for *rejection*) was not obtained. Thus, in a pathetic division, the Council became hostage to its own procedural laws; the result of the voting would have obliged the Council to keep on working with a text that an absolute majority of the participants had rejected. Pope Paul VI's intervention followed; he reassigned the topic to a joint committee to be headed by cardinals Ottaviani and Bea and simply postponed the topic to be (eventually) discussed at a later time.

Two years later, in the fall of 1965, on the last session of the Council,

7. See Antonio Romeo, "The Encyclical *Divino Afflante Spiritu* and the *Opiniones Novae*," *Divinitas* 4 (1966): 378–456.

at a time many people thought that this topic would never be addressed again, *Dei Verbum* was presented to the plenary session at the pope's request. It was symptomatic that, in spite of a new and vastly improved text, controversy was reignited immediately, first about inspiration and then, more passionately, about inerrancy. The drafters of *Dei Verbum* hoped to skirt a new controversy by avoiding the word *inerrantia*, since they considered it altogether negative. Yet, if for no other reason than the uproar that had been caused by Cardinal König's unforgotten intervention, a vocal minority of the Council insisted that the document states full absence of errors in the Bible. They were willing to replace "inerrancy" with "truth in the Bible" only if the text clearly stated that the Bible was free of any error. Eventually the committee gave in and inserted into no. 11 the two words *sine errore*. By this time, however, for contemporary theology the term "inerrancy" had lost its pedigree and it is now usually shunned in an effort to replace it by a kind of politically correct speech: the postconciliar parlance avoids "inerrancy" and speaks only of "the truth" or "truthfulness" of the Bible.[8]

Thereafter, another controversy broke out about the rest of the sentence in no. 11, in which *sine errore* was inserted. The historical details have been described several times.[9] The dispute required another intervention of Pope Paul VI. This way the expression *veritas salutaris* describing the truth of the biblical texts was found wanting by a substantial minority. Many Council fathers thought that this term was suggesting a restriction of inspiration and thus implying that truthfulness was guaranteed for only those biblical passages that referred to salvation. The ambiguities of the text were difficult to extricate from the suspicion that it suggested the idea, previously rejected by the *Magisterium*, that truth was assured only when a text was dealing with salvific or, in more theological terms, soteriological (doctrinal, moral, theological, religious) matters. After long debate, the Council's Theological Commission was entrusted over the matter. At its proposal, the term *veritas salutaris* was discarded, and the rewritten sentence obtained the endorsement of the

---

8. This reticence about the word "inerrancy" was purposefully broken in three essays in Hahn, *For the Sake of Our Salvation*; Pitre, "Mystery of God's Word," 6:47–66; Germain Grisez, "Inspiration and Inerrancy of Scripture," 6:181–90; and Joseph C. Atkinson, "The Interpenetration of Inspiration and Inerrancy," 6:191–22.

9. See my rendition: Farkasfalvy, "Dogmatic Constitution on Revelation," 86–87.

pope and—with a sense of relief, and even enthusiasm—of a preponderant majority of the Council. Yet, soon after the Council, this enthusiasm began to diminish and vanished as new ambiguities in the text surfaced with conflicting interpretations brought to light. The official English translation was used as an egregious witness to the text's ambiguity. In my translation, both here and elsewhere, I point out that the Latin text speaking of *veritas* must be translated with a definite article (and capitalized) as "the Truth" as it was done in other languages: la Vérité, die Warheit, la Verità, la Verdad.[10] When translated in English as "that truth," the text is no longer in agreement with what was accepted, after long discussion and a moment of impasse, by the Council and the pope.[11]

This sentence has become the Achilles's heel of the document. After article no. 11 was dragged through many disputes at various forums, including the Synod of Bishops in 2008, Pope Benedict XVI assigned to the Congregation for the Doctrine of the Faith (CDF) the task of providing an authentic interpretation of *Dei Verbum* concerning biblical inspiration and its implications with regard to the truth of the Bible. The subsequent year, under the direction of the CDF, the pope commissioned the Pontifical Biblical Commission (PBC) to spend the next five years in preparation of a document on the interpretation of *Dei Verbum*. After five successive plenary assemblies, the PBC handed over a finished document to Cardinal Mueller, who, in 2013, with his preface and with the authorization of Pope Francis, the newly elected pontiff, published it. The official version of the text was in Italian.[12] We will say much more about this document in the next chapter.

10. At the Vatican website the official texts in all these languages use the definite article, and several capitalize "Truth." Only in English do we read *that truth*, which suggests several kinds and forms of truth, of which then, allegedly, not all are inerrantly expressed in the text.

11. The so-called liberal interpretation, adopted most famously by Raymond Brown, says that the conciliar document covers (restrictively) *that truth* which, in a given scriptural text, obtains written expression for the sake of our salvation. Of course, in the Latin text is found, instead of "that truth," simply *veritatem* without the demonstrative pronoun. The footnotes to the text and the conciliar discussions would support as a more precise and correct translation the following: "*the T(t)ruth* which God wanted to be put into sacred writings for the sake of salvation." Yet, I must admit, even in this form the text remains opaque so that, without careful reading *in context*, it can be endlessly discussed—as it was by the PBA in March 2017—on behalf of opposite partisan interpretations.

12. This time the language of the document makes a difference because, when understanding the traditional phrase *Deus Auctor Scripturae* as *Dio è l'autore della Scrittura*, the PBC unwittingly

The Balance

In what sense and in what way did *Dei Verbum* succeed or fail to renew the Catholic theology of revelation and inspiration? The document was apparently still working with the assumption that "the truth of the Bible" was the most important consequence of inspiration. This mindset betrays little awareness that the document's new concept of revelation is incompatible with the assumption that inspiration affects only and all the formal assertive sentences of the biblical text, providing the human author with an a priori (and ahistorically conceived) conformity with an abstractly defined measure of truthfulness in each of his humanly construed affirmations. Discarding the word *inerrantia* might have appeared as a merely semantic break with a traditional terminology and offered the impression that, when *inerrantia* was replaced by *veritas sine errore*, nothing really changed, because only cosmetic remedies were being introduced. To explain why and how inspiration implied truthfulness, a more nuanced notion of inspiration was needed. Paragraph no. 11 sounded extremely simplistic: "Everything asserted by the inspired authors or sacred writers must be held to be asserted by the Holy Spirit." By itself, this sentence sounds extremely severe, but the Council could not afford to skip it, for, after all, it had been pronounced on the highest level of authority.[13] However, the Council tried and succeeded in softening its apparent harshness (the implication that in every biblical statement human and divine authority coincide) and replaced it with a succinct statement, which then, after heated debates and several amendments, became increasingly contorted and even cryptic—manifestly the product of a compromise. This is how the following passage was born: "The books of Scripture must be acknowledged as teaching solidly, faithfully, and without error the Truth which God wanted to be put into sacred writings for the sake of salvation." On the one hand, the omission of the term "salvific truth" (*veritatem salutarem*) gave a bland and non-

---

overlooked the broader connotations of the word *auctor* (from Tertullian to the papal encyclicals!) and turned it into *scriptor* (writer, *Verfasser* or literary author).

13. The footnote quotes for this principle seven sources form Augustine, Thomas, the Council of Trent, Leo XIII (*Providentissimus*) and Pius XII (*Divino Afflante*), showing that it was, indeed, nonnegotiable.

committal tone. On the other hand, the last words of the sentence produced uncertainties about how one may excoriate from the biblical text "the Truth [in the official English version: 'that truth'] which God wanted to be put into sacred writings." The conciliar text certainly does not tell from which *sources other than scripture itself* the exegete can figure out the truth (the Truth or that truth) God had wanted to be put into written form in the Bible. Soon after the Council, these last words were lifted from context to demonstrate that "the Truth put in writing" in the Bible was not meant to imply the truthfulness of "everything asserted by the inspired authors," but only texts containing *some kind of* (the) truth: truth that God want to be expressed in scriptural documents. Even if, under pressure by the pope and a significant minority of Council fathers, the term "salvific truths" was excluded from the document, after the Council numerous Catholic exegetes continued to claim that, in a nutshell, Vatican II asserted that the Bible lacks error only in those texts that contain "salvific truths."[14] How far this could go was illustrated by Raymond Brown's exegetical experiment applied to Mary's virginity.[15] Brown wanted to see if a seemingly nonnegotiable truth could become negotiable if one proves that it is not "salvific"—that is, not indispensable for salvation. Although at the Council many votes were cast in favor of *Dei Verbum* in a belief that the old frontier of inerrancy remained unchanged, the final formulation of no. 11, softened by translations and interpretations, soon became used in a sense that was explicitly excluded at the Council. *Dei Verbum* became blurred, leaving behind a burdensome legacy. The simple fact that complaints at the Synod of Bishops of 2008 prompted the pope to turn to the CDF for an authoritative interpretation of no. 11 of *Dei Verbum*, a text accepted forty-four years earlier with an overwhelming majority, proves this. At the pope's request, the Pontifical Biblical Commission, an international group of twenty biblical

14. Brian W. Harrison, "The Truth and Salvific Purpose of Sacred Scripture According to *Dei Verbum*, article 11," *Living Tradition* 59 (1995). See also the discussion of the "misinterpretation" of *Dei Verbum*, no. 11, by Brant Pitre, "The Mystery of God's Word," in Hahn, *For the Sake of Our Salvation*, 6:52–53.

15. Brown, *The Critical Meaning of the Bible* (New York and Ramsey, N.J.: Paulist Press, 1981), 36–37. See the severe judgment on Raymond Brown's exegetical experiment penetrating "our Catholic doctrinal patrimony at a very deep level" by Harrison, "Restricted Inerrancy and the 'Hermeneutic of Discontinuity,'" in Hahn, *For the Sake of Our Salvation*, 6:240–42.

scholars and the consultative organ of the CDF, began a five-year study to clarify and possibly complete the teaching of *Dei Verbum*.[16]

16. The CDF employs the International Theological Commission and the PBC as consultative resources. Before Benedict XVI became pope, he headed the CDF for twenty-seven years and knew personally each member of the PBC. He was personally involved in choosing all members before they were appointed to the commission. Yet he resigned before the PBC and the text was approved and published under the authority of Pope Francis I.

6 ✝ THE PONTIFICAL BIBLICAL
COMMISSION'S DOCUMENT ON
INSPIRATION AND TRUTH
IN THE BIBLE

The 2008 Synod of Bishops "On the Word of God in the Life and Mission of the Church" submitted to the pope in proposal no. 2 the following request:

> The Synod proposes that the Congregation for the Doctrine of the Faith clarify the concepts of "inspiration" and "truth" in the Bible, along with their reciprocal relationship, in order to better understand the teaching of *Dei Verbum* 11.

At the following General Assembly of the Pontifical Biblical Commission the pope directed its new president, William Cardinal Levada, that the PBC undertake the study of this matter and prepare a document. The pope was not only fully aware of how *Dei Verbum* came about, but after the Council consistently worked on promoting its reception,[1] he also knew the PBC better than any previous pope because, as its president since 1981, he was personally involved in its history and the appointment of all its members for decades. He must have realized, however, that a large majority of the PBC studied inspiration in rather inadequate courses of systematic theology (most often in Fundamental Theology) and might not have acquired any expertise in this matter. To

---

1. Joseph Ratzinger, "Origin and Background," commentary on *Dei Verbum*, 3:155–98.

put it more dramatically but with historical accuracy, when the wish of the pope was communicated to the PBC that it prepare a document on inspiration, there was an audible murmur in the meeting room: "We are exegetes; we know little about this; this is a theological topic." Pope Benedict XVI might have been aware of this fact but probably trusted that the current secretary of the PBC, the German Jesuit Fr. Klemens Stock, with wide background in the traditional theology of inspiration, would bring this task to completion. Indeed, credit goes mostly to the secretary for leading the PBC to finish this assignment within the allotted time period.[2]

Authorship as Provenance

The document was finished on time, although with considerable difficulties. To start with a global remark of criticism, it reads as a patchwork by twenty (maybe in effect only fifteen or fewer) individual contributors. However, its naively fresh approach and improvised methodology explains not only its deficiencies, but its success in avoiding confrontations with those problems that were simmering in the last several decades. The commission has never bothered to discuss a recent bibliography on the topic and behaved like the Council did almost forty-five years earlier: heated discussions were reserved for inerrancy and what the PBC ended up calling "the biblical truth."

The PBC created a theology of biblical inspiration that is neither brilliant nor consistent but, for many reasons, quite independent of the classical textbooks. The merit of the document consists of its obviously close ties with the experience of contemporary exegetes who had worked with individual books of the Bible. Although most members of the commission lacked in-depth familiarity with the corresponding chapters of Fundamental Theology or the sporadic postconciliar literature about

2. The pages that follow chiefly rely on the English text, translated from the official Italian version of the PBC; Thomas Esposito, OCist, and Stephen Gregg, OCist, *Ispirazione e Verità della Sacra Scrittura* (Rome: Libreria Editrice Vaticana, 2014); rev. Fearghus O'Ferghail: Pontifical Biblical Commission, *The Inspiration and Truth of Sacred Scripture: The Word That Comes from God and Speaks of God for the Salvation of the World* (Collegeville, Minn.: Liturgical Press: 2014). In addition, I used much information from my personal participation in the PBC; yet, to the largest extent possible, I am trying to avoid mentioning the names of the individual members.

inspiration, the document as a whole approaches biblically very human books, which, however, are treated in the church with utmost reverence: texts into which these men (at that time the PBC consisted of men only) invested their entire lives.

The document was designed to consist of four parts. The first part treats inspiration and the canon, the second discusses the Truth (or truthfulness) of the Bible, and the third attempts to interpret those "challenging" texts that might raise doubts about the Truth (or truths, in fact the "inerrancy") of the Bible. At the end, a fourth part draws summary conclusions from the document's main points. Here we are mostly interested in the first two parts.

Instead of wrestling with the customary opening chapters of the traditional treatises on inspiration (*De existentia inspirationis*), the committee chose to start with a survey of the biblical books,[3] examining how they express an awareness of their own *divine provenance*. In the traditional theology of inspiration, such an initial approach (the *auto-testimonianza* of the individual books, as the secretary called the content of the first part) would not be deemed legitimate. In traditional apologetics you do not prove the inspiration of the Bible from the Bible itself, or at least not from the Bible presupposed to be an infallible source of revelation. But this objection was well prevented by the assumption that, in this introductory part, we deal with the fact of inspiration only phenomenologically by showing how the biblical writers (whoever they were) express their consciousness that in their books they express, in some sense, God's word. At the secretary's initiative this phenomenological investigation was to be carried out without any further pretension in each book of the Bible. Thus, in a truly cooperative manner, each member doing his homework between the first two yearly general assemblies brought about a lengthy study consisting of a total of forty-two sections, covering both testaments book by book in search of self-referential comments by the scriptural authors or last redactors, material endowed by divine provenance and/or authority. The committee quickly realized that only in two short passages (2 Tm 3:16 and 2 Pt 1:20–21) do biblical texts speak of inspiration in a comprehen-

---

3. The choice came from Fr. Stock as secretary, with very little participation by the members in devising a methodology to follow.

sive sense. It also assembled a vast dossier in which the biblical authors express an awareness of a divine initiative behind each book, aiming, in some sense, at the transmission of God's word to his people.

In this way, practically all books of the Tridentine canon (including the deuterocanonicals, as the presence of the book of Sirach testifies) were sifted through, and the phenomenon of their authors' awareness of the books' divine provenance was described. At that point, the bold conclusion was made that God is for all these books the divine author. Of course, the sentence was written mostly *in Italian* (or French or German or Spanish), not in Latin. The members of the PBC showed little awareness that, ever since Fr. Augustinus Bea's article of 1943, the neo-Thomistic literature *de inspiratione* assumed that God was each book's *literary* author. The relaxed phenomenological style with which the PBC kept on identifying divine authorship (in the sense of the Italian term *autore*) with divine provenance in a broad sense suddenly blossomed into a full-fledged statement that quotes *Dei Verbum* (no. 11, p. 54) that God was believed to be, indeed, as the *auto-testomonianza* or self-witnessing of each biblical author illustrates, the author (*autore*) of each book, and covering the composition with divine authority. Consequently, in spite of its length (forty-two paragraphs: forty-four pages), the document's phenomenological first part bypassed the burning issue of Rahner's famous distinction between *Urheber* (initiator) and literary *Verfasser*, so that the problem Rahner had raised and Alonso Schökel wrestled with and *Dei Verbum* left undecided remained unresolved. One would like to say that a crucial problem, which *Dei Verbum* discreetly avoided, was now unwittingly stumbled over and left behind by the PBC.[4]

At first this phenomenological approach appeared to be eminently fit and fruitful for work in committee: the biblical books were re-

---

4. The document of the PBC uses the term *autore* very sparingly. It uses *autore* only when quoting *Dei Verbum* (in the preface, in paragraphs no. 3, 6, 55, 63, and 139) or says explicitly in no. 10 that authorship means "provenance" (*proviene*). Twice we find an explicit comment that God's authorship is *mediated*: *attraverso uomini* (v. 6) and *mediante uomini* (v. 10). In the body of its text, the document speaks of a "double authorship" in terms of "God and the human author" (not "divine and human authors") then preponderantly, after paragraph no. 10 almost exclusively, the word *autore* is used only in reference to the *human* author. If we try to assess the collective mindset of the committee, we can say without reservation that in this document *Deus Auctor Scripturae* means the divine provenance of scripture and, consequently, the point that Augustinus Bea wanted to make in 1943 has been addressed only as if by accident; but in reality, it was ignored.

searched one by one, each by a different individual member, possibly always by someone who was an expert in a particular book. Since plenary sessions took place only once a year, each person worked alone in his field of competency and communicated his findings to the secretary via e-mail. Although there was an a priori consensus about the divine provenance (called at the end "divine authorship" in a nonspecific sense), it soon became obvious that this meant for each biblical text a different reality. Thus, the resulting concept of divine provenance or authorship was, by implication, in no way univocal or uniform, but analogous by a large radius of diversity. Thus this concept of divine provenance succeeded in including a wide variety of texts, literary genres, and authorial intents all used by divine inspiration when channeling God's word into writing. It also became clear that these diverse forms of divine provenance were ultimately a common feature of *the texts* rather than indicators of identically experienced charisms imparted to the human *authors*. In other words, the objective aspect of inspiration was emphasized with the subjective side suffering more neglect. But, for better or worse, at no point did the PBC introduce a conceptual distinction between inspiration of texts and inspiration of authors in the Bible.

This much-too-easy initial method employed by the commission became the chief cause of its defects. In reciting the most significant references to *some* kind of divine provenance in the various biblical books monotony was hard to avoid, but the resulting concept of inspiration as divine provenance was blurred and rather loose. At this point an analytical study of the divine provenance (or authorship) of the biblical books implied in these texts would have had to be performed to investigate if and how a specific concept of divine authorship of both testaments had developed in the church in the same sense in which the idea appears in neo-Scholastic textbooks. Unfortunately, all this is missing from the document; instead, in no. 51 a claim is being stated of a synthesis about the divine authorship of the Bible in its entirety. The postulation is made that each human author of the Bible claimed that through him "God was acting" and that this divine authorship is "analogously the same" for all books of the Bible.[5] This suddenly achieved synthesis turns out to be

---

5. See PBD, *Inspiration and Truth of Sacred Scripture*, no. 52, page 55.

nothing but a preconceived model with no convincing or compelling evidence from previous paragraphs.

Next comes a definition-like statement about inspiration that is clearly prefabricated but is not from a neo-Thomistic textbook; rather, it was practically lifted from *Dei Verbum* with a somewhat looser terminology (see the hazy concept of a special relationship) and a casual style so that even the reference to God as an author appears to be inserted as an afterthought, this time directly copied from no. 11 of *Dei Verbum*:

According to the biblical writings[6] inspiration presents itself as a *special relationship with God (or with Jesus) whereby he grants to a human author to relate— through the Spirit—that which he wishes to communicate to human beings.* In this way what no. 11 of *Dei Verbum* asserts is confirmed: the books are written by the inspiration of the Holy Spirit; *God is their author,* because he employs chosen persons acting in and through them; these, however, write as true authors.[7]

The seemingly abundant material was collected by individual members in two years. Two years' efforts yielded only meager results, reminding one of Horace's famous line: "Mountains are in labor to give birth to a laughable mouse."[8] Indeed, this text was born with little substantive result although at a price of arduous labor by detailed research covering the majority of the biblical books.[9]

In no. 53 of the document, a new discourse begins under the title "How to Receive the Inspired Books." This appears to be a new beginning, treating the following topics but in little continuity with the previous paragraphs:

---

6. This phrase indicates the connection with the first forty-four pages in which "the biblical writings" were examined about their divine provenance.

7. PBD, *Inspiration and Truth of Sacred Scripture,* no. 52, page 54; all italics are mine.

8. "Parturiunt montes, nascetur ridiculus mus"; Horace, *Ars Poetica* I.137.

9. This quick transition from phenomenology to a formal definition lifted from *Dei Verbum* is hard to defend. But, at this point, the PBC had no choice. The members worked on the first part in almost full isolation, restricting themselves to individual biblical books. From there no path could lead to the patristic synthesis of *Dei Verbum.* The commission would have needed a crash course on selected texts by Irenaeus, Origen, Augustine, Bernard, and de Lubac; in no other way could the commission provide a logical transition to the patristic synthesis that Congar, who was apparently the chief drafter of *Dei Verbum,* had published immediately before the Council.

(a) *The Writings of the New Testament Attest the Inspiration of the Old by Their Christological Interpretation*;

(b) *Proof* of this thesis from the canonical gospels

(c) *Explanation* of this thesis from 2 Tm 3:16 and 2 Pt 1:21

(d) A second subtitle: *The Process of the Literary Formation of the Biblical Writings and Inspiration*

(e) The next subtitle: *Toward a Two-Testament Biblical Canon*

In step (e) (no. 56) this document managed to break loose from the conceptual trap of the double authorship (as well as the preconception that God is a literary author, producing books by using human writers).[10] At this point it finally becomes clear that the meaning of "divine inspiration of scriptures" cannot be found in God's literary authorship of the canonical books. The reason is simple: revelation is not a matter of mere words, nor even of mere suggestion or infusion of concepts, images, words, or ideas to human minds, followed by an additional push to the hagiographic will endowed by grace and moving the human author mentally and physically to express in written words "that which God wants to put in writing." The rich and wide meaning of revelation of chapter I of *Dei Verbum* required a broader concept of inspiration.

Here the PBC had to abandon a tempting image for a committee consisting, to a large extent, of retired university professors, subconsciously thinking about the hagiographer as a doctoral student who, under the tutelage of his divine mentor (the divine *Inspirator et Auctor*), tries to put into writing "all and only that" (see *Dei Verbum*, no. 11), which his divine "dissertation director" intends to see "put in writing" by him. Fortunately, a different concept of inspiration emerged from the biblical texts as a process intimately linked with divine revelation: a process in which God's Holy Spirit was speaking, as he was providing power and might through words and deeds, setting in motion and moving ahead an economy of salvation with a chain of human transmitters, endowed with insight, understanding, and authority to speak God's word, in continuous progress and development, while God's words took shape, by expanding the incarnation of the Son, and resounded through the

---

10. "God is their author, because he employs chosen people, acting in and through them; these, however, write as true authors"; *Dei Verbum*, no. 53, page 51.

centuries, was remembered, transmitted, and recalled until enshrined and preserved in written works.

The Primacy of Two Biblical Verses, the Book of Revelation and the Unity of the Testaments

At this point the document joins a longstanding tradition that recognized and maintained that, strictly speaking, only two verses of the New Testament, 2 Timothy 3:16 and 2 Peter 1:21, provide explicit attestation to the inspiration of the Bible. Both belong to pseudepigraphic apostolic letters, one Pauline and the other Petrine. If we do not object in principle to pseudepigraphy in the Bible,[11] we might learn to appreciate both the pastoral letters and 2 Peter in their role of closing the canon of the apostolic letters of the New Testament. The book of 2 Timothy is a retrospective composition: a literary monument erected in honor of Paul's martyrdom and apostolate. A collection of his letters that closes with this piece would hardly admit another later addition. Similar is the impact that 2 Peter makes. Attached to Peter's first letter, it helps create a parallelism between Peter and Paul in their respective role of building up the church. In the way 2 Timothy does, 2 Peter also evokes the apostle's martyrdom (1:12–15) and recalls his role as Jesus' immediate disciple and eyewitness of the manifestation of his divinity in the transfiguration (1:16–18). While both letters of Peter appear to be, in some important way, imitations of the Pauline epistles, 2 Peter is not only chronologically the latest of the New Testament documents, but is the first Christian piece of literature, manifesting a fully developed canonical conscious-

---

11. The members of the PBC seemed to follow the majority of exegetes who consider both the pastorals and 2 Peter as documents written after the death of both apostles. "Pseudepigraphy" may not be the best term, because its use in reference to these apostles seems to imply deception by falsely attesting Pauline, respectively. Petrine authenticity to 2 Peter or the pastorals. For the literature and the trends on this issue, see David G. Meade, *Pseudonimity and Canon: An Investigation into the Relationship of Authorship and Authority in Jewish and Earliest Christian Tradition* (Grand Rapids: Eerdmans, 1986); Terry Wilder, *Pseudonimity, the New Testament, and Deception: An Inquiry into Intention and Reception* (Oxford and Lanham, Md.: University Press of America, 2004); Ellis, *Making of the New Testament Documents*, 293–303, 406–25. By references to these chief apostles' martyrdom, insistence on the authenticity of their apostolate and the allusions they contain about the possession of their letters by the churches, these documents signify an advanced stage in the formation of the New Testament canon.

ness. It claims the Christians' possession of the Hebrew scriptures as their rightful heritage; it refers to the synoptic story of the transfiguration and is aware that the Christian church possesses a collection of Paul's letters.[12]

Exceptionally excellent is what the PBC's document says in a lengthy section about the book of Revelation's doctrine of inspiration, written by an expert who had authored a fine commentary on the book.[13] He shows that Revelation is a decidedly retrospective document that provides a synthetic vision of the twelve apostles (Rv 12:14) chosen by Jesus and describes the way the Lamb "opens the book" of salvation history (Rv 5:6–9), as if taking into possession the Old Testament, and shows the church to be the New Jerusalem descending from heaven at the end of history (Rv 21:2). Moreover, this uniquely prophetic book of the New Testament stands out by its emphasis on writing and testimony. At the same time, the book echoes all that had been said about the word of God throughout the Old Testament and in the gospels.[14]

Although, when defining inspiration, the PBC chose not to mention the decrees of the Council of Trent and the papal encyclical, those documents of the *Magisterium* also attributed key importance to 2 Timothy 3:16 and 2 Peter 1:21 as the most explicit passages about the action of the Spirit, creating inspired texts. Nonetheless, the importance of nos. 55–61 of the PBC document (pages 55–68) consists in the way the paragraphs point to the importance of linking canon with inspiration.

As we have remarked, when starting the document with the *autotestimonianze* of biblical books, the PBC employed questionable methodology. This led to a pseudo-definition of biblical inspiration, only loosely related to the preceding inquiry, while copying the definition from *Dei Verbum*'s no. 11 with some vestiges of the neo-Thomistic Roman theology of the twentieth century. We must add, however, that, once the document turns to the topic of the canon, the correct path reemerges: we read again about revelation as divine self-disclosure, producing not only both factual and audible, but also written manifestations to endow the community of salvation (Israel and afterward the church) with per-

12. More will be said on the canonical importance of 2 Pt 10 in chapter X.

13. Vanni, *Lettura del Apocalipsis* (Navarra: Verbo Divino, 2005).

14. Rv 1:11, 1:19, 2:1, 2:8, 2:12, 2:18, 3:1, 3:7, 3:14, 10:4, 14:13, 19:9, 21:5.

manent records of God's word that had created salvation history. This reflects the correct idea that only such a theology of revelation can lead to a correct theology of inspiration capable of treating in a single, unified process the formation of the Christian Bible and the emergence of a biblical canon.

Consequently, much of what Karl Rahner tried to state in 1958 as the thesis in his book is vindicated here, probably more convincingly and with less complexity, although with insufficient precision.[15] Briefly, the inspiration of scripture is regarded here as a constitutive element of that salvation-historical divine act by which God constitutes the church: scripture is essential to the process in which the church came to exist as the institution of salvation by extending the efficacious presence of the incarnate Logos who had inserted himself into history for the sake of mankind's universal salvation. This means that, in the way the process of revelation leads to incarnation and incarnation to passion and glory, so does it also lead further to a verbal and written form of expression of God's active presence, which addresses the world effectively as "divine word," demanding the response of faith. To be sure, scripture does not constitute "another," a "concurrent," or a "parallel" form in which the Logos would penetrate and sanctify the world. Rather, scripture is an extension of the one and same coming and arrival of that single incarnation, which the Logos undertook into the realm of human existence and permanently continues in the form of written words. The dogmatic presuppositions that the previous statements involve pertain to a larger context of Christology and ecclesiology. They relate to three areas of study: the oneness or uniqueness of the incarnation; the full eschatological significance of Jesus' death and resurrection; and the completion of God's work of salvation in Christ and the eschatological nature of the church. Of course, the PBC was not expected to explore these topics, yet moved on with the perspective of a universal salvation history having at its center the mystery of Christ.

15. Rahner, *Inspiration in the Bible*, 50–51.

Biblical Truth

In its second part (pages 69–122), the PBC's document attempts to grapple with inerrancy in the terminology it inherited from *Dei Verbum*. Interestingly, in the drafting of the document (and its English translation) hesitations between "Truth of the Bible" and "Truth in the Bible" finally led to the term "biblical truth." This phrase appears amidst efforts to find a substitute term for the unlucky *veritas salutaris*, which at the last session of the Council caused so much trouble that it was finally eliminated. The intricate Latin phrase that took its place certainly did not refer only to some truths but *the truth as God teaches it* for our salvation everywhere in Bible, although in various different ways, forms, and literally genres.[16] Here the PBC document quotes for the ninth time no. 11 of *Dei Verbum* to narrate the way the Council replaced by this phrase previous versions of its statement about salvific truth. After rejecting an interpretation that would introduce material distinctions between texts with and without salvific import, the Council finally states that in all texts the truth is to be understood from the point of view of its revelatory content, insofar as God reveals himself for a soteriological purpose: "for the sake of our salvation" (no. 63, on pages 69–71).

Whether this interpretation of *Dei Verbum* is effective enough to define the theological foundations of Catholic exegesis remains to be seen. In any case, it is disheartening to notice that afterward, in nos. 63 and 64, the PBC document itself becomes rather ambivalent. Not only is the "truth for the sake of salvation"[17] nothing short of a replica of the *veritas salutaris*, but the document incorrectly affirms that this phrase in the text is "*a parenthetical clause* (page 70) referring to 'truth.'" If that were true, its function would be to specify (and thus logically limit) and reduce the extent of truth to salvific content. However, neither in the Latin text of *Dei Verbum* nor in the original Italian text of the PBC's document can the notion be found that "in view to our salvation" is a

---

16. Veritatem, quam Deus nostrae salutis causa Litteris Sacris consignari voluit.

17. The Italian text of the PBC reads, "L'inciso 'in vista della nostra salvezza' si riferisce a 'verità,' ciò significa che quando si parla di 'verità della Sacra Scrittura,' si intende quella verità che riguarda la nostra salvezza." The Italian word *inciso* does not mean precisely (only very broadly) "parenthetical clause." It means a "phrase included"—namely, in the text.

"parenthetical clause" that refers to "the Truth." Ultimately the PBC document misinterprets the role of *salutis causa*, for, in fact, this term modifies the predicate *consignari voluit* [wanted to be put] as a complement of purpose and does not restrict "the Truth" to some special kind of "salvific truth." This was pointed out at the last session of the PBC, but the drafter of the paragraph declared his disagreement, and so the text remained unchanged.[18]

Moreover, this ambivalence of the PBC's interpretation fully surfaces in a paragraph dedicated to explaining in detail *Dei Verbum*'s footnote no. 21, which quotes St. Augustine (*De Genesi ad Litteram* 2.9.20) and St. Thomas (*De Veritate* q. 12, a. 2).[19] Here the PBC's document asserts that these two quotations in *Dei Verbum*'s footnote "exclude from biblical teaching all that is not useful for salvation."[20] This is a very harsh statement and does not do justice to St. Augustine's thought but signals a return to the ambiguities of *veritas salutaris* that the Council rejected. More troublesome is the fact that now in no. 64 (page 71), for the first time, an expression appears meaning nothing else than a substitute for *veritas salutaris*: what the Council had decidedly eliminated, now the PBC revives. In Italian, "verità in vista della nostra salvezza" (with the English translation "truth for the sake of our salvation") is an explicit and exact retroversion of *veritas salutaris*.[21] We can summarize. After

18. My English translation of no. 11, published formerly in Farkasfalvy, *Inspiration and Interpretation*, 226–27, is endorsed explicitly—with a similar grammatical analysis—by Pitre, "Mystery of God's Word," 6:53, no. 24.

19. The inconsistency of the text directly refers to the fact that the PBC's text reflects several contributions and amendments by different members, which the final version of the text simply juxtaposed without establishing consistency. The story of this short paragraph in *Dei Verbum*, no.11, and its explanation by the PBC well demonstrates the whole pathetic story that made the problem come about. First, "inerrancy" was eliminated, and "truth without error" replaced it; then "salvific truth"—eliminated much earlier by the Council—came back in the language of the PBC as "truth for the sake of salvation" and has finally obtained the name of "biblical truth" as its new passport for further circulation. Semantics changed, but ambiguity persisted.

20. For the sake of a precise interpretation of footnote no. 21 in *Dei Verbum*, the following must be said: the text it quoted from Augustine should have been left out of *Dei Verbum*. Without the context of the whole sermon, it is confusing, and, once *veritas salutaris* is eliminated, it becomes pointless. St. Thomas's text is also misleading, for it is not about biblical truth. As its Latin text and its translation in the PBC's document show, Aquinas says that "those things which cannot pertain to salvation are alien to the matter of *prophecy*." But "prophecy" is not the same thing as "biblical truth."

21. Moreover, the Italian term *in vista* is much more cautious (and correct). It does not mean "for the sake of," but "in view of."

having narrated how the term *veritas salutaris* failed to obtain the support of the Council, the PBC's document examined the footnotes of *Dei Verbum*'s two quotations, one from Augustine and the other from Aquinas,[22] and *used them as proof texts to reintroduce the previously eliminated term* veritas salutaris *in a barely disguised form.* The English version of the PBC's text, "truth for the sake of our salvation," is even more obviously nothing short of the *veritas salutaris* as a phoenix reborn from its ashes in splendid ambiguity.

The next forty paragraphs (pages 71–121) undertake the task of applying this understanding of "the biblical truth" to various biblical passages of the two testaments. The result is a monotonous listing of the books of the Bible to show that their main content was to put into writing the truth for the sake (or in view) of salvation. This survey of the Bible takes the form of an unstructured litany of salvific truths in the Old and New Testaments (pages 73–93 and 94–121, respectively). In the PBC document, the primacy of the New Testament and of the gospels is mentioned together with the Christological unity of the two testaments. Again, the paragraphs about the book of Revelation (no. 99–101 on pages 109–17), while lengthy, constitute impressive but poorly integrated passages.

The last four pages of this same document want to summarize the lengthy examination of what "biblical truth," or "the truth in the Bible," means. We cannot call it a synthesis because the chapter ends on three disparate notes: (1) The Old Testament expresses God's truthful revelation of himself in history; (2) In the New Testament Jesus reveals the Father; and (3) There is canonical unity and even "canonical logic" in the whole Bible. These points are postulated as a conclusion of the previous forty pages, but they do not seem to follow from them.

The PBC's document, *The Inspiration and Truth of Sacred Scripture*, was completed and published under Pope Francis with low-level publicity. Its reception and ability to penetrate Catholic exegesis, and biblical theology at large, remain to be seen. The best news it obliquely conveyed was that the neo-Scholastic inspiration treatises, pushed out of circulation by *Dei Verbum*, never made a comeback. The most unsettling aspect of the document is its methodological disarray. Consequently, it was un-

---

22. In my opinion, these were left in the text by an editorial accident: when eliminating *veritas salutaris*, the editors failed to delete the footnotes accompanying this phrase.

able to expand *Dei Verbum* and provide the outline of a new theology of inspiration. As far as the Truth of the Bible was concerned, it could not shed the ambiguities associated with *Dei Verbum*; nor could it go beyond the idea of biblical truths as salvific communications mixed with nonsalvific assertions, like grains buried by piles of chaff. In short, the document could not convey a clear vision about where the Truth in the Bible lies or explain what "biblical truth" specifically means.

7 ✣ HOW TO COMPLETE
THE THEOLOGY OF
INSPIRATION?

We must now go back to some earlier phases of our inquiry to advance some questions about the theology of inspiration, which *Dei Verbum* left incomplete. The unfinished topics are the following:

1. Scriptural authorship (divine and human)
2. The linkage of revelation and inspiration in the mystery of the incarnation
3. Inspiration and its relationship to the church
4. The church's role in defining the biblical canon
5. Inspiration as an analogous concept covering the Bible's authors, texts, and readers

Deus Auctor Scripturae and Its Ultimate Meaning

Let us repeat the basic facts in chronological order. In 1943, Augustinus Bea stated that *Deus Auctor Scripturae*, understood in the sense of a literary authorship, is the foundation stone of any Catholic theology of inspiration.[1] In 1958, Karl Rahner made a strong case that *auctor* in

---

1. Bea, *Deus Auctor Sacrae Scripturae*, 16–31. The term "dogmatic constitution" means a document dealing with a doctrinal question on the highest level of authority by the pope in unity with the College of Bishops. It does not mean a document that defines a dogma that had not been previously stated; its focus is doctrinal (as opposed to pastoral) and intends to clarify a matter in

this phrase cannot be taken in the sense of a literary author but only as "originator." In 1964, after lining up more patristic texts, Alonso Schökel went beyond Rahner's research, showing that the testimony of tradition is much more complex than either Bea or Rahner had suspected. In the same year, with the authority of an Ecumenical Council, *Dei Verbum* used the traditional terms by calling God "the *auctor* of the scriptures."[2] However, by applying the two-term expression *inspirator et auctor* only to God and by calling only the human author *verus auctor*, this document showed awareness that the divine and the human authors of the scripture are not to be called *auctores* in the same sense. In 2008, however, Benedict XVI's *Post-Synodal Exhortation* called God (and only God) *verus auctor*, creating thus a slightly different impression about the meaning of the term. In the same year, the pope charged the Pontifical Biblical Commission to write a document to interpret *Dei Verbum* about inspiration and truth in the Bible. Once finished, this document was submitted to Pope Francis and was published under his authority in 2014. Remarkably, now, some fifty years after *Dei Verbum*, in the collective perception of the PBC, the divine authorship of the scriptures appears hardly distinguishable from its divine provenance. The question about God's literary authorship seems to have been fully forgotten, although in the PBC's document, written in Italian, *autore* could have been interpreted to mean "literary author." But nothing appears in the document to support this specific meaning, for the text keeps on talking about the scriptures' divine provenance in the sense of a divine originator (in Rahner's language, *Urheber*) and not as literary *Verfasser* or writer. From all these documents the summary conclusion is this: God is the divine *auctor* of scripture not only as an ultimate Cause or the Creator but in the same sense in which he sets in motion and keeps under control the inner-worldly history of salvation—that is, in the sense he is the cause of the incarnation and the entire process centered on it. As the primary cause of both creation and salvation history he brought about literary works, written through human authors, and is, therefore, *auctor*

dispute. The Dogmatic Constitution *Dei Verbum* covers matters about revelation and tradition left open at the councils of Trent and Vatican I.

2. Vatican II promulgated only two dogmatic constitutions, *Dei Verbum*, about divine revelation, and *Lumen Gentium*, about the church.

scripturae but not a literary author. God was not writing or publishing books.

Nonetheless, Alonso Schökel was right, even if the PBC did not seem to have taken notice: "divine provenance" does not tell enough about God's authorship. Something else must be said that would specifically characterize his authorship without bringing down his role to the level of human activities. Now, in the following paragraphs, we ought to see in what sense his authorship differs from that of human authors.

Personal Authorship

Biblical and patristic sources typically refer to the divine author in personal terms as the Holy Spirit who speaks through Moses and David and, in general, through "the prophets and the apostles." The Nicene Creed says that the Spirit is the one "who has spoken through the Prophets" (*qui locutus est per Prophetas*). Traditionally, the apostolic preaching owes its origin to the descent of the Spirit at Pentecost, when he turned Jesus' chosen disciples into qualified messengers of the gospel. Irenaeus vigorously defends an anti-Gnostic thesis: that both *apostolic preaching and apostolic writing* were fruits of Pentecost.[3] The apostles became qualified first to preach and then to write only after acquiring from the Spirit an understanding of Jesus' deeds and words. Irenaeus uses the Acts of the Apostles not randomly, but explicitly, because he understands that the first chapters of Acts must be read in continuity with the conclusion of Luke (chapter 24) to establish theological connection between the risen Christ and the Spirit he sent from the Father, as he had promised, to constitute the church through the apostolic preaching.

The role of the Holy Spirit is well attested in *Dei Verbum*, but, in the presentation of the traditional teaching on double authorship, it is God who is said to be author or "inspirer and author" (no. 16), with no references to the Spirit or to a trinitarian context. Only sporadic remarks call attention to the fact that divine authorship aims at establishing personal ties between the divine author and the readers of the Bible in a sense of *actuality and immediacy* that, even in the case of the strongest claims for literary authorship, cannot be accomplished by a human writer.

---

3. Irenaeus, *Adversus Haereses* III, Preface.

In the PBC's document the language about the divine provenance of the scriptures is even more pale and impersonal than in *Dei Verbum*. First, the document fails to point out that in biblical texts the most important paradigm is that of divine *speech* and not of divinely induced writing. Since the PBC did not discuss God's purported literary authorship, it does not contribute to the theology of biblical inspiration with regard to the term "divine authorship."

Authoring Words "Living and Effective" (Hebrews 4:12)

Inspiration in the Bible must mean something more than divine provenance. How much more and in what way? The dispute about divine literary authorship provides no answer, in spite of some authors' insistence on a univocal application of the term *auctor*,[4] for a closer look always reveals more dissimilarity than similarity.[5] Nor does transcendental authorship, in a metaphysical sense, provide a solution, because the key concept for the inspired scriptural word is not only the transcendence of the divine author but also the permanence of the inspired result: God who inspires the scriptures is "the God of Abraham, the God of Isaac, and the God of Jacob. He is God not of the dead, but of the living" (Mt 22:32; Mk 12:24; Lk 20:38). It is God who speaks through the Bible, while the human author is defunct. The (human) author who appears under the magnifying glass of a historical-critical investigation is a person of another epoch and is by now long gone. God is not like the human authors whose personal words pass into oblivion; He is the living God. He is supratemporal and as such, speaks to us in various and sundry ways through patriarchs, prophets, apostles, and hagiographers, while he himself remains permanently and personally accessible (and able to personally access us) at any time. He remains *free to approach us directly*, not only by signs and words as if *from without*, but also *from within* when he directly moves us

---

4. This appears most clearly in Bea's essay as he says, "In the usage of the Church Fathers the term *auctor*, applied (*angewendet*) to the hagiographers, becomes *transferred* (*übertragen*) to God"; Bea, *Deus Auctor Sacrae Scripturae*, 27–28.

5. God cannot be called a literary author *in sensu proprio*, as a user neither of a human idiom (God is not an ancient author of Hebrew or of *koine* Greek) nor of a literary form (as if God was the author of a creation epic). God does not follow a discursive path of thinking; he does not experiment with style; he does not fail to express what he intends to say; he does not manifest his changing moods, his inner conflicts, tensions, unresolved dilemmas, etc., as a human author would.

by grace. The immediacy and efficacy by which God speaks to all human beings in the hidden realm of the conscience and one's self-awareness are unparalleled to what external human speech can accomplish. The Spirit speaking in the scriptures is the same one who can speak to us at any time. Not only *can* he do so, but he *does*. The One who inspired the biblical authors *can and does* inspire the reader. In the intimacy of the soul, the Spirit can approach even the illiterate and those who have no access to biblical texts. Besides speaking to individual conscience, God paved a special way to man through a history of salvation, in which he addresses man in a community of salvation; his people is the church, formed in concrete assemblies and worldwide convocations. Whenever the scriptures are read in the church, the biblical word is *actualized*; therefore, "*Thus says the Lord*" is an utterance that refers to both the past and the present. Here we touch upon a neglected sentence of *Dei Verbum* by which the document recognized continuity between inspired writing and inspired reading of the biblical books: "Holy Scripture must be read and interpreted in the same Spirit in which it was written."[6] That Spirit is the One who congregates the Body of Christ and addresses mankind as it walks the pathways of history.

What has just been stated implies that, besides a divine provenance of the biblical word, we must speak of a divine presence that has permanently accompanied the biblical word ever since it was written down. Divine provenance *through* inspired human authors refers per se to a transient action that may be explored in terms of instrumentality, though that alone cannot explain the inspiration of the Bible by a God who is *Auctor et Inspirator*. For the inspired *texts*, this divine provenance means a permanent effect, ready to become at any time a personal communication addressing the reader's mind and soul, so that God's word shows itself as an actual reality, sacred and supratemporal. This is what is meant by the Dominical *logion* found identically in each synoptic gospel:

Heaven and earth will pass away, but my words will not pass away. (Mt 24:35; Mk 13:31; Lk 21:33)

---

6. This is in *Dei Verbum*, no. 12, with a footnote referring to St. Jerome, *In Galatians* 5.19–20 (Patrologia Latina 26, 417 A). The English text on the Vatican website carried for years a misleading typo: "in the sacred spirit" instead of "in the same spirit."

When the modern term of "canonical meaning" was introduced into biblical exegesis, this aspect of inspiration was also reassessed. Of course, speaking of "the Bible" as a generic term presupposes some concept of a canon. God's word is permanent in its written form, but the interconnectedness of the books and their interpretive framework as a salvation history become more manifest through the establishment of the canon. The very fact that today and over the past 2,000 years of Christianity the biblical books have been interpreted against the background of the history of Israel, the person of Jesus, and the history of the early church suggests that this ensemble of the Bible was not the result of fiction or of a random process of networking between isolated or arbitrarily connected literary products. While the historical-critical method interprets each book by itself against its immediate historical background, seeking mostly the authorial intent behind specific literary works or units, canonical interpretation insists on the historical interconnection of the biblical books. For some scholars this may be relevant only with respect to the social context or the cultural background of a book; others insist on the biblical authors' ideas about larger units of a sacred history, while typically, only faith-based interpreters work for a theological understanding of the history of revelation. In any case, it is extremely important to also understand inspiration against the background and in the perspective that the biblical canon presupposes. Such an outlook brings us to the conclusion that biblical faith assumes not only the Bible's divine provenance, but also an authorial intent on God's behalf, the ultimate context in which the Truth of the Bible can and must be affirmed. A substantial portion of the patristic and medieval heritage saw scripture in this way when speaking of its spiritual meaning, regardless of the diverse methods by which ancient exegetes tried to appropriate such a meaning.[7]

7. We cannot speak of a spiritual meaning of the Bible without assuming the presence of the Spirit in both the human author and the reader or, as the book of Revelation says, trying to "hear" what the Spirit is saying to the church. It may be helpful to quote here a less often quoted New Testament text, 1 Pt 1:10–12, about the inspiration of both reader and writer in reference to revelation, inspiration, and the unity of the two testaments: "Concerning this salvation, the *prophets* who prophesied of the grace that was to be yours made careful *search and inquiry*, inquiring about the person or time that the *Spirit of Christ within them* indicated when it testified in advance to the sufferings destined for Christ and the subsequent glory. It was *revealed* to them that they were *serving not themselves but you*, in regard to the things that have now been announced to you through *those*

Here we probably find the reason ancient authors, when writing about inspiration, wrote more about the inspired texts than about the inspired authors, although later, when the theology of inspiration began to be forced into the narrow system of double authorship, many of their insights fell into oblivion.

Individual and/or Collective Inspiration

While traditional doctrine dealing with inspired human authorship routinely uses models of individual inspiration, there is no reason to forbid the possibility of more complex scenarios that modern biblical studies propose by pointing to multiple stages of development and the participation of several authors and redactors, in the process by which various biblical books came about.

Dei Verbum itself presupposes a model of gradual development for both revelation and inspiration by pointing to the stages of oral dissemination and transmission as a chain connecting the Revealer with the inspired writer. This way of thinking about the origins of scriptures goes back to the works of Irenaeus, whose texts greatly influenced *Dei Verbum*. Since, according to *Dei Verbum*, the role of oral transmitters precedes the activities of the inspired writers, one must conclude that in whatever form or fashion we speak of inspiration as an individual charism, we cannot disregard continuity between oral and written transmission. In fact, when dealing with such matters as the Mosaic authorship of the Pentateuch or the developmental analysis of the prophetic books, exegetes of all persuasions assume a chain of oral transmitters, even if in the Bible the titles of the books attribute their origin to one person. Most often it is assumed that prophetic preaching was originally oral and only later, through consecutive stages, was channeled into written documents. For example, the book of Jeremiah contains many explicit references to the dramatic stages through which Jeremiah's oral message passed before becoming written word.[8]

---

who brought you good news by the *Holy Spirit* sent from heaven—things into which angels long to look!"

8. "Then the king sent Jehudi to get the scroll, and he took it from the chamber of Elishama the secretary; and Jehudi read it to the king and all the officials who stood beside the king. Now the

We must refer also to the patristic notion of divine pedagogy, attributed by many church fathers to God's relentless effort of moving forward with salvation history.[9] Both revelation and inspiration are a process through centuries, involving God's gradual self-disclosure and moving from a less perfect to a more perfect expression of revealed truth. These approaches to scriptural origins necessarily imply an extended notion of inspiration with a plurality of persons involved. On a larger scale, if we follow the traditional attribution of the Old Testament to "Moses and the Prophets" or speak of "the apostolic gospels" or "apostolic writings" or recognize their apostolicity by secondary claims (even if calling them "pseudepigraphs"), we make references to several persons and roles in this process. When speaking of a Johannine School or a School of St. Matthew or Pauline Circles (which may or may not be an arguable process in all cases), we consistently assume that the charism of (subjective) inspiration involved several persons with various roles in producing the inspired text.

In other words, the charism of inspiration, in whatever context we think of it, must be spoken of as part of the whole process that links revelation as words and deeds to the end products—that is, the books of written words in the two testaments. This notion brings us to a clearer understanding that, indeed, God spoke in a multiplicity of forms of expression—according to the Vulgate *multifarie multisques modis* (Heb 1:1)—until he deigned to speak through an individual human nature in which his Son assumed flesh, died, and was raised according to the testimony of the prophets and the Son's acts and words were committed to oral and written expression through his disciples. Because of the variety of ways in which inspiration involves a multiplicity of human beings into authoring biblical books, the understanding we describe here obliterates most efforts, which in the past concentrated on a single, generic, psychological process as a type of *continuum* between the abstractly conceived divine author and one individual's intellect and will, who then eventual-

---

king was sitting in his winter apartment (it was the ninth month), and there was a fire burning in the brazier before him. As Jehudi read three or four columns the king would cut them off with a penknife and throw them into the fire in the brazier, until the entire scroll was consumed in the fire in the brazier"; Jer 36:19–23.

9. *Dei Verbum*, no. 15.

ly wrote or dictated the biblical text. In reality, inspiration moves human persons to obtain insights and understanding, retain and evoke memories, and formulate concepts or compose narratives by a variety of human activities, through which God's word reaches its audience in finally crystallized written documents.

There is no reason for assuming a uniform pattern through which each part of the Bible came to its canonical variety of results. Instead, each individual book must be regarded as having had its own story (*habent sua fata libelli*):[10] in the Bible also, each literary unit is created by a limited number of responsible authors and editors who brought the text to its final form under divine inspiration and so assured transmission for the word of God into a stable, readable, and rereadable form, accessible for all people versed in a particular idiom. With the caution that all this happened in the context of human frailty and imperfection, we must assert that authors and redactors are *veri auctores*—that is, they made their contributions with their understanding of what they were doing, even if their understanding was limited, incomplete, and imperfect.

Clearly, therefore, individual authorship is not indispensable for someone to be called "inspired author." By projecting a chain of successive individuals, who all participated (even if only anonymously) in the process leading to the production of a book, one must not necessarily make the concept of an inspired author vanish by a fragmentation of the scriptural books into discontinuous layers with a disarray of authorial intents. Such an understanding of human authorship would render inspiration pointless: at the end of the process we would not know what the Spirit is telling the church (see Rv 2:7, 2:11, 2:17, 3:6, 3:13, 3:22). If, however, we assume that the text, issued under inspiration, preserves and transmits God's word through a process that is providentially guided and protected, we learn to value the reception and preservation of the canonical books by the church as an important and necessary complement to inspiration, whereby the Spirit's speech obtains lasting perma-

---

10. This is part of a hexameter, an often-quoted line from a fragment of a work by Terentianus Maurus, a Latin grammarian of the late second century A.D.: [*Pro captu lectoris*] *habent sua fata libelli* (l. 1286). I quote it in its common interpretation: "[according to the measure of the readers,] all books have their [own] destinies."

nence amidst other writings entrusted to the care of the community of believers. This line of thought will enable us, in the last chapter of this book, to treat the essential links that connect inspiration and canon. But first we look at another central preoccupation of *Dei Verbum* and of the PBC document studied previously.

8 ✝ TRUTH AND TRUTHFULNESS

MOVING BEYOND *DEI VERBUM*

Shortcomings in the Conciliar Text

Inerrancy or Truth without Error?

Replacing *inerrantia* by *veritas sine errore* was probably just a sideshow in the birth of *Dei Verbum*. It was sad to see the Council take refuge in semantics by introducing some sort of political correctness in the way a new brand of theologians began to speak exclusively about "the truth of the Bible" and relegate the expression "inerrancy" to conservatives or evangelicals; but the *Relator* of the committee, presenting *Dei Verbum* under the pressure of a vocal minority, agreed to insert "sine errore."

By itself, the term "the Truth of the Bible" had little to offer. Neither the Council nor the drafting committee intended to break continuity with the dogmatic tradition or the modern papal encyclicals that frequently spoke of inerrancy. The neo-Thomistic textbooks' teaching about inerrancy did not forget to mention that in *Providentissimus Deus*, Pope Leo XIII rejected Cardinal Newman's proposal to allow errors to enter the biblical texts by terming them *obiter dicta* ("casual" or "side remarks"). The pope's thesis was consistently upheld in subsequent papal documents.[1]

---

1. "For all the books which the Church receives as sacred and canonical, are written wholly and entirely, with all their parts, at the dictation of the Holy Ghost"; *Providentissimus*, no. 20. Most scholars considered the term "dictation" exaggerated or inappropriate; only a minority were aware

Some might have felt that inerrancy was an unsolvable problem from the earliest times, and it was for this reason that symbolic or spiritual interpretations kept returning to exegesis because of certain texts like that of the world's creation in six days or of Adam from mud and of Eve from Adam's rib, mankind's fall into a sinful state because their ancestors ate a piece of fruit, Jonah surviving for three days in a whale. A global negative judgment about the church fathers' search for a spiritual meaning in such narratives has been refuted many times.[2] Yet it is more important to insist that, for decades before Vatican II, the esteem of patristic exegesis made a significant comeback by those who saw that attention to the literary genre of the biblical narratives solves many such issues.[3] For *Dei Verbum*, however, immediate magisterial context was provided by *Divino Afflante* and the literature that it had prompted. But *Divino Afflante* tried to vindicate the truth of the Bible's *literary meaning* on the basis of the literary form (or *genus litterarium*) of each textual unit, a framework that raised unexpected problems.

Truth in Accordance with the Literary Genre

As it is often noted, prior to *Dei Verbum*, while the terminology of inerrancy still reigned, a relaxation of strict rules for plenary inerrancy took place only at one occasion: the publication of *Divino Afflante*, which stated that the true meaning of a biblical text cannot be established without taking into account the *literary genre* that an author adopts. As the encyclical admits, this approach has been used before, but now it was

---

that in Latin *dictare* is linked to the present-day German verb *dichten*, meaning to "compose"; see Jean Leclercq, *L'amour des lettres et le désir de Dieu: Initiation aux auteurs monastiques du Moyen Âge* (Paris: Cerf, 1957), 72–73.

2. An excellent essay is found about the interpretation of poetic and narrative texts by Francis Martin and Sean McEvenue, "Truth Told in the Bible: Biblical Poetics and the Question of Truth," in *The International Bible Commentary*, ed. William R. Farmer (Collegeville, Minn.: Liturgical Press, 1998), 116–30.

3. See the summary by Vawter, *Biblical Inspiration*, 119–31, describing the many positive features of Catholic exegesis between the two Vatican Councils as it focused on the literary forms or literary genres for determining the truth value of various texts. Vawter rightly points out the merits of M. J. Lagrange, *La méthode historique* (Paris: Gabalda, 1903), and F. von Hummelauer, *Exegetisches zur Inspirationsfrage* (Freiburg: Herder, 1904) by using a correct approach to the question of inerrancy with regard to texts coming from a prescientific milieu.

also projecting that many issues could finally be put to rest: the book of Job takes place within the framework of a fictitious story; Jonah is not a historical prophet; the books of Judith, Esther, and Tobit and large parts of Daniel belong to the genre of historical fiction, with many additional easy solutions offered, mostly for problems belonging to biblical history and geography.

Much too soon, however, Catholics realized that new challenges from the new approaches of literary criticism came with strong emphasis on the literary genre but threatened to subvert the foundations of the Christian message. The study of literary forms by the relatively new method of *Formgeschichte* (in English, *Form Criticism*) was initiated right after the First World War by Martin Dibelius, Karl Ludwig Schmidt, and Rudolf Bultmann in relative isolation from Catholic biblical studies.[4] This new methodology, however, quickly began to penetrate Catholic biblical studies after World War II, first in Germany, then almost everywhere in Western Europe. *Formgeschichte* claimed to possess new tools for deciding the historicity of religious narratives by analyzing and classifying the literary forms of the texts. While for many it appeared attractive, it raised strong suspicions in others, including all those who had mixed feelings about the relaxed standards for historicity in *Divino Afflante*.[5] Especially under the influence of Bultmann, who coupled his use of form criticism with philosophical ideas of existentialist tendencies and ideas stemming from the school of "history of religions" (*Religionsgeschichtliche Schule*), the new method was quickly coupled with the thesis that most ancient religious texts must be considered cultic myths whose historicizing content must be first eliminated and only their cultic or liturgical content retained. Bultmann's influential program of demythologization swept through the continent as an aggressive agenda that distilled and discredited the mythological elements from the biblical accounts while dismissing

4. After Vatican II, Catholic biblical scholarship revised its stance on the form-critical method while remaining critical of its philosophical presuppositions and especially of Bultmann's theory and practice of demythologization. A summary of the Catholic experience with the *Formgeschichte* is well documented in the Pontifical Biblical Commission's document *The Interpretation of the Bible in the Church*, published in 1993 (Rome, Edizioni Vaticane: 1993); see Joseph Fitzmyer, *The Biblical Commission's Document "The Interpretation of the Bible in the Church,"* Subsidia biblica 18 (Rome: Pontifical Biblical Institute, 1995).

5. The content and impact of this encyclical by Pope Pius XII (1943) is well described by Vawter, *Biblical Inspiration*, 84–85 and 101, with references to post–Vatican II literature.

their historical credibility altogether. For papal authorities, exercising an oversight of Catholic teaching, fighting Bultmann's growing popularity meant a return to the antimodernist battle that they continued until the eve of Vatican II. As early as 1950, this new problem had greatly influenced Pope Pius XII's encyclical *Humani Generis*, which practically froze the climate of Catholic biblical scholarship by introducing a new era of defensiveness and suspicion.

As mentioned earlier, *Divino Afflante* was originally welcomed as a papal encouragement to explain the biblical texts' apparent lack of historicity by establishing their literary genre so that the true authorial intent behind a text could be truthfully ascertained and problems of inerrancy eliminated or at least reduced. It was hoped that the exegete, in addition to using linguistic and grammatical tools, also used the tools of modern literary criticism and succeeded in vindicating the *real authorial intent* behind the text *and its truthfulness*. Now, suddenly, the euphoric mood of the Catholic biblical movement was chilled. The similarities between literary criticism encouraged by *Divino Afflante* and Bultmann's movement of the *Formgeschichte* became a source of confusion. It has also become increasingly clear that the new trend of demythologization was based on a Protestant theological outlook that questioned the historic nature of biblical revelation altogether and raised systematic doubts about the historicity of most gospel narratives. By its strongly conservative push, Pope Pius's new encyclical *Humani Generis* began again to stir up the basic questions of biblical inerrancy with respect to both testaments. The document was decried as "resetting the clock" by several decades, for, just as in the early period of the antimodernist controversies, it cautioned against reducing the biblical stories—from the first chapters of Genesis to all miracle stories of both testaments—to religious myths. Some systematic theologians rightly perceived that the ultimate issue was, indeed, not the use of modern literary criticism but the factual nature of revelation. At the opposite side, exegetes became afraid that the "progress" achieved by *Divino Afflante* would be suddenly reversed and their newly granted liberties curtailed. It seems, however, that little attention was paid to the thesis, by now routinely assumed by Catholics, that God was the literary author of the biblical texts. However, this assumption was the ultimate reason every conclusion obtained by the use of literary criticism was automatically elevated to theologi-cal significance.[6] If God were a literary author, the literary imperfec-tions (or to be more explicit, misperceptions of primitive minds, non-sequiturs introduced by unskilled authors, vicissitudes of transmissions and redactions) would have to be seen as authored and not only allowed by God. In retrospect, there appears an eerie similarity between Bult-mann's revolutionary movement, linking the *Formgeschichte* of the liter-ary forms with demythologization, and the Catholic position pointing out the decisive importance of the texts' literary genres ascribed to the divine literary author and the inerrancy of their truth content.

It was ironic—and confusing—that *Humani Generis* continued to champion, as *Divino Afflante* had, the progressive view of the prima-cy of the authorial intent (by the *human author*) as the one that alone tells the true meaning of the text, while cautioning against those newly emerging trends that urged the incorporation into Catholic exegesis the rediscovered patristic views on the spiritual sense hidden in the text.[7] With this, *Humani Generis* defended, in fact, the claim of the historical-critical exegesis that the true meaning of the text coincided with what critical exegesis designated as its proper territory of expertise: the science of discovering the authorial intent behind a text. In this new context, the discussion about the literary meaning of the text kept supposing that the human and divine authors were *auctores* in the same sense of the word and that, consequently, their intent was coextensive. The exegete was trapped in an unsolvable problem. He was expected to maintain that the valid and solid meaning of the text was to be found in a demonstrable authorial intent and to assume at the same time that *this* state of mind of a human being was lacking any error. Otherwise he would attribute to God (the principal literary author) some degree of error or ignorance.

6. The sudden jump from the concept of God as author of the scriptures to inerrancy is a clear indicator that, although not openly declared, a literary authorship is being meant: "To return, how-ever, to the new opinions mentioned above, a number of things are proposed or suggested by some even against *the divine authorship of Sacred Scripture*. For some go so far as to pervert the sense of the Vatican Council's definition that *God is the author of Holy Scripture*, and they put forward again the opinion, already often condemned, which asserts that *immunity from error* extends only to those parts of the Bible that treat of God or of moral and religious matters. They even wrongly speak of a human sense of the Scriptures, beneath which a divine sense, which they say is the only infallible meaning, lies hidden"; Pius XII, *Humani Generis*, no. 22.

7. See the last sentence in the previous note.

The scheme of double authorship thus became a conceptual straitjacket, limiting the divine author's communications by means of the actual intent of the human author. This perception of the status of Catholic biblical scholarship was the true background of that embarrassing scene of Vatican II, at which Cardinal König attempted to speak up on behalf of the liberties of the Catholic exegete by proposing to the Council a public recognition of the presence of errors in the Bible.[8] This is also why, when the concept of inerrancy (in terms of *sine errore*) had made its way back to *Dei Verbum*, some concluded that the church was hopelessly stuck with its traditional teaching, or—as Raymond Brown suggested in a footnote—it was addicted to ongoing doubletalk and was unable to face the errors of its past.[9] In any case, it can be said today that inerrancy remains explicitly on the program of the church as a main concern with regard to biblical interpretation, but, unfortunately, no sufficient clarity has been reached about what inerrancy would exactly entail.

What I described earlier may finally bring to the reader's attention another set of circumstances that accompanied the first attempt of the Council to deal with the topic of revelation in its first failed document, *De Fontibus Revelationis*. While the Council was evenly divided about the topic of revelation and inspiration, the papal organs of the *Magisterium* (basically the Holy Office under Cardinal Ottaviani) continued to fight its battle against the trends of Bultmannian exegesis rapidly spreading among Catholic exegetes. As late as 1964, between the first two ses-

---

8. The cardinal avoided the word "error," yet he used the equivalent expression *a veritate deficere* (= being defective with respect to truth).

9. "Essential to the critical interpretation of church documents is the realization that the Roman Catholic Church does not change her official stance in a blunt way. Past statements are not rejected but are requited with praise and then reinterpreted at the same time. It is falsely claimed that there has been no change towards the Bible in Catholic Church thought because Pius XII and Vatican II paid homage to documents issued by Leo XIII, Pius X and Benedict XV and therefore clearly meant to reinforce the teaching of their predecessors. What really was going on was an attempt gracefully to retain what was salvageable from the past and to move in a new direction with as little friction as possible. To those for whom it is a doctrinal issue that the Church never changes one must repeat Galileo's *sotto voce* response when told that it was a doctrinal issue that the earth does not move: 'E pur si muove' (Nevertheless it moves). And the best proof of movement is the kind of biblical scholarship that would not have been tolerated for a moment by church authorities in the first forty years of this century"; Brown, *Critical Meaning of the Bible*, 18–19n41. (The whispered words of Galileo are—according to historical critics—legendary; they were never said.)

sions of Vatican II, an interim Pontifical Biblical Council published a new document in defense of the historicity of the Gospels: *De Historica Veritate Evangeliorum* (often quoted as *Sancta Mater Ecclesia*).[10] *Dei Verbum* was strongly influenced by both *Divino Afflante* and this much later document, *De Historica Veritate Evangeliorum*. In no. 12, the conciliar document preserved the encyclical's positive tone by encouraging Catholic scholars to engage in every form of biblical research:

To search out the intention of the sacred writers, attention should be given, among other things, to "literary forms."[11] For truth is set forth and expressed differently in texts which are variously historical, prophetic, poetic, or of other forms of discourse. The interpreter must investigate what meaning the sacred writer intended to express and actually expressed in particular circumstances by using contemporary literary forms in accordance with the situation of his own time and culture. For the correct understanding of what the sacred author wanted to assert, due attention must be paid to the customary and characteristic styles of feeling, speaking and narrating which prevailed at the time of the sacred writer, and to the patterns men normally employed at that period in their everyday dealings with one another.

At the same time, *Dei Verbum*'s chapter V (no. 18–19), by a lengthy treatment of the apostolic provenance of the canonical gospels, echoes the 1964 document with specific references to a set of nonnegotiable positions concerning the historical reliability of the canonical gospels:

The Church has always and everywhere held and continues to hold that the four Gospels are of apostolic origin. For what the Apostles preached in fulfillment of the commission of Christ, afterwards they themselves and apostolic men, under the inspiration of the divine Spirit, handed on to us in writing: the foundation of faith, namely, the fourfold Gospel, according to Matthew, Mark, Luke, and John.

10. Pontifical Biblical Council, "The Historicity of the Gospels," *Acta Apostolicae Sedis* 56 (1964): 712–18. This is often regarded to be the last document of the old Pontifical Biblical Commission that still functioned as an organ of the Magisterium, speaking in the name of the pope. But, in fact, the Latin text refers to it as the "Instructio Sancta Mater Ecclesia," produced by an interim entity called *Pontificium Consilium Studiis Bibliorum Provehendis* (Pontifical Council for Promoting Biblical Studies). See its English text, translated by Joseph A. Fitzmyer, in *Theological Studies* 25 (1964): 386–408.

11. Here the term "literary form" does not mean the use of Bultmann's method of the *Formgeschichte*, but Pius XII's *genus litterarium* as proposed in his Encyclical *Divino Afflante*.

Holy Mother Church[12] has firmly and with absolute constancy held, and continues to hold, that the four Gospels just named, whose historical character the Church unhesitatingly asserts, faithfully hand on what Jesus Christ, while living among men, really did and taught for their eternal salvation until the day He was taken up into heaven (see Acts 1:1). Indeed, after the Ascension of the Lord the Apostles handed on to their hearers what He had said and done. This they did with that clearer understanding which they enjoyed (Acts 1:3) after they had been instructed by the glorious events of Christ's life and taught by the light of the Spirit of truth (Acts 1:2). The sacred authors wrote the four Gospels, selecting some things from the many which had been handed on by word of mouth or in writing, reducing some of them to a synthesis, explaining some things in view of the situation of their churches and preserving the form of proclamation but always in such fashion that they told us the honest truth about Jesus (Acts 1:4). For their intention in writing was that either from their own memory and recollections, or from the witness of those who "themselves from the beginning were eyewitnesses and ministers of the Word" we might know "the truth" concerning those matters about which we have been instructed (see Luke 1:2–4).[13]

We have here additional evidence that *Dei Verbum* was born under unusual tensions between forces not fully understood in their intensity by the members of the Council, while the pope, the Roman Curia, and the theological experts lacked the resources (and ran out of time) for bringing under full control all burning issues.

As has been emphasized repeatedly in this book, an unqualified adherence to the concept of God's *literary* authorship perpetuated the problems of inerrancy. While *Divino Afflante* asserted the importance of literary genres and emphasized the primacy of literary meaning and *Humani Generis* resumed the severe tone of the antimodernist controversies, Catholic exegetes found themselves trapped in a dilemma. If the literary sense is decisive and God had to be thought of as a literary author, one can hardly avoid the conclusion that, in some sense, inspiration guides the human author in choosing literary genres. Yet here again one should remember Rahner's vehement objection against *this* model of the double authorship: "God does not write letters to Philemon!" In other

---

12. This phrase (in Latin: *Sancta Mater Ecclesia*) is an explicit reference to the 1964 document *The Historicity of the Gospels*, which starts with these words and contains the teaching of the paragraph.

13. *Dei Verbum*, nos. 18–19.

words, God and the human author cannot be considered authors in the same sense and on the same level, nor can they be thought of as authors by joint choices.

From Literary Genre to Salvific Truth

It may be surprising that, in the way *Dei Verbum* quotes *Divino Afflante*, the literary genres seem to pertain exclusively to the realm of human authorship.[14] Is this a corrective? *Divino Afflante* did not categorically state that God was not a literary author and certainly did not derive the literary genres in the Bible from God's authorship. Yet by comparing *Dei Verbum* and *Divino Afflante* a shift appears, leading to uncertainties or even inconsistencies. In what sense is the truth, as intended by God, to be found, revealed or veiled, expressed or hidden, behind the literary form? Is the literary genre only an obstacle that the exegete removes to access and excoriate the meaning of the text, or does it play a positive role when presenting the divinely intended content in literary clothing? The medieval concept of *involucrum* (meaning "wrapped" content) attributes a positive role to the literary form, of which the spiritual meaning remains inseparable. By references to "divine pedagogy" or "condescendence," both *Dei Verbum* and *Divino Afflante* refer to the biblical texts' human characteristics (including their imperfections), but still as willed by their divine "author and inspirer," because they play the important role of accommodating the human recipient and lead him to the core of what God intended to say.

Divine Intent and Canonical Context

A further remedy to the ambiguities left behind by *Divino Afflante* and *Humani Generis* might be found in *Dei Verbum* in the sentence that concludes paragraph no. 12:

14. This is certainly the way *Dei Verbum*, no. 12 (with an explicit reference in footnote 8) applies the following text of *Divino Afflante*: "The interpreter must investigate what meaning the sacred writer intended to express and actually expressed in particular circumstances by using contemporary literary forms in accordance with the situation of his own time and culture. For the correct understanding of what the sacred author wanted to assert, due attention must be paid to the customary and characteristic styles of feeling, speaking and narrating which prevailed at the time of the sacred writer, and to the patterns men normally employed at that period in their everyday dealings with one another."

But, since Holy Scripture must be read and interpreted in the same Spirit, in which it was written, for, in order to explain the meaning of the sacred texts, no less careful attention must be given to the content and unity of the whole of Scripture *with due attention paid to the living tradition of the whole Church and the Analogy of the Faith.*[15]

Here a counterweight is placed against the preponderance of a mere literary interpretation of the biblical texts as presented by *Divino Afflante.* For it is obvious that the unity of the scriptures, and thus the ultimate meaning of the biblical texts, must be sought in a wider canonical context, a context that had been at least partially hidden from each human author. God alone knows the whole context of salvation history; the human author is not aware, even in the highest forms of prophecy, of the full canonical context into which his text is about to be inserted. Only in the mind of God does the meaning of the divine words and deeds of salvation history coalesce into a unified salvation history. "Biblical truth," a term fabricated by the PBC to designate *the Truth* "that God wants to be assigned to writing in the Bible," is available to the human mind only in the total context of the scriptures, because that was not available before the one mediator between God and man, the man Jesus Christ had manifested it (see 1 Tm 2:5).

The reception of *Dei Verbum* did not proceed in the direction that would have been friendly to a canonical or spiritual exegesis. A good example of the document's twisted reception is found in the distinction introduced by Raymond Brown between the text's critical and ecclesial meanings. To resolve tensions between the two, he began to distinguish between what the Bible "meant" and what it "means." Brown must have been aware that in practical terms a much longer list of distinctions was needed: the authorial intent (what a biblical writer or redactor had in mind), the meaning that the text obtained when included in a scriptural canon, and the meaning of the text when interpreted by its liturgical use or when quoted in theological disputes or homiletic and catechetical contexts. When Brown opted for replacing all the aforementioned

---

15. My text follows closely the Latin text that the official English translation, widely spread (for example, in most copies of the Catholic *New American Bible*), only loosely renders: "Sed, cum Sacra Scriptura eodem Spiritu quo scripta est etiam legenda sit et interpretanda sit, ad recte sacrorum textuum sensum eruendum, non minus diligenter respiciendum est ad contentum et unitatem totius Scripturae, ratione habita vivae totius Ecclesiae Traditionis et analogiae fidei."

meanings by a single formula separating what the text *means* and *meant*, he launched a simplistic parlance that became popular in American Catholic seminaries, colleges, and universities. With no philosophical epistemology and hermeneutics to undergird it, he gave the impression that the theological or ecclesial meaning of a text might be regarded as fluid. At the same time, the exegete felt encouraged to securely pursue his program of critical exegesis by claiming that the original meaning was locked in the (human) authorial intent, which was allegedly accessible (only) through historical-critical studies.

It seems to me that Brown's system is nothing more than a mutation of neo-modernism, mostly interested in providing some space for policies of living and letting live for all who are using various kinds of approaches in biblical studies. In this system, the biblical experts stay anxiously fenced off in a VIP section reserved for the elite, consisting of those who know Hebrew and Greek and thus can ponder the nuances of ancient texts and consider themselves to be the ones who practice scientific studies of the Bible. Others concentrate on what the Bible "means" for the church in various theological or devotional perspectives. This split was originally created and cultivated by the modernists and has reappeared in the last decades of the twentieth century.

The Trap of the Salvific Truth and the Authorial Intent

The truth of the Bible cannot be dissolved into an amalgamation of polyvalent uses of a text. If we follow *Divino Afflante* with an exclusive interest in the original authorial intent, we certainly remain faithful, at least implicitly, to two principles, both rooted in the wisdom of early Christianity, to admit no compromise: (1) the text has a literal meaning upon which all other (derived or accommodated) meanings are built and (2) the literal meaning cannot be obtained with sufficient precision unless the tools of language (linguistics and grammar) are combined with the approach of literary analysis, specifically the issue of the *genus litterarium*. However, these principles need to be completed by a third one opening a wider horizon: the intent of the primary *auctor/originator* who is the living God and the Holy Spirit. Although we must deny that God is a literary author, we must affirm his *personal* authorship, which cannot be restricted by the perspective or intent of the human author who, although a truly literary author, is limited by time, culture, history, and literary genre.

After such lengthy preliminary remarks, we may see both the wisdom and the problematic features of *Dei Verbum*, no. 11, concerning scripture's truthfulness, a statement that resists so many attempts at interpretation.[16]

According to my proposed translation:

The books of Scripture must be acknowledged as teaching solidly, faithfully and without error the Truth which God wanted to be put in Sacred Writings for the sake of our salvation.

After the sixty years that elapsed since the last conciliar discussion of *Dei Verbum*, one may still be perplexed about what the drafters of *Dei Verbum* had in mind when, for the first time, they were proposing and defending the expression *veritas salutaris*.[17] A quick search in the Patrologia Latina can show that this expression does not belong to patristic vocabulary, or even to the theological language of the Middle Ages. However, in the acts of the Council of Trent, the gospel is said to be proclaimed first by Jesus and then preached by disciples over the whole world "as the fountainhead of all salvific truth and moral discipline" (tamquam fontem omnis et *veritatis salutaris* et morum disciplinae). Apparently, in a context about the purity of the gospel, the expression *veritas salutaris* means the totality of the Christian doctrine, distinguished from moral teaching. Here it is used in the singular but in a universal sense. Did the drafters of *Dei Verbum* lift this term from its context? If they did, they introduced a slight alteration so that it obtained the

16. In Latin: "Scripturae libri veritatem quam Deus nostrae salutis causa Litteris Sacris consignari voluit, firmiter, fideliter et sine errore docere profitendi sunt." In the (assumedly "official") English translation, propagated in largest number among the faithful by the *New American Bible*: "The books of Scripture must be acknowledged as teaching solidly, faithfully and without error that truth which God wanted put into sacred writings for the sake of salvation."

17. Here I am, as an eyewitness of each session of the PBC 2008–13, trying to figure out the authorial intent of a *collective* human author—namely, the Pontifical Biblical Commission, which, in a way contrary to its official intention to clear away the ambiguities attached to *Dei Verbum*, no. 11, produced a text with two conflicting understandings of that paragraph and, again, in the Italian rendition of the commission's document, adhered to divergent translations of the Latin passage of *Dei Verbum*.

meaning of "doctrinal teachings about both faith and morals." This unclear vocabulary indicated a slippery slope so that the protesting minority had a legitimate concern, for, no matter what the *relator* of the drafting committee had said, the text was ambiguous. What followed during
the last fifty years, including the PBC's latest document, confirmed the
suspicion that the lack of clarity was not only a matter of semantics but
was residing in the minds of those drafting the text.

The 2013 document of the PBC, *The Inspiration and the Truth of Sacred Scripture*, is the best proof that a large number of Catholic exegetes
demanded that the Bible be read without any a priori claim of inerrancy
(errorless truths) but also with the admission that, in nonreligious matters, the biblical text reflects the mentality of past ages, with a great deal
of ignorance in matters of historical, geographic, natural, and political
sciences. Yet, supposing such a broad concept of the limits to the truths
of the Bible may not suffice. Today's average student, enrolled to study
the Bible, is easily shocked by much of what he learns. For example, many
historical critics deny that Abraham ever existed, that the Exodus ever
took place; they also question if Moses was a historical figure and, in general, hold in doubt whether numerous important events narrated in the
Old Testament have ever happened. One might seek consolation in the
fact that the history narrated in the gospels is not assailed with similar
ease. In fact, the words and deeds of Jesus are more readily taken up by
historical or archaeological research. New Testament history is practiced
with more openness to verify the data of the texts. This is, however, not
so much a reflection of some remaining belief in the Bible's inerrancy, but
rather of a present-day fatigue due to the various "quests" of the historical
Jesus: their results are suspicious not only to the uneducated faithful but
to many college-educated laypersons, even after a cursory college course
about the Bible as literature.

In my opinion, the sad truth is that the concept of salvific truth was
eliminated by the Council from the text of *Dei Verbum*, but not from
the minds of Catholic biblical scholars as the PBC's apparent comfort
with the expression "Biblical Truth(s)," a code word for *veritas salutaris*,
eloquently proves.

As long as we are fixated on thinking about propositional truths
and force upon ourselves the notion of equating what the (human) au-

thor has in mind with what God is asserting, we remain trapped within the human author's perspective, pondering the truthfulness of often banal culturally and historically conditioned statements. It seems that even at Vatican II, the discussion about the Truth of the Bible was too narrowly restricted to the Bible's literary meaning and was identified with the human author's intent. This perspective was then mistakenly assessed as needing further *material* restrictions. The specifically salvific character of God's word does not proceed (only) from the truthfully expressed conceptual content that the biblical text transmits, but from an encounter with Christ through the Spirit, which the inspired word may initiate and further. Had the Bible not expressed in written form a revelation that truly happened in God's incarnate word, it would not be able to express salvific events. In other words, the Bible cannot contain salvific truth without making concrete references to salvation history centered on Christ, just as the most edifying paragraphs of the Code of Hammurabi cannot save us, regardless of how closely they may at times agree with passages of the Pentateuch. Once the written words are cut off from their salvation-historical relationship with Christ, they do not contain or communicate the Truth God revealed for the sake of our salvation.

Inspiration covers each book and all its parts, but not because the human author is granted some kind of superhuman knowledge or judgment that would allow all his authorial intent to exceed his cultural barriers. The purpose of inspiration coincides with that of the economy of salvation: God approaches man to teach him the Truth, who is Christ, for the sake of leading man to know and love him (God) as well as to know and love himself and other human beings. The purpose of revelation is not to provide a shortcut or a substitute for history that is the necessary framework for man's journey of discovering the world, to develop his faculties or the laws (physical and human) of nature, or to accumulate ways and means by which to master the world, exploit the potential of technology, and explore the secrets of his own rationality. If we explore the Bible by treating it as if God were its literary author, then we are making false assumptions by seeking its value in comparison to other human works, as if they were on the same level. Doing so would lead to treat the Bible as we treat classical texts of various cultures, like the Odyssey or the Bhagavad-Gita, by attributing their value to the high esteem they enjoy in their cultural context. However, if we separate the Bible from the living Christ, in whom its ultimate meaning consists, and from the power of the Holy Spirit, in whom God personally address-es us in the scriptures' inspired words, we will not find in it the Truth. Even when the human author of a biblical book adopts the genre of his-toriography, in either the ancient or modern sense of the term, the bib-lical book must not be considered as divine historiography. Nor are the biblical books that employ other genres to be read as expressions of the Holy Spirit's states of mind, as though the divine author, when inspiring human authors, became locked in space and time. The Bible is the writ-ten record of God's word addressing man in the course of man's ongoing search for God. When addressing man, God's word calls him to him-self for conversion, repentance, self-knowledge, moral knowledge, and self-transcendence—ultimately for the purpose of encountering God become man. Of course, the Bible also tells man about the ways God ap-proaches him in uniquely historical *events*, which are, however, paradig-matic and therefore universally applicable to every individual life. The Bible's Truth surpasses the historical framework in which it has been delivered, but its Truth cannot be separated from history, even if man's historical knowledge is full of imperfections. The epistemological gaps between our minds and the physical or historical reality we explore do not justify the denial of any part of this reality, but only caution against overestimating the precision of our knowledge.

God, the divine author speaking through the Bible reveals himself through history, but also transcends history. Yet his inspired word, doc-umenting "the words and deeds" of revelation in writing, conveys an outlook, purpose, and context in which the human authors participate when rendering their own talents and potential to express these words and deeds. The human authors cannot fully comprehend revelation be-yond the limits of that historical existence within which their human lives run their course. This applies to all mediators of revelation from Abraham to Moses and to the prophets. Jesus' case is, however, an excep-tion because of the hypostatic union that uniquely unites him with the Father: the personal subject of his acts and words is the divine person of God's only Begotten Son. But even in the story of Jesus, we see an individual human being's history that takes place running from *a beginning* (ἀρχὴ; see Jn 1:1) to an *end* (τέλος; see Jn 21:30) and form a unique *destiny*; his human consciousness perceives concepts, formulates questions, moves from topic to topic, expresses, by putting into actions and words only what the Father wants the Son to reveal in his earthly life. Only when he is raised from the dead is the Lord given power over all things created, material and spiritual (see Mt 28:20).[18]

Fullness of Truth in the Spiritual Meaning

According to the neo-Thomistic doctrine of inspiration, the main effect or consequence of divine inspiration is inerrancy. When this was replaced by "truth without error," one expected a shift of meaning to occur. But then the statement was made that "scripture must be read in the same Spirit in which it was written." This sounded like a *manifesto* passing far beyond the inspiration/inerrancy model of the neo-Thomistic textbooks. Unfortunately, it received much less attention than it deserved.[19] Yet it is also noteworthy that the traditional neo-Scholastic treatises, when moving from inspiration to inerrancy (as errorless truth), also manifested a twist in the discourse; from speaking about subjective inspiration (*inspired author*) they switched to objective inspiration and began to speak of the *inspired text* with no notice of this change. The implied logic could be explained in this way: as in the first chapter of the treatise on inspiration *God is defined as the literary author of scripture*, in the next chapter we may come to the conclusion that all scriptural statements are truthful in an absolute sense because their (literary) author is God who cannot lie or err. However, if the premise is false, then the conclusion does not follow.

18. These acts of Jesus are fully historical on account of Jesus' human nature, but they are, on account of his divine nature and personhood, potentially suprahistorical and, indeed, become such in his glorification.

19. The original Latin text capitalizes *Spiritu* to show its reference to the Holy Spirit: "Sacra Scriptura eodem Spiritu quo scripta est etiam legenda et interpretanda sit"; *Dei Verbum*, no. 12; see Ignace de la Potterie, "Reading Holy Scripture 'in the Spirit': Is the Patristic Way of Reading the Bible Still Possible Today?," *Communio* 13, no. 4 (1986): 3–4; de la Potterie, "'Interpretation of the Holy Scripture in the Spirit in Which It Was Written' (*Dei Verbum* 12c)," in *Vatican II: Assessment and Perspectives Twenty-Five Years After (1962–1987)*, ed. René Latourelle (New York: Paulist Press 1988), 1:220–66.

The *composition* of the *text* is the fruit of a human authorial function and thus can (in fact, does) carry in itself unmistakable signs of limitations, typical of human cognition and self-expression not applicable to God.

Dei Verbum extends its definition of revelation and inspiration to include both history and message (words and deeds) in their concreteness and avoids running into the neo-Scholastic conundrum between God's literary authorship and the absolute inerrancy of the resulting text. The encyclical *Divino Afflante* was unable to do the same and thus created a strange atmosphere of negativity toward cultivating the mystical sense of the Bible:

> By making such an exposition, which is above all, as we have said, theological, they [the interpreters] will efficaciously reduce to silence those who, affirming that they scarcely ever find anything in biblical commentaries to raise their hearts to God, to nourish their souls or promote their interior life, repeatedly urge that we should have recourse to a certain spiritual and, as they say, mystical interpretation. With what little reason they thus speak is shown by the experience of many, who, assiduously considering and meditating the word of God, advanced in perfection and were moved to an intense love for God; and this same truth is clearly proved by the constant tradition of the Church and the precepts of the greatest Doctors. Doubtless all spiritual sense is not excluded from the Sacred Scripture. (*Divino Afflante*, no. 25)

This diagnosis of the preconciliar theology of inspiration helps; however, the twenty-first-century reader understands why *Dei Verbum*, a document about revelation, inevitably cracked open problems that in 1964 the theologians at the Council were still not ready to tackle.

In retrospect it is, however, clear that some theologians could have provided better insights. According to Henri de Lubac, had you asked Origen what inspiration's main effect was, he would not have spoken of inerrancy but of the unfathomable depth of meaning in each text, the Christological sense of every part, the presence of the Spirit, and, in this sense, the Truth of scripture in the way Jesus spoke of himself as "the Way, Life and the Truth." This is also the sense in which the biblical Truth is salvific or redemptive. As Jesus said, "The Truth will set you free" (Jn 8:32). De Lubac has also shown that, while on the one hand, the Origenian thesis about the omnipresence of a spiritual sense in the Bible goes back to apostolic tradition, on the other hand, surviving as a teaching of the church until the end of Middle Ages, it started fading in modern times.[20]

This book is not the place to fully treat this thesis or to specify the spiritual meaning of scriptures. Yet we must remain committed to the patristic vision of *Dei Verbum* without compromises. We will attempt to look at this matter and mention its implications in what follows.

1. For providing biblical texts to serve the church through the centuries, the Holy Spirit has not only prompted and guided writers to produce the biblical books, he has also continued speaking through the church by proclaiming Christ and transmitting his knowledge (see 2 Cor 2:14) through both the written instruments of the Bible and assuring Christ's own personal presence in all functions of the Body of Christ.

2. The "truth of the gospel" (Gal 2:5, 2:14), which is "message and proclamation" (see 1 Thes1:5, 2:2, 2:4, 2:9, 3:2; 1 Pt 4:6), and the meaning of "all the scriptures" (Lk 21:22, 24:27)[21] imply the Christological fact of the incarnation and the ecclesiological fact of the living Christ, risen and glorified, manifesting himself alive to his believers, both individually and collectively. Therefore, the truth of the Bible cannot be decomposed into a finite set of truthful sentences with no reference to a higher, comprehensive reality: the living and glorious Christ, who "once raised, dies no more, for death no longer has power over him" (Rom 6:9).

3. The Truth of the Bible connotes a fullness that is where scripture, sacrament, and the assembly of the believers invoke the events of the salvific history of God's interaction with man. This truth of the Bible is identical with the "two-edged sword" by which the Epistle to the Hebrews characterizes God's word (4:12). There are two essential aspects of the incarnation that cannot be reduced to a single dimension: God's word is both historical and yet ever "living and effective." Just like every human word uttered in history, it fades into the past as soon as it is pronounced. Yet "the plan of the Lord stands forever" (Ps 33:11): his word is

---

20. This is what we find amply explained and proven in chapter 8 in de Lubac's *Histoire et Esprit*, 336–55, with references to texts by Origen and the posterity that drew from him, mostly in the Latin Church, including Jerome, Ambrose, Augustine, and many medieval authors.

21. These are two different expressions: πάντα τὰ γεγραμμένα (Lk 21:22) and ἐν πάσαις ταῖς γραφαῖς (Lk 24:27); both are forerunners of the New Testament concept of the canon, that we will treat further.

ready to address us now as it did in the past and will in the future. While God's salvation history moves on to its completion, Christ is "the one who is and was and is to come" (see Rv 1:4, 1:8; 4:8) so that his risen existence remains actual and, by speaking his words, the Bible is the salvific source for both communities and individuals.

The text of *Dei Verbum* tried to convey this lofty outlook of the Bible's truth as the risen Christ, but the disputes that surrounded it both at the Council and in postconciliar debates (including those in the PBC) obscured these issues time and again by their anxious preoccupation with the texts being error-free. Focusing on the absence of errors in the Bible and calibrating the various propositional truths of human assertions, the disputes misled many exegetes. For in such a perspective, scriptures are not regarded as serving "the church of the living God, the pillar and foundation of truth" (1 Ti 3:15) but become subject to a scrupulous inquiry that attributes to God the role of composing literary products perfectly free of (human) errors. Seeking the Truth of the Bible in its salvific context must not result in defining it as *veritas salutaris*—that is, a truth found only in more narrowly restricted texts, according to their topic and purpose, while still seeing in the scriptures' Truth as the expression of Christ, authored and inspired by the Spirit, the agent in whom it was written and is to be interpreted within. This full canonical context is not to be defined in literary terms as from Genesis to Revelation but in terms of the fullness of revelation as the reality of God's words and deeds from creation to eschatology.

These thoughts about inerrancy and the Truth of the Bible invite further inquiry in two directions. First, revelation must be looked at as a progression from the less perfect to the more perfect; second, every stage of this historical process needs to be seen in the context of its whole development, producing its purpose and fruit at the fullness of time. In recent times such thoughts motivated the reappropriation of the patristic view of the unity of the Bible, in which there is place for both continuity and imperfection, God's working with man as a *paidagogos* or educator and leading him out of ignorance and sinfulness to knowledge and friendship. Meanwhile, a canonical exegesis began to emphasize that no theological understanding of the Bible is possible without an understanding of the Bible as a sequenced collection of texts possessed by a community of salvation—that is, men and women responding in faith to God's self-disclosure through the words and deeds deposited in biblical texts.[22] These two approaches encourage us to take steps forward in the next chapters, first investigating revelation and inspiration as divine condescension and then sketching a theology of the biblical canon.

22. Mark S. Gignilliat, *A Brief History of Old Testament Criticism: From Benedict Spinoza to Brevard Childs* (Grand Rapids: Zondervan, 2012); see also Martin, *Sacred Scripture*, 234; Christopher R. Seitz and Kent Harold Richards, eds., *The Bible as Christian Scripture: The Work of Brevard S. Childs* (Atlanta: Society of Biblical Literature, 2013). Pope Benedict XVI (Joseph Ratzinger), in his *Jesus of Nazareth* (New York, Doubleday: 2006), xix, also endorsed Childs's approach of reading "the individual texts of the Bible in the context of the whole."

9 ✢ INSPIRATION AND TRUTH
IN THE CONTEXT OF DIVINE
CONDESCENSION

The Meaning of Condescension

Dei Verbum, no. 13, refers to the analogy between inspiration and incarnation by using the term "condescension."

> In Sacred Scripture, therefore, while the truth and holiness of God always remains intact, the marvelous "condescension" of the eternal Wisdom is clearly shown, "so that we may learn God's unspeakable kindness, and what measure of adaptation he applied to his speech on account of a thoughtful concern for our weak human nature."[1]

This quotation comes from a homily by John Chrysostom.[2] *Humani Generis* used this term, quoting several other passages by the same church father.[3] The term συνκατάβασις that Chrysostom used is for-

---

1. "In Sacra Scriptura ergo manifestatur, salva semper Dei veritate et sanctitate, aeternae Sapientiae admirabilis condescensio, ut discamus ineffabilem Dei benignitatem, et quanta sermonis attemperatione usus sit, nostrae naturae providentiam et curam habens." I provided my translation to make fully clear that here the reference to God's Wisdom has a personalized and trinitarian meaning.

2. *In Gen.* III.8; Hom. 17.1 (PG 53, 134). The conciliar text uses two Latin words to approximate the Greek συνκατάβασις: "adtemperatio" and "condescensio."

3. "For as the substantial Word of God became similar to men in all things 'except sin' so the words of God, expressed in human language, are made similar to human speech in every respect except error. In this consists that 'condescension' of the God of providence, which St. John Chrysostom extolled with the highest praise and repeatedly declared to be found in the sacred

tuitous, because it evokes, on the one hand, a keyword (καταβάς) of the incarnational and Eucharistic language of John's Gospel, speaking of the Son of God as Bread descending from Heaven into the world (see Jn 6:51, 6:54, 6:58; see also 3:13), and combines it with two Greek prepositions. The first, syn-, connotes association, and the second, kata-, indicates a downward movement. The Latin text uses two terms to render the rich connotations: *condescensio* and *adtemperatio*. The first conveys the meaning that, when assuming a creaturely condition, God relinquishes his transcendental superiority; the second refers to an accommodation of God's speech to man's ability to hear and understand. For the sake of emphasis, the word "human" is used within the last sentence of no. 13 with (*homo*, respectively *humanus*) four times: "God speaking to *man* assimilates his word to *human* language and *human* speech to help the weakness of the *human* flesh." Although John Chrysostom is known to have belonged to the Antiochian school of patristic exegesis, the term of συγκατάβασις is not specific to that tradition. The source may be Origen, the first and most important thinker connecting the scriptures with the incarnation of the Logos. Due to the Latin translation of many of Origen's works, these thoughts of his permeated centuries of Latin tradition (Augustine, Gregory the Great, Bernard of Clairvaux), emphasizing that "the human flesh"—the *assumpta caro* of which the conciliar text speaks—both veils and reveals, tempers and helps to transmit the divine light of revelation. Like a shade or a screen, the humanity of Christ reduces the brilliance of divine truth to both protect the human eye and allow man to perceive what shines through. Similarly, God's word cannot address man unless it configures man's capacity of perceiving and comparing revealed truth with analogous ideas, obtained through ordinary knowledge, so that man may come to an understanding of what God is saying.

These ideas of the patristic tradition show that a theology of inspiration presupposes *reflection* on religious epistemology in general. The idea that God personally approaches the human being implies that he initiates a kind of descent to man, resulting in commonality between

---

books"; *Divino Afflante*, no. 37. A footnote in the encyclical lists the following references: *In Gen* I.4 (PG 53, col. 34–35); *In Gen* II.21 (*PG 53, col.* 121); *In Gen* III.8 (PG 53, col. 135); *Hom.* 15 *in Jn* 1:18 (PG 59, col. 97–98).

God and man in a personal encounter. Thus, in the context of Christian revelation, already at the beginning of salvation history, we detect, on the one hand, man's anticipatory participation in the incarnate life of Jesus on earth, and, on the other hand, we see in Jesus' human life (acts and words) on earth, God's incarnate presence, anticipated in the Old Testament, come to fullness at a particular time in Jesus' individual human nature. Only in his risen existence does Jesus move beyond the dimension of history. Only in virtue of the identity of the divine person, by which Jesus' individual human nature and eternal divinity are fully and entirely joined, on a fully experienced, not merely ontological level of exalted glory, and thus again we see Jesus' words vindicated:

Heaven and earth will pass away, but my words will not pass away. (Mt 24:35; Mk 13:31; Lk 21:33)

Remarkably, the three synoptic gospels preserved this saying *in a verbatim identical form and in a common context* of the eschatological discourse. We see in this sentence, as in a synthesis, the permanence of God's word that addresses man not just as written or printed word but also as "living and effective" (Heb 14:2).

The Imperfections of Inerrancy

Since revelation is historical and progressive, it constitutes God's truthful word. Yet its truth becomes only gradually comprehensible and thus, at any given point in time, it is always imperfectly and incompletely understood. This could have been a good reason for *Dei Verbum* to abstain from the perfectionist term of inerrancy without rejecting it altogether in a theological sense. When including the term *sine errore*, the Council succeeded, expressing its continued commitment to the concept of errorless scriptures, but the rest of the conciliar discussions continued to ignore the need for further nuancing this concept. We can, however, move further to explain how the idea of an errorless documentation of revelation is compatible with imperfections and, if one may say, with chronic incompleteness of the truth in any human literary production.

Several understandings of the word "truth" surface in this connection. Interestingly, exegetes appear more preoccupied with the least disturbing and easiest biblical passages, for which traditional wisdom has brought many solutions. For example, geographic or historical terms are usually not erroneous unless the literary or narrative context requires a high level of precision. Moreover, the gospel narratives must be respected for their literary genre when transmitting popular accounts of historical events within a less restricted radius of exactness. Herod Antipas is called "king" in Mark 6:14–26, although his title was only "ethnarch" (ethnic ruler), but in Mark's text the story of the Baptist's execution must not be expected to rise beyond popular narratives, circulating as oral tradition in Galilee among the disciples of John and Jesus. Matthew 27:9 cites Jeremiah but attributes the quotation to Zechariah; however, in the Matthean context, Zechariah 11:12–13 is fused with Jeremiah 18:1–4, and the text also evokes Jeremiah 32:6–9, so that again the mentioning of only one prophetic name (the one who was better known) must not raise eyebrows.[4] How this is to be interpreted, in the context of Matthew's general thought about the fulfillment of prophetic texts, is another question that remains currently under dispute. But Matthew is not in error naming Jeremiah instead of Zechariah.[5] These kinds of

4. Compare the four texts: (1) The chief priests gathered up the money, but said, "It is not lawful to deposit this in the temple treasury, for it is the price of blood." After consultation, they used it to buy *the potter's field* as a burial place for foreigners. That is why that field even today is called the Field of Blood. Then was fulfilled what had been said through Jeremiah the prophet, "And they took the thirty pieces of silver, the value of a man with a price on his head, a price set by some of the Israelites, and they paid it out for the *potter's field* just as the Lord had commanded me" (Mt 27:6–10).

(2) I said to them, "If it seems good to you, give me my wages; but if not, let it go." And they counted out my wages, *thirty pieces of silver*. But the LORD said to me, "Throw it in the treasury, the handsome price at which they valued me." So I took the thirty pieces of silver and threw them into the treasury in the house of the LORD (Zec 11:12–13).

(3) This word came to Jeremiah from the LORD: "Rise up, be off to the *potter's house*; there I will give you my message." I went down to the *potter's house* and there he was, working at the wheel. Whenever the object of clay which he was making turned out badly in his hand, he tried again, making of the clay another object of whatever sort he pleased (Jer 18:1–4).

(4) This message came to me from the LORD, said Jeremiah: "Hanamel, son of your uncle Shallum, will come to you with the offer: *Buy for yourself my field* in Anathoth, since you, as nearest relative, have the first right of purchase." Then, as the LORD foretold, Hanamel, my uncle's son, came to me to the quarters of the guard and said, "Please *buy my field* in Anathoth, in the district of Benjamin; as nearest relative, you have the first claim to possess it; make it yours." I knew this was what the LORD meant, so *I bought the field* in Anathoth from my cousin Hanamel, paying him the money, seventeen silver shekels (Jer 32:6–9).

5. This is one of the errors alleged by Cardinal König at the Council.

imputed biblical errors do not constitute serious issues with regard to inerrancy or biblical truth except for the literalist or the scrupulous.

A much more important set of problems is constituted by texts that seemingly attribute to God the ordering of immoral actions or describe such actions taking place with implied divine approval. For example, many authors would mention polygamy, presented in Genesis as an apparently normal arrangement in the lives of the patriarchs or narratives about the prophets (for example, Hosea) or the Middle Eastern arrangements of harems in the royal court. A customary solution is to refer to the idea of divine pedagogy by stating that polygamous relationships in royal courts were considered normal and part of the international politics of the times. In any case, throughout the Old Testament, from Abraham to Moses, God shapes a nation according to his standard as it gradually emerges from paganism. Neither the morality of the Ten Commandments, as interpreted in today's church, nor present-day concepts of monotheism should be retrojected as fully understood and enforced in the decades that followed the Exodus. Speculating about the revelation of the Decalogue in terms of a natural-law morality is correct and needed, but presupposing that such considerations were common in early Israel is anachronistic; a fully developed formulation and practice of the Mosaic Law with a moral code of purity must not be postulated for Israel's wanderings in the desert.

More serious are those issues connected with the biblical accounts of the occupation of the Promised Land, especially when a divine command of complete destruction is being given in connection with the determination that the Israelites would not take over pagan cult and culture, specifically the Canaanites' idolatrous practices, and would abstain from intermarriage and religious syncretism. This precept is repeatedly formulated in terms of absolute intolerance, forbidding any mercy or sparing of survivors.

When Yahweh your God has brought you into the country that you are going to make your own, many nations will fall before you: Hittites, Girgashites, Amorites, Canaanites, Perizzites, Hivites and Jebusites, seven nations greater and stronger than yourselves. Yahweh your God will put them at your mercy and you will conquer them. You must put them under the curse of destruction (*kherem*). You must not make any treaty with them or show them any pity.

You must not intermarry with them; you must not give a daughter of yours to a son of theirs, or take a daughter of theirs for a son of yours, for your son would be seduced from following me into serving other gods; the wrath of Yahweh would blaze out against you and he would instantly destroy you.

Instead, treat them like this: tear down their altars, smash their standing-stones, cut down their sacred poles and burn their idols. For you are a people consecrated to Yahweh your God; of all the peoples on earth, you have been chosen by Yahweh your God to be his own people. (Dt 7:1–6)

The Hebrew term *kherem*, often translated by the Septuagint as *anathema*,[6] means the obligation to fully destroy all sacred objects of a given foreign cult and the refusal to take any booty during a military operation in course of a "holy war"—that is, to be carried out by the Israelites under divine command as a sacred duty. To a large extent, texts like the one just quoted deal with a primitive concept of fighting for survival on behalf of and under the protection of a national or tribal deity. This concept is reflected in the Bible for conveying a teaching about the Israel's privileged destiny and the idea that their monotheistic religion admits no compromise. However, the references to *kherem* in the Bible must not be translated into our present-day understanding as a system of divinely sanctioned genocide. Recent archaeological finds confirmed that this biblical command was hardly a practice followed at the occupations of the Promised Land, but a retrospective idea, introduced into the texts by the editors of the Pentateuch during the Exile, whom they wanted to show how Israel had lost its original heritage by assimilating to a pagan lifestyle. Consequently, texts about *kherem* hardly reflect a divine instruction received as revelation by God to Moses, but rather in a retrospective view of the past. These texts about *kherem* express a principle of cultic and religious separation rather than a command to practice merciless religious warfare. In Deuteronomy, Joshua, Judges, and 1 Samuel (15:21), *kherem* appears in terms of a reproach condemning greed and selfishness as well as the Israelites' proneness for dispossessing and exploiting the nations they conquered while taking over their culture and wealth: cities, temples, customs, agricultural practices, and religious beliefs. The biblical texts that involve the command of *kherem* retroject an *ideological* position of religious isolationism in line with the deuter-

6. Lv 27:28; Nm 21:3; Dt 13:18; Jo 6:17–18, 7:22–23; Jdg 1:17.

onomistic revision of the historical books for the sake of explaining how the Israelites *sinned* against their monotheistic ancestral faith *by dispossessing the Gentiles out of greed while being unfaithful to the Mosaic Law.* Instead, they married the wives and daughters of their previous enemies, kept their captives as slaves, learned to use magic incantations, began worshipping astral deities and other polytheistic cults, and performed various forms of fertility rituals, including the sacrifices of children—held to be an abominable practice throughout the Bible, although detectable in the religions of most agricultural societies, including those of the ancient Middle East.[7]

When God engages man in dialogue, divine condescension means God's willingness to approach his people in spite of their moral and cultural deficiencies. The command of *kherem* appears to be a regrettable facet of the sacred warfare practiced throughout history on both sides of violent ethnic conflicts. Such practices and mentality were apparently an inevitable part of the history within which God approached the sons of Israel, intending to form a people of his own, practicing merciful tolerance toward them, as he had generally addressed the human being in various stages of his fallen condition.

Man's initial imperfection must not be understood only in temporal terms. A second dimension surfaces when we realize that God accommodates himself to man's *finite* nature by teaching him *partial* truths and *incomplete* notions. Here we deal with man's ontological imperfection in terms of his altogether limited understanding of spiritual and divine truth.

Faithful, Firm, and Inerrant Truth in the Bible

It may be helpful to further examine what the three expressions in no. 12 of *Dei Verbum* mean when applied to the Truth in the Bible: *fideliter, firmiter,* and *sine errore.* While the idea that the Bible speaks about a multiplicity of truths in truthful and correct sentences is hard to avoid in the context of inerrancy, that kind of approach is usually misleading. More correct would be to state that God's living word communi-

---

7. The literature on this topic is extensive. For general orientation, see Thomas A. Heath, Jeremy Evans, and Paul Copan, eds., *Holy War in the Bible: Christian Morality and an Old Testament Problem* (Downers Grove, Ill.: IVP Academic, 2013).

cates the Truth—that is, the living Christ—like a river overflowing with abundant water, transmitting its abundance to all who hear and receive it with faith. A distributive meaning of "the Truth" as a multiplicity of truthful sentences would project the idea of God speaking in broken human sentences as if he were no more than his messengers. Here we again recall the patristic tradition on Ps 62:12 (Vulgate 61:12), already quoted, once in its compact formulation by St. Bernard:

"God spoke only once," once because always; for He is one single, uninterrupted and eternal speech.[8]

On God's side there is but one speech-act: the eternal Word. He accompanies mankind's journey; this began with his act of creation and continued by condescending and accommodating all along human history. As the theology of revelation of *Dei Verbum* proposes, inspiration transmits God's word so that man may hear and comprehend it. God's speech-act takes a written form in the scripture to constitute a text that is accessible in a stable manner. This is one of the meanings of *firmiter* (firmly). But *firmiter*, together with *fideliter* (faithfully), ultimately refers to an eternal, never-changing truth, expressed in Hebrews 13:8: "Jesus Christ is the same yesterday, today, and forever." The truth of scripture consists in the way it signifies Christ, but not just in a narrow, narrative sense by preserving human memories about the historical Jesus. The gospel narratives do more than just faithfully and truthfully (according to contemporary usage, "objectively") tell what Jesus actually did and taught. The gospel texts do not come from unengaged and unbiased reporters, but from disciples, who, though experiencing doubts, failures, enlightening events, and crashing defeat, were ultimately confirmed in their faith by the Holy Spirit. In these writings, which came about in the closest vicinity to the incarnate Word, the truth of the scriptures cannot be reduced to unbiased and detached witnessing by people who, like the Roman historian Tacitus, pretended to have narrated *sine ira et studio* (with no emotion or bias) all that they had witnessed. The truth of the

8. "Semel locutus est Deus. Semel utique quia semper. Una enim et non interpolata sed continua et perpetua locutio est." *Sermones de diversis* 5.2; Leclercq and Rochais, *Sancti Bernardi Opera Omnia* VI.1, 99. This verse of the Psalms has been commented on in a similar way by St. Augustine and others. In my opinion, Bernard was the first to say that God's *personal* word—that is, his Son— is an ongoing and never-ending speech addressing the human being.

gospels is the truth of the apostolic faith. The evangelists were certainly believers and in that sense biased because they loved and suffered for Jesus, whose story they narrated or wrote. They worked against considerable odds to reproduce in an understandable and, in some sense comprehensive, (synthetic yet nonexhaustive) way what the church had to hear about Jesus, satisfying not merely humanly assessed needs but obeying divine commands from the risen Christ. Paul saw the truth of his message as based on his encounter with Christ, which he called revelation: "I did not receive it from a human being, nor was I taught it, but it came through a revelation of Jesus Christ" (Gal 1:12). The apostolic church read and held as its own the Hebrew scriptures because it believed that the scriptures were inspired by the same Spirit who spoke from Christ. The Truth of the scriptures is not the truth of well-informed historians or moralists of good judgment or religious writers of authentic genius, but the Truth of the revelation they transmit. The writers of the scripture were, in an original or extended sense, "Prophets and Apostles," participating in prophetic and apostolic charisms of enlightenment and guidance of the same Spirit.

The human process by which revelation becomes written word is accommodated to human nature, culture, and history. This is so not because we need an excuse for all the evidences of human crudeness, cruelty, ignorance, lack of literary skills, and time-bound conceptual understanding (or lack of understanding) appearing in the Bible, but because God could not effectively communicate with us unless he addressed us according to our limited capabilities and notions. Only a well-educated person realizes that our knowledge is always finite and, no matter how far we progress, our ignorance remains infinite. If the human authors are *veri auctores*, then the biblical text transmits the Truth—namely, Christ—without error, but not in perfect human literary products of omniscient minds. Even if man grows in knowledge and understanding of his world and his past, at no point in time does his cognition reach perfection. Knowledge that is perfectible is necessarily imperfect.

In a more explanatory and verbose manner, some of the oldest patristic sources—much older than John Chrysostom—spoke of God's condescension in terms of a divine pedagogy. Here we quote a most insightful text from the late second century by Irenaeus:

Thus it was, too, that God formed man at the first, because of His munificence; but chose the patriarchs for the sake of their salvation; and prepared a people beforehand, teaching the headstrong to follow God; and raised up prophets upon earth, accustoming man to bear His Spirit [within him], and to hold communion with God: He Himself, indeed, having need of nothing, but granting communion with Himself to those who stood in need of it, and sketching out, like an architect, the plan of salvation to those that pleased Him. And He did Himself furnish guidance to those who beheld Him not in Egypt, while to those who became unruly in the desert He promulgated a law very suitable [to their condition]. Then, on the people who entered into the good land He bestowed a noble inheritance; and He killed the fatted calf for those converted to the Father, and presented them with the finest robe.[9] Thus, in a variety of ways, He adjusted the human race to an agreement with salvation. On this account also does John declare in the Apocalypse, "And His voice as the sound of many waters." For the Spirit [of God] is truly [like] many waters, since the Father is both rich and great. And the Word, passing through all those [men], did liberally confer benefits upon His subjects, by drawing up in writing a law *adapted and applicable to every class* [among them].[10]

This concept about God adapting his speech to our limitations must be combined with what *Divino Afflante* says about God letting his word be shaped according to literary genres so that it become accessible for his human audiences:

Nevertheless no one, who has a correct idea of biblical inspiration, will be surprised to find, even in the Sacred Writers, as in other ancient authors, certain fixed ways of expounding and narrating, certain definite idioms, especially of a kind peculiar to the Semitic tongues, so-called approximations, and certain hyperbolical modes of expression, nay, at times, even paradoxical, which even help to impress the ideas more deeply on the mind. For of the modes of expression which, among ancient peoples, and especially those of the East, human language used to express its thought, none is excluded from the Sacred Books, provided the way of speaking adopted in no wise contradicts the holiness and truth of God, as, with his customary wisdom, the Angelic Doctor already observed in these words: "In Scripture divine things are presented to us in the manner which is in common use amongst men" (*Commentary to Hebrews*. chapter I, 4). For as the substantial Word of God became like to men in all things, "except sin,"

---

9. This alludes to the parable of the Prodigal Son (Lk 15:22–23).
10. Irenaeus, *Adversus Haereses* IV.14.2, in Roberts and Donaldson, *Early Christian Writings*, 204.

(Heb 4:15) so the words of God, expressed in human language, are made like to human speech in every respect, except error. In this consists that "condescension" of the God of providence, which St. John Chrysostom extolled with the highest praise and repeatedly declared to be found in the Sacred Books. [See *In Gen.* I.4 (PG 53, col. 34–35); II.21 (PG 53, col. 121); III.8 (PG 53, col. 135); *Hom.* 15, *in Joannem,* ad. I.18 (PG 59, col. 97–98).]

From such an understanding it follows that the Truth that the Spirit deposited into inspired writings for the sake of salvation does not belong to a special *kind of truths* discernible in scripture by the exegete who then separates it from other kinds of truths because of his diagnosis that it falls under the protective umbrella of inspiration and is, in this sense, free of error: *sine errore.* Nor are we dealing with the truth in such a way that it can be exegetically verified (through its literary genre) to pertain to the human author's intent and automatically ascribed to the primary divine author. The truth of the inspired text is what the community of salvation has learned, continues to learn, and, under the guidance of the Spirit, recognizes as *taught from that Spirit who does not cease forming God's holy people.* This is why *Dei Verbum,* no. 13, is at pains to keep the elements of inspired authors and inspired texts, as well as inspired church (and in that sense, inspired readership) linked together.

Authorial Intent and Truth

In the majority of publications, biblical scholarship tries to achieve little more than to establish what the human author(s) of a text had in mind when creating a particular text. As I suggested, *Divino Afflante* had greatly promoted this tendency by emphasizing the primacy of the literal meaning, a meaning intended by the human author.

Perhaps in the past (right after the Council) the exegete still felt equipped to establish the intent of the human author, but today's exegesis is more cautious and less sure of itself. Consequently, a theology of inspiration has better chances to be correct when it convincingly states that the authorial intent never exhausts the meaning of the text. Revelation is God's pedagogical enterprise: in his condescension and accommodation he teaches man to listen to him in order to understand the meaning of his words, both past and present. Scripture as a written document is created so that man may recall his history and see both how his own sinful failures have marred his past and how God provided hope for the future. Even in the human history of Jesus there is a pedagogical process. Both his call to repentance and his unspeakable condescension to the abyss of human suffering and death unfold in progression. We read the key concepts in Matthew's Gospel: "I desire no sacrifice but mercy" (Mt 9:13) and yet, "This is my blood to be poured out for you and for many for the forgiveness of sins" (Mt 26:28). The progression of sacred history makes later learning elevate and clarify earlier learning, but later insights do not destroy the importance and validity of earlier utterances, because man's progressive learning is reproduced anew in every age and in every personal journey. Both individually and collectively, man is a work in progress. The documentation of his past must remind him of his failures, the incompleteness of his redemption, and the records of his hopeful but fragile redeemed existence. If scripture is a documentation of man's journey with God, then it shows the drama of redemption in terms of both success and failure. De Lubac's *Exégèse médiévale* recalls the patristic principle that, in the course of salvation history, the Bible speaks at once of our collective and individual story. Ancient authors say that what "once had been accomplished for the sake of us all" continues to take place repeatedly in our personal histories *quotidie*: "every day."[11] This is the basis of an ongoing reading of the Bible in the liturgy and in one's personal life.

The Transcendence of the Divine Truth

Divine condescendence can never go as far as to allow that God's word would either lie or deceive. But the question remains: can it coexist in the human mind with a measure of ignorance or lack of understanding? When becoming a man, God chose to be an *infans* at his birth—that is, speechless and apparently (and in human terms truly) ignorant.[12] Other-

---

11. See de Lubac, *Medieval Exegesis*, 2:134–43. The idea finds its marvelous classical expression by St. Bernard: "Hoc semel contulit universitati: hoc quotidie singuli in nobis actitari sentimus" [This happened once for all mankind, this we every day experience individually happening inside of us]. *Sermones super Cantica* 16.2, in Leclercq and Talbot, *Sancti Bernardi Opera Omnia* I:90.

12. "Infans quidem est, sed Verbum infans, cuius ne quidem; infantia tacet" [He is an infant but the infant is the Word who cannot be silent even in his infancy]; St. Bernard's *Sermo in Nativitate* V.1, in Leclercq and Rochais, *Opera Omnia*, IV:266.

wise he could not have grown in knowledge and wisdom. Yet "Jesus increased in wisdom and in years, and in divine and human favor" (Lk 2:52). In fact, he grew in knowledge as he learned to speak, memorized texts like the Psalms, realized rational links between concepts, collected information, obtained training in discursive thought, and was validly corrected when mispronouncing words, forgot names, or failed to understand foreign words.

It is most apparent in the incarnate Son that, by his condescension, God adjusted himself to our level of knowledge and participated in the ways man knows and feels, even by experiencing various instances and forms of human ignorance. This does not reduce or deny in the least Jesus' full divinity in both nature and person but rather manifests his *katabasis* or descent into the realm of a human mode of knowledge that classical theology always affirmed when speaking of Jesus' vulnerable and mortal humanity, susceptible to physical and psychological suffering. Since the incarnation is a descent into "passibility" and "mortality," and thus there corresponds to it a temporary, free withdrawal from fully experiencing the consubstantial union that links him to the divine nature, while experiencing human nature in an unaided, postlapsarian form ("similar to us in all except sin"; see Heb 4:15), incarnation logically implies the experience of ignorance with a corresponding gradual growth of human knowledge and the experience of a discursive mode of thinking by forming concepts and learning to proceed by logical steps. If this is what incarnation and human development (from embryo to maturity) means for Jesus, the *primum analogatum* of an inspired (Spirit-filled) revealer on behalf of the Father, then, all other prophets, hagiographers, and apostolic witnesses must be seen as fully human and thus persons who are only partly knowledgeable while remaining partly ignorant.

In cosmology we cannot conclusively prove the "Big Bang Theory," and it therefore remains a scientific hypothesis. Its exact meaning may be unclear not only to one who is not trained in physics but also to scientists with no philosophical training. In comparison with scientific theories, the statement "At the beginning God created heaven and earth" (Gen 1:1) is more accessible for all people who know the commonplace meaning of "beginning" and the dictionary definition of the word "God" and realize that "heaven and earth" expresses a "two-stage" universe: both the habitat of the human race with its surroundings and the rest of reality beyond our direct perception. Although there are an endless number of questions we can ask about Genesis 1:1, it successfully conveys the simple truth that no existence, physical or spiritual, antedates God. In other words, both what is available to our senses (*visibilia*) and what is beyond them (*invisibilia*) owe their origin to him.

There are many similar examples that illustrate that God speaks to us on the level of our capabilities, yet such examples leave many questions unanswered. God successfully speaks to the human being, and the truth of his statements is reliable, though they do not eliminate all of our false notions. Through unexpected turns in salvation history he surprises us, and much of what he says leaves behind unexplained loose ends. In the biblical narratives, we encounter features of popular storytelling more frequently than not. This fact indicates that the literary genres of most historical texts assume a simple audience. Gaps and seemingly contradictory details can be found time and again indicating lack of precision in the way a narrator aimed to tell his story. In some sense, there are notorious errors that exegetes notice in terms of grammar and composition; in spite of all efforts of textual criticism we often cannot tell which errors had been committed by the author and which by a copyist. Similarly, the seemingly unusual grammatical structure in the Hebrew, Greek, and Aramaic texts may not always come from error because the original texts might have been copied, read, stored, and transmitted through many centuries, during which the language in question (in most cases Hebrew) went through significant changes. Scribes not only copied the ancient texts but introduced efforts of updating many texts so that they may appear less obsolete or obscure. There are in the Bible many cultural peculiarities: popular or contrived etymologies that modern linguists reject, but that usually carry some theological reference or geographic names obscured by lack of standardized spelling (or simply because the place has vanished and archeologists have not yet found it). Since ancient authors delighted in the use of symbolism, there is a long list of biblical passages that historians may reject, but, in the eyes of theologians, these passages have important significance while also reflecting prescientific thinking about natural phenomena. There are also gaps in the stories, lack of plausible motives for actions, mistaken identifications, and awkward cross-references; one might go on listing other kinds of imperfections, for they are numerous. God condescends to writers of the various historical periods and adjusts his speech to both worldly topics and religious or moral messages, yet he remains the speaker. By the way God speaks, his holiness and truth, though veiled in some sense, become revealed without being compromised (*salva semper veritate et sanctitate*: *Dei Verbum*, no. 13).

The PBC's document *The Inspiration and the Truth of Sacred Scripture* fills its entire third section (pages 123–56) with the interpretation of parts of scriptures that offer challenges for us in terms of the Bible's inspiration and truth. This section of the document first surveys "contradictions, historical inaccuracies, implausible narratives" in historical texts (which mostly involve miraculous events of both testaments), and "social and ethical challenges" in the manifestations of the divine Will (in the way they seem to condone or order polygamy, or tolerate prostitution, the oppression of minorities or women). The selection is quite dated; the church fathers, especially those who were involved in apologetic debates with pagans and were facing controversies as bishops overseeing their flock, repeatedly dealt with many of them centuries ago.[13]

As we read in Psalm 12:6, "The words of the LORD are pure, like silver tried in a furnace of earth, purified seven times." This verse expresses a certain maximalist ideal of God's inspired words, yet, the metallurgical metaphor is remarkable. The Hebrew text uses here the dual form of the word *seven* to indicate an ongoing process of purifying silver, as the *New Living Bible* skillfully puts it, "like silver refined in a furnace, purified *seven times over*." Traditional Jewish and Christian exegesis is based on a deep awareness that human words are never pure enough to express worthily the word of God; they always sound tainted by our sinful humanity. We do not understand authentically what God reveals unless our faculties are cleansed by fire, as Isaiah learned at his call:

Then I said, "It's all over! I am doomed, for I am a sinful man. I have *filthy lips*, and I live among a people with *filthy lips*. Yet I have seen the King, the LORD of Heaven's Armies." Then one of the seraphim flew to me with a *burning coal* he

13. See a short survey in Farkasfalvy, *Inspiration and Interpretation*, 120–39. An excellent update of Henri de Lubac's teaching on patristic and medieval exegesis can be found in Peter Casarella's introduction to de Lubac's *Scripture in the Tradition* (New York: Crossroad, 2000), xi–xxii.

had taken from the altar with a pair of tongs. He *touched my lips* with it and said, "See, *this coal has touched your lips. Now your guilt is removed, and your sins are forgiven.*" (Is 6:5–7)

It seems that divine condescension and absence of error from the inspired word means much more than interpreting the human author's original intent according to the literary genre or the cultural context and/or pointing out mistakes and misunderstandings that entered the text during its transmission.

Other fascinating evidence for man's compulsive inclination to pollute God's word is explained from man's inclination to anthropomorphism or *mythopoieia*, resulting in mixing traditional beliefs of ancient religions, primitive myths, and poetic imagination. A biblical text can be reduced by translators or exegetes to chains of platitudes, but by doing so the "divine intent" would be eliminated together with the mystery of man's call to rise to the dignity of a partner in dialogue with the Absolute Being.

In this way we detect an unsolvable mystery that underlies the basic paradigm of revelation and scripture: "God speaks to man." Why does he? This question points to the ultimate unsolvable issue of inerrancy. The ultimate issue is not raised by incongruities of historical details or conflicting data in the biblical texts when compared to Egyptian sources or Assyrian and Babylonian tablets. Even the question of believing in miracles is only loosely dependent on the human dilemma of accepting or dismissing altogether natural explanations. While all these issues merit attention, the true problem lies elsewhere. God's word speaks of salvation, but salvation consists of being cleansed from sin and entering into union with God. While God condescends ("comes down") to man and man tries to ascend to him, there is always the danger that we think of him as a finite being, limited by space and time—"just another guy"— and construe of him an idol whom we misrepresent when affixing on him his own words taken from the Bible.

Although it might be said that the Truth of scripture is the most important consequence of inspiration, this Truth does not mean chiefly the correctness of propositional truths contained in isolated passages and applied to finite physical beings or events. Many sentences can be selected and quoted outside of their context so that their truth can be legitimately questioned. Such a reading of the biblical texts might lead to absurd conclusions, as the following examples (many of them classical) show.

In the Bible God is believed to be a physical being: "The man and his wife heard the sound of *Yahweh God walking* in the garden in the cool of the day." (Gen 3:8)

God commands child sacrifice: "God said, 'Take your son, your only son, your beloved Isaac, and go to the land of Moriah, where *you are to offer him as a burnt offering* on one of the mountains which I shall point out to you.'" (Gen 22:2)

God creates evil: "I form the light and I create the darkness, I make well-being, and *I create disaster*, I, Yahweh, do all these things." (Is 45:7)

God acts with hatred: "I shall bless those who bless you, and *shall curse those who curse you.*" (Gen 12:3)

God commands genocide: "So, devour all the peoples whom Yahweh your God puts at your mercy, show them no pity." (Dt 7:16)

I doubt that even these few examples can be dealt with under the same common heading or be resolved with one single scheme of interpretation.[14] The PBC's document of 2013 has a much larger selection of difficult passages but is still limited. Such items need to be resolved in the context of a canonical interpretation. This concept is of relatively recent origins in American Protestantism and still insufficiently integrated into contemporary exegetical practice.[15] In the pre–Vatican II Catholic biblical renewal, almost identical ideas and terminology had already emerged, mostly in French literature that followed the pioneer work of Celestin Charlier: *La lecture chrétienne de la Bible*, published in 1947 by a Belgian Benedictine of Maredsous.[16] This trend was influential for about twenty years, but faded away from the bibliographies of the postconciliar years and has never been replaced in recent decades. Brevard Childs, professor of Old Testament at Yale, has, however, accomplished much not only by reinventing this model in a creative manner, but also by developing a new focus of research on canon and canonicity. The

---

14. I just mention here a recent book on this topic that I have not been able to sufficiently consult for this publication: Matthew Ramage, *Dark Passages of the Bible: Engaging Scripture with Benedict XVI and St. Thomas Aquinas* (Washington, D.C.: The Catholic University of America Press, 2015).

15. Seitz and Richards, *Bible as Christian Scripture.*

16. Celestin Charlier, *La lecture chrétienne de la Bible* (Maredsous: Editions de Maredsous, 1947); English translation: *The Christian Approach to the Bible* (London: Sands, 1961).

present-day canonical approach vigorously demands a more theological exegetical practice. Although the trend of a canonical exegesis is today not yet in smooth conversation with contemporary historical-critical groups, both sides greatly profited from new discoveries and insights concerning the history of the canon of both testaments. In the same context, interest has grown in the theology of inspiration, and the theology of the canon has also been promoted, the latter to be investigated in the next chapter.

10 ✝ INSPIRATION LEADS
TO CANON

Inspiration and Canon Linked in Luke/Acts

In Christian parlance, canonical texts are inspired. This implication is not strictly logical, yet it follows from the history of the Christian canon. The Greek word "canon" (κανών) means "norm" or "measure." Both the word and the concept are present in St. Paul's letters, signifying a norm of conduct or limit to behavior (2 Cor 10:13, 10:15, and 10:16) or, in the combative context of Galatians, a doctrinal norm about circumcision (6:16). "Canon" even refers specifically to a standard of behavior with regard to the Mosaic Law in instances in which it was required by the Gospel of Christ. In the Pauline letters and in early patristic usage, this word certainly does not signify a list of normative books; however, in Christianity, the concept (although not the finalized list) of sacred books was part of the Jewish heritage.[1]

The first Gentile Christians who learned about Jesus and believed in him did not have to convert to Judaism, but it was part of their faith in Jesus to adhere to the inspired scriptures of Judaism because what they learned about Jesus from the apostolic kerygma—his life, teaching, death, and resurrection—took place according to the scriptures. These scriptures were accessible by then for quite some time in the Greek translation of the Septuagint (LXX). This was a collection somewhat wider

---

1. I assume in this chapter the majority opinion: Luke and Acts were written by the same writer before the end of the first century.

than Jewish canon, finalized only later, after the destruction of Jerusalem in the First Jewish War (68–70 A.D.). All books of the LXX had a Jewish background, but a few written originally in Greek were included. Jesus' preaching and theological message laid emphasis on the "fulfillment of the scriptures";[2] he referred to the scriptures as "the Law and the Prophets." The term "scriptures," frequently mentioned in the earliest Christian writings, like Paul's authentic letters, was well enough defined in the first century for both Judaism and nascent Christianity, but it did not yet officially designate a precise set of canonical books.

It is in such a context that the early church's proclamation of Jesus death, burial, and resurrection "according to the scriptures" (see 1 Cor 15:3–5) implies the acceptance of a set of holy books. Thus, what the apostolic church said about revelation and inspiration (God speaking to and through Moses and the prophets) constantly referenced written sources as lasting deposits of God's word; "canonical scriptures" meant that God has not only spoken to his people but that his words were being preserved in inspired books. Meanwhile, by the first century A.D., in post-Maccabean Judaism, there appeared a sense that a cessation of prophecy occurred (see 1 Mc 9:27) and thus, in general, inspired scriptures belonged to a distant past. We can see this reflected in Luke's Gospel referring to "the Law and the Prophets" as belonging to a distant sacred past: "The law and the prophets were in effect until John came; since then the good news of the kingdom of God is proclaimed, and everyone tries to enter it by force" (Lk 16:16).

According to the same writer, who also composed Acts, the disciples of Jesus began announcing their faith in the risen Christ as well as preaching his words and deeds in intimate connection with God's word just as their Lord instructed them:

He said to them, "These are *my words that I spoke to you while I was still with you*—that everything written about me in the *Law of Moses, the Prophets, and the Psalms* must be fulfilled."

---

2. Just to serve as reminders, I quote here from the canonical gospels: "But let the scriptures be fulfilled" (Mk 14:49); "Have you not read this scripture?" (Mk 12:10); "But all this has taken place, so that the scriptures of the prophets may be fulfilled"(Mt 26:56); "Do not think that I have come to abolish the law or the prophets; I have come not to abolish but to fulfill (Mt 5:17)"; "These are my words that I spoke to you while I was still with you—that everything written about me in the Law of Moses, the prophets, and the psalms must be fulfilled" (Lk 24:44).

Then he opened their minds to *understand the scriptures*, and he said to them, "Thus it is *written*, that the Messiah is to suffer and to rise from the dead on the third day, and that repentance and forgiveness of sins is to be proclaimed in his name to all nations, beginning from Jerusalem. You are witnesses of these things. And see, I am *sending upon you what my Father promised*; so stay here in the city until you have been clothed with power from on high." (Lk 24:44–49)

The italicized words in this passage constitute evidence that the early church, when explaining its teaching, argued from two sources: the Jewish scriptures and the Dominical tradition (words and deeds of the Lord), transmitted through Jesus' disciples as they understood it through the enlightenment of the Holy Spirit. In Luke's reconstruction of the beginnings of the primitive church, what we called in previous chapters "inspiration" constitutes a living continuum of God's speech transmitted through writings called "the Law and the Prophets," the incarnate Son's words and deeds (Luke's first volume), which are enlightened by faith in Jesus' resurrection and transmitted by the apostolic preaching. Luke's understanding of the church's kerygmatic origins is the oldest documentation of how inspiration and canon are linked. Through Jesus, the Old Testament is connected with the apostolic message, the latter of which Lucan texts present as a *living word*, not only because of its original oral delivery, but also because of its direct origins from the Holy Spirit, through whom the prophets (Moses included) had spoken.

The attribution of *inspiration* to the *Holy Spirit* is consistently shown as present throughout the process, which leads "from revelation to inspiration and to canon"; the Spirit's active presence is emphasized in most theologically weighty passages of both Luke's Gospel and Acts:

1. He first describes Jesus' infancy stories as taking place under the influence of the Holy Spirit in order to fulfill the scriptures (see Lk 1:15, 1:17, 1:35, 1:41, 1:47, 1:67, 1:80, 2:25–27).

2. He then continues describing Jesus' ministry as prompted by the Holy Spirit (see Lk 3:16, 3:22, 4:1, 4:14–21).

3. He begins Acts with the apostolic group's universal mission launched by the Holy Spirit (see Acts 1:5, 1:8, 1:16, 2:4–33).

4. Finally, if we compare the short prologue of Luke's Gospel (1:1–4) with the opening sentences of Acts, we see how the author considers his own first volume as a written narration of Jesus' deeds and words

(Acts 1:1), furthered by a similar documentation about "the apostles," whom Jesus chose to carry the same message in the power of the Holy Spirit from Jerusalem "to the ends of the earth" (1:8).

It is also noteworthy that in these passages, references to oral communication (by Jesus and the apostles) and to written records (texts of the Old Testament and Luke's own text) are carefully knitted together with repeated references to the ongoing presence of the Holy Spirit. Three examples might be helpful:

1. "He unrolled the scroll (βιβλίον) and found the passage where it was written: '*The Spirit of the Lord* is upon me, because he has anointed me to bring glad tidings to the poor. He has sent me to proclaim liberty to captives and recovery of sight to the blind, to let the oppressed go free, and to proclaim a year acceptable to the Lord.'

Rolling up the scroll (βιβλίον), he handed it back to the attendant and sat down, and the eyes of all in the synagogue looked intently at him.

He said to them, 'Today this *scripture* (βιβλίον) is *fulfilled* in your hearing.'" (Lk 4:17–21)

2. "*You will receive the power of the Holy Spirit* which will come on you, and then you will be my *witnesses* not only in Jerusalem but throughout Judaea and Samaria, and indeed to earth's remotest end." (Acts 1:8)

3. "In *my earlier work*, Theophilus, I dealt with *everything Jesus had done and taught* from the beginning until the day he gave his instructions to *the apostles he had chosen through the Holy Spirit.*" (Acts 1:1–2)

While Luke clearly sees a temporal shift between the two testaments (the first already written at the time he writes and the second first expressed by oral delivery), he is mindful of *the sequence of fulfillment* from the Old to the New. Thus, in revelation he recognizes a two-phase sequence: the Old Testament, now possessed in written records (βιβλία) comes to fulfillment through "Jesus' acts and words," which then come to be channeled into the oral preaching of the apostles and are finally deposited in written form. Luke's text presents this model *in concreto* in four movements that determine his two-volume work:

1. The *words* of *Isaiah*, transmitted in his book (βιβλίον); see Lk 4:17–18;

2. are to be *read* aloud by *Jesus* declared as fulfilled in his deeds and words; see Lk 4:19;

3. they are then to be preached orally by *the apostles* throughout the world; see Acts 1:8;

4. and are put into *written form* by (*apostolic*) *ministers of the word*; see Lk 1:2, Acts 1:1–2.

There can be little doubt that Luke was the first to express this systematic understanding of the chain "revelation/inspiration/transmission." We find his own self-understanding as attached to the chain, because Luke is himself also a "minister of the word." What he presents is an alternating sequence with oral and written expressions from Old Testament to Jesus and from Jesus to the apostolic church. This chain indicates the place of the sacred texts "of old," which the church inherited from its Jewish past and continues reading. It indicates the place of the two books Luke is putting into the hand of *Theophilus*, the recipient and/or sponsor of both volumes (Lk 1:3 and Acts 1:1).

The structure of Luke-Acts is far from being merely formal. It is linked by a larger unifying theme from the incarnation of the Word in Mary's womb through the Spirit (Lk 1:35) all the way to the narrative of the descent of the Spirit upon the reconstructed group of the twelve apostles (Acts 2:4); the *same Spirit* determines the beginnings of Jesus' human existence, his ministry (Lk 4:1, 4:14), and the ministry of the apostles. This Spirit completes the fulfillment of Isaiah's text at Jesus' first preaching in the synagogue of Nazareth (Lk 4:18) and arches over to the descent of the same Spirit as a "Promise from Above" (Lk 24:49; Acts 1:8), endowing the disciples with the gift of speech (Acts 2:4). References to the Holy Spirit in Luke's two volumes constitute theological continuity for the narratives as one of his most significant theological contributions. Thus Luke not only provides us with a tool for understanding the literary genre of the gospels as a presentation of "words and deeds" with which Jesus began his ministry (ὧν ἤρξατο ὁ Ἰησοῦς ποιεῖν τε καὶ διδάσκειν in Acts 1:1), but also incorporates into one comprehensive vision Jesus' ministry, the empowering of the eleven (expanded at the beginning of Acts to twelve), and their initial ministry, extended in the geographic outline of the book from Jerusalem to Rome. The gospel marches from a narrowly Jewish context into the center of the empire; at its end, the book of Acts documents the church's conscious embracement of a new future in Paul's conclusive statement: "Let it be known to you that this salvation of God has been sent to the Gentiles; they will listen" (Act 28:28).

The dating of Luke's writings—and sometimes even the thesis that the two books were originally intended as one single two-volume composition—is under dispute and further exploration. However, literary analysis of the two books leaves no doubt about the identity of both books' author. The two volumes constitute, in fact, a prophetic anticipation of the New Testament canon. Their outline represents an exceptionally insightful understanding of the Christian enterprise that, after the Jewish war, was quickly evicted from Jerusalem, but, while facing the pressures and persecutions of a new political environment, it willingly accepted its worldwide mission.

Canonical Perspectives in the New Testament

Luke versus Marcion

It would be misleading to begin a review of our certainties and uncertainties about the dating of Luke and Acts and to argue on behalf of the majority view that claims the priority of Luke (and of his vision) to Marcion's work, which was, in fact, traditionally interpreted since the late second century, as using and transforming Luke. The traditional thesis that Marcion copied and falsified Luke while rejecting Acts is nowadays disputed by a revisionist theory that claims that Luke's work was contemporary to or possibly produced in reaction against Marcion.[3] The two camps are more separated than ever. While all agree that we do not possess a single authentic sentence from Marcion's hand, two attempts have already been published as "critical editions" of Marcion's Bible with

---

3. See Joseph B. Tyson, *Marcion and Luke-Acts: A Defining Struggle* (Columbia: University of South Carolina Press, 2006); Jason D. BeDuhn, *The First New Testament: Marcion's Scriptural Canon* (Salem, Ore.: Polebridge, 2013).

the claim that its two volumes, *Euaggelion* and *Apostolikon*, constitute the first Christian canon, antedating Luke's double work.

The rediscovery of Marcion as the first inventor of a Christian canon is not a brand-new idea. After Adolf von Harnack's full-scale effort to revive Marcion as a positive hero of early Christian history,[4] Hans von Campenhausen took the next step by attributing to Marcion the creation of the first New Testament canon and the idea of a "Christian Bible."[5] Although Marcion's importance with respect to the development of the Christian canon cannot be underestimated, we must not go as far as to rehabilitation. Because of the scarcity of reliable historical sources, extreme caution is in order.

Here we will only argue for the priority and originality of the Lukan theology of a Christian canon (it may be regarded as a "pre-canon") in opposition to Marcion's elevation of his *Euaggelion* and his Pauline *Apostolikon* as the only reliable apostolic writings. As it is generally admitted, Marcion's position on scriptures consisted of three elements:

a. In a book (by now lost), under the title of *Antitheses*, Marcion enumerated the inconsistencies of the Jewish scriptures and its contradictions with the teachings of Jesus. Allegedly, on this basis he concluded that the God of the Old Testament is not the same as the Father of Jesus Christ, whom he denied to have been the creator of matter and cause of evil. Unfortunately, all this is known only secondhand.

b. Thus, while rejecting the scriptures of the Jews, Marcion proposed two sacred books, the *Euaggelion* and the *Apostolikon*. Although disputed for its origin, the first is quite similar to Luke's Gospel, but is quite a bit shorter, possibly on account of a number of editorial changes. The second is a ten-letter collection of Pauline letters, similar to the present-day canon of Paul's epistles but without the three pastoral letters and Hebrews.

c. It is a widely spread conviction among experts that, to a large extent, Marcion's success was due to his position on scripture. We do not

4. Adolf von Harnack, *Marcion: Das Evangelium vom fremden Gott; Eine Monographie zur Geschichte und Grundlegung der katholischen Kirche* (Leipzig: J. C. Heinrichs, 1924); compare David Balás, "Marcion Revisited," in *Texts and Testaments*, ed. W. Eugene March (San Antonio: Trinity University Press, 1980), 95–108.

5. Hans von Campenhausen, *Die Entstehung der christlichen Bibel* (Tübingen: Mohr, 1968); trans. as *The Formation of the Christian Bible* (Philadelphia: Fortress, 1972).

know if and how Marcion argued about other options for apostolic gospels or letters and their authenticity. In possession of a canon that he claimed to be complete and closed, Marcion easily evaded the difficult disputes other Christians faced.

Marcion's early detractors, of whom Tertullian and his five-volume *Contra Marcionem* stand out most famously, accused Marcion of falsifying (by abbreviating and editing) Luke's Gospel and rejecting Acts and the non-Pauline apostolic letters, while also eliminating three of the four apostolic gospel books used in the church.

Those who, for the past hundred years, fought for rehabilitating Marcion accused Tertullian's book as hopelessly biased, mixing fact and fiction for the sake of creating a distorted image of Marcion as an arch-heretic. The effort to restore Marcion's reputation went parallel to the thesis that the four-gospel canon was produced in the second century in reaction to Marcion's pioneer position of a "gospel canon" by which he had claimed his *Euaggelion* as the only authentic narration of Jesus' life and teaching. A positive view of Marcion's Gospel would mean to rank it among the earliest attempts to reduce the confusing multiplicity of competing gospels or to show that it was a sober and viable "single-gospel option," which, in the course of history, lost out against authoritarian figures occupying the major episcopal sees of the empire.

Without going into too many further details, we enumerate the three main arguments that show that Marcion did not represent an authentic tradition but a novel position of an innovator, working with great talent for organization but with false premises.

First, one must realize that what the unity of the two testaments, referring to the authority of "Prophets and Apostles," antedates Marcion. It reaches back to the earliest Pauline letters and antedates the composition of the earliest gospels. Christianity was born in possession of the Hebrew scriptures while granting not just equal but higher authority to Jesus' words and deeds. The oldest traces of oral tradition about the Apostle Paul are constantly interspersed with references to the scriptures of old and to Jesus and his first disciples, who were models for Paul.

Second, the tensions and controversies, traceable to the second century, about Paul's apostolic ranking and the authority of his teaching all *presuppose* that Paul's brand of Christianity was initially closely linked to the Palestinian movement that Paul once persecuted (see 1 Cor 15:9; Phil 3:6), but that he later joined and remained loyal to, leaving behind clear testimonies of sharing that faith. Even if Paul repeatedly contested the practices of the first Christian communities and leaders with regard to Mosaic Law (and possibly never fully settled this dispute), he fully recognized the authenticity of Cephas and those "who were apostles before" him, including Cephas (Gal 1:17). Paul's references to Peter and the twelve (1 Cor 15:5), with whom he compares his "apostolate" (Gal 2:8), apostolic title, and message (see 1 Cor 9:2; Rom 1:5; 1 Cor 15:9), are particularly important because they prove that Marcion's contention that Paul was Jesus' only truthful disciple, while Peter and the twelve had betrayed him and ended up as Judaizers, cannot be verified in the sources; it was entirely Marcion's invention.

Third, the apostolic character of the Christian message, expressed in both the title of Marcion's *Apostolikon* and the role of Peter and the twelve present in the earliest gospel texts, is a presupposition that Marcion and his opponents (in particular, the Church of Rome) held in common. It is helpful to recall Harry Gamble's remark that Marcion's central thesis was not a closed canon but his claim of asserting Paul's exclusive apostolicity.[6] This thesis, however, stands no historical scrutiny. What linked the two parts of Marcion's canon was his belief that his *Euaggelion* (which was, by any reckoning, some archaic and/or strongly edited form of Luke's Gospel) was a gospel coming from Paul, while the other gospels circulating in the church supported Peter and the twelve, who had betrayed Jesus and his original message. This supposition patently contradicts even Marcion's version of the *Euaggelion*.

Regardless of whether we trust Tertullian's judgment, our sources on Marcion sufficiently prove that it was Marcion who de facto relinquished the apostolic tradition when championing *an exclusive apostolicity*. Thus, in sharp contradiction to Marcion, the sources vindicate Luke's vision of linking revelation and inspiration and thus lay foundations for a two-testament Christian canon. The New Testament canon continues and completes Luke's vision as it bases the future of Christian theology

---

6. Harry Y. Gamble, *Books and Readers in the Early Church: A History of Early Christian Texts* (New Haven, Conn.: Yale University Press, 1995).

on the unity of the two testaments, asserting the prophetic character of the Old and the apostolicity of the New Testament.

Closure of the Pauline and Petrine Epistles

Luke's vision was not isolated, but is found in many late writings of the New Testament. The two most important passages on inspiration, 2 Timothy 3:16 and 2 Peter 1:21, treated earlier, about the two testaments should be dealt with in a similar vein as the passages quoted from Luke. Another verse in 2 Peter refers with near explicitness to the two testaments as "Prophets and Apostles" and places Christ in the middle of them:

to recall the words previously spoken by the holy *prophets* and the commandment of the Lord and Savior through your *apostles*. (2 Pt 3:2)

The context of this quote is a New Testament document that, a few lines further down and for the first time in history, speaks of a collection of Pauline writings, approved by the apostle Peter in full awareness that some passages of the Pauline letters are difficult to interpret:

And consider the patience of our Lord as salvation, as *our beloved brother Paul, according to the wisdom given to him, also wrote to you*, speaking of these things as he does *in all his letters*. In them there are some things hard to understand that the ignorant and unstable distort to their own destruction, just as they do *the other scriptures*. (2 Pt 3:15–16)

Dated most commonly to the first quarter of the second century, this passage betrays a *canonical thinking in close connection with the concept of apostolicity*, assuming that the reader also thinks in a similar way. The unity of the scriptures, referenced by a word that, in earlier Christian writings, mean at this time normally the Old Testament, is here paralleled with a Pauline collection of letters. At the same time, the passage also implies that Paul's letters are comparable to a twosome "collection" of Petrine letters. For in Peter's second letter there is an intentional reference to 1 Peter, although this fact is often overlooked. Not only does the apostle write here for the *second time* (2 Pt 3:1), but with this reference to his approaching *death*, Peter, the purported author, instead of providing an autobiographic side remark, inserts a note for the sake of excluding the possibility of any future attributions of a later letter to Peter as their author:

I think it right, as long as I am in this "tent," to stir you up by a reminder, since I know that I will soon have to put it aside, as indeed our Lord Jesus Christ has shown me. (2 Pt 1:13–14)

By this feature, 2 Peter must have helped the reader recognize an intention of closure imposed on the Petrine letters that, however, also further reinforces the parallelism between Peter and Paul.[7] The reference to Peter's association with the Lord on the "holy mountain" of the transfiguration in some sort of mystical experience may become well contextualized if we recall Paul's self-image as a mystic in 2 Corinthians 11:16–12:5, and we realize that, here again, 2 Peter is the document that balances the record between the two apostles:

When we told you about the power and the coming of our Lord Jesus Christ, we were not slavishly repeating cleverly invented myths; no, *we had seen his majesty with our own eyes.* He was honored and glorified by God the Father, when a voice came to him from the transcendent Glory, "This is my Son, the Beloved; he enjoys my favor." *We ourselves heard this voice from heaven,* when we were with him on the holy mountain. So *we have confirmation of the words of the prophets;* and you will be right to pay attention to it as to a lamp for lighting a way through the dark, until the dawn comes and the morning star rises in your minds. (2 Pt 1:16–19)[8]

Moreover, the same canonical imagination we mentioned earlier is displayed again in this passage of 2 Peter: *Jesus'* words and deeds are said to be attested by *apostolic* witnesses with Peter's testimony in the forefront and the Pauline letters in the background (quoted with Peter's endorsing words) in a role of confirming the "words of the *prophets*"—the Hebrew scriptures. This provides a remarkable summary of Luke's synthesis, expressing similar views.

---

7. As we mentioned previously in connection with 2 Timothy, "pseudepigraphy" is used here for defending authentic documents and for preventing a mushrooming of an irresponsible practice of further such works. Of course, the expression "all his [Paul's] letters" in 2 Pt 3:1 already introduced parallelism between Peter and Paul.

8. The summary of the transfiguration in 2 Pt 1:16–18 additionally reinforces the authenticity of Peter's apostolate as well as that of the apostolic narrators in general (see the word "us" in v. 18 as an apostolic plural). It is noteworthy that 2 Pt 1:20 identifies the scriptures with prophecies, for which the Christian church possesses the Holy Spirit as a principle of interpretation.

Inspiration and Canon in the Second Century

There is enough evidence from extant works of the early second century that the tripartite division of God's word was omnipresent in Christianity.[9] The writers of the sub-apostolic age, usually called "the apostolic fathers" and dated to the first half of the second century, defend and promote Christian teaching with frequent references to the (Jewish) "scriptures." Scriptures were read and interpreted in close connection with teachings received from or about Jesus through his disciples, globally referred to as "the apostles." These are named rarely, most often in reference to Peter or Paul (rarely to John). Today we can quote these texts (quoting the "scriptures" as coming from prophets and apostles), from well-studied critical editions in relatively recent modern translations. They include Clement of Rome,[10] Ignatius of Antioch,[11] Poly-

---

9. See the discussion in chapter 1.

10. "The *apostles* have preached the Gospel to us from the Lord *Jesus Christ*; Jesus Christ [has done so] from God. Christ therefore was sent forth by God, and the *apostles* by Christ. Both these appointments, then, were made in an orderly way, according to the will of God" (1 Clem 42). "Let us take the noble examples furnished in our own generation. Through envy and jealousy, the greatest and most righteous pillars [of the church] have been persecuted and put to death. Let us set before our eyes the illustrious *apostles*. *Peter*, through unrighteous envy, endured not one or two, but numerous labors, and when he had finally suffered martyrdom, departed to the place of glory due to him. *Paul also* obtained the reward of patient endurance, after being seven times thrown into captivity, compelled to flee, and stoned. After preaching both in the East and West, he gained the illustrious reputation due to his faith, having taught righteousness to the whole world, and come to the extreme limit of the West, and suffered martyrdom under the prefects. Thus was he removed from the world, and went into the holy place, having proved himself a striking example of patience"; 1 Clement 5, in Roberts and Donaldson, *The Early Christian Writings*. "Look carefully into the *Scriptures*, which are the true utterances of the Holy Spirit"; 1 Clement 5.45. "Take up the epistle of the blessed *Apostle Paul*"; 1 Clement 5.47. "You understand, beloved, you understand well the *Sacred Scriptures*, and you have looked very earnestly into *the oracles of God*; 1 Clement 5.5.

11. "The *prophets* were His servants, and foresaw Him by the Spirit, and waited for Him as their Teacher, and expected Him as their Lord and Savior, saying, 'He will come and save us'"; Magnesians 9:2.

"Study, therefore, to be established in the doctrines of the Lord and the apostles, that so all things, whatsoever ye do, may prosper both in the flesh and spirit; in faith and love; in the Son, and in the Father, and in the Spirit"; Magnesians 13:1.

"I do also love the *prophets* as those who announced *Christ*, and as being partakers of the same Spirit with the *apostles*"; Philadelphians 5:2.

"He who disbelieves the *Gospel* disbelieves everything along with it. For the *archives* [i.e., writing of the Old Testament] ought not to be preferred to the Spirit. 'It is hard to kick against the pricks'; it is hard to disbelieve *Christ*; it is hard to reject the preaching of the *apostles*"; Philadelphians 8:3.

carp of Smyrna,[12] and other mostly anonymous works like the Letter of Diognetus, the Didache,[13] the Letter of Barnabas,[14] and the so-called Second Epistle of Clement, attributed to Clement of Rome.[15] From the middle of the second century we can add Justin Martyr and Tatian, but the writings of these two church fathers signal the advent of a new reflection on the Christian faith with a change of focus and vocabulary.[16] A very early, but not precisely datable, personality of this time period is Papias, bishop of Hierapolis in Asia, whose extant fragments are still under dispute.

None of these writers manifests awareness of a New Testament canon or provides or assumes a list of sacred books. Although for quite some time studies of the early history of the Christian canon usually began canvassing the evidence of these church fathers' use of the various New Testament books, such an approach does not produce significant results. Collecting sporadic, alleged quotations from various early gospels or Pauline epistles proves very little about the process of an emerging canon, which most scholars assume to be the way the New Testament canon

12. "Let us then serve *Him* in fear, and with all reverence, even as He Himself has commanded us, and as *the apostles* who preached the Gospel unto us, and *the prophets* who proclaimed beforehand the coming of the *Lord*"; Letter of Polycarp to the Philippians 6:3.

13. "But concerning the *apostles* and *prophets*, according to the decree of the *Gospel*, thus do. Let every apostle that cometh to you be received as the Lord"; Didache 11:3–4.

14. "*The prophets*, after having obtained grace from Him, prophesied concerning Him. And He (since it behooved Him to appear in flesh), that He might abolish death, and reveal the resurrection from the dead, endured what and as He did, in order that He might fulfill the promise made unto the fathers, and by preparing a new people for Himself, might show, while He dwelt on earth, that He, when He has raised mankind, will also judge them.... But when He chose His own *apostles* who were to preach His *Gospel*, He did so from among those who were sinners above all sin, that He might show He came 'not to call the righteous, but sinners to repentance.' Then He *manifested Himself to be the Son of God*"; Letter of Barnabas 5:6–9.

15. "I do not, however, suppose ye are ignorant that the living Church is the body of *Christ*; for the *Scripture* says, 'God made man, male and female.' The male is *Christ*, the female is the Church. And the *Books* and the *Apostles* plainly declare that the Church is not of the present, but from the beginning"; 2 Clement 14:2.

16. The vocabulary of "Prophets and Apostles" as inspired authors of the two testaments reaches its full development in Irenaeus and Tertullian; in their footsteps the rest of the theological tradition expands. A sharp awareness of the unity of the two testaments appears in the following text by Tertullian: "Tam enim apostolus Moyses quam apostoli prophetae, aequanda erit auctoritas utriusque officii ab uno eodem domino apostolorum et prophetarum" [For so is Moses an apostle as the apostles are prophets; the provenience of both offices being from the one and the same Lord of apostles and prophets]; *Contra Marcionem* IV.24.8–9, Corpus Christianorum, Series Latina I, 609.

came about. In most cases, these quotations or allusions are made from memory and with a lack of precision so that no valid conclusions can be obtained about the status of these texts. Even less can be said about permanent collections of sacred books and their explicit use as a source for liturgy, teaching, or theology or especially as criteria for orthodoxy.

However, it can be established with relative ease that, when facing doctrinal controversy and experiencing a need for authoritative sources, these writers refer with impressive unanimity to the Old Testament as "scriptures" or "prophets" or to the "gospel," preserved in the memory of the church as the teaching of the Lord and his apostles.[17] This theological outlook is hardly different from what we had said previously about the late writings of the New Testament: on the one hand, there is clear awareness that the Christian message has appropriated the Jewish scriptures, but, on the other hand, there is the remembrance of an authoritative dissemination of Jesus' words and deeds through the church by the original disciples. The latter aspect becomes expressed by texts speaking of the apostles in a generic sense. The sources show that to express the nascent church's self-understanding in terms of doctrinal identity, a growingly uniform vocabulary was used. Meanwhile, the inconsistencies in the use of the word *apostolos* by the earliest written documents of the New Testament disappeared. In the second century, in authors like Irenaeus and Tertullian, a more unified vocabulary tends to wash together previously diverse early notions of who the apostles were.[18]

While the apostles are mentioned with ongoing references to the twelve whom Jesus selected as a tightly knit group of disciples and missionaries,[19] their personal identities and their life stories fade so quickly that, in early Christian literature, very little reliable information can be found about them individually, except for Peter and Paul. It is puz-

17. Farkasfalvy, "'Prophets and Apostles': The Conjunction of the Two Terms before Irenaeus," in March, *Texts and Testaments*, 109–34; Farmer and Farkasfalvy, *Formation of the New Testament Canon*.

18. It seems that in Irenaeus and Tertullian the concept of apostleship stands closest to Luke's Gospel: "And when day came, he called his disciples and chose twelve of them, whom he also named apostles" (Lk 6:13).

19. Mk 3:14; Mt 10:1; Jn 6:67–71; 1 Cor 15:5; Rv 21:12–14. However, the use of the term "apostle" in Acts 14:14 (applied to Barnabas) or Rom 16:7 (applied to Junias and Andronicus) or in the generic expression "apostles and prophets" (Eph 2:20, 3:5; Rv 18:20) reveal a less tidy use of the word "apostle." We read only in Lk 6:13 that Jesus, when choosing the twelve, named them "apostles."

zling that in the Johannine tradition the word "apostle" as applied to the twelve is entirely missing, although the twelve stand out as a most important group (Jn 6:67, 6:70, 6:71, 20:24); in this sense the term is absent also from the Epistle to the Hebrews.[20] Similarly, this criterion of an apostolic origin for a doctrine becomes independent of the question, whether it was transmitted orally or in writing. This feature may offer another piece of evidence that the concept of apostolicity predated the spread of authoritative written documents. The comment that apostolicity is a *theologoumenon*—that is, a simplified conceptual construct distilled by primitive Christian memory,[21] created in the second century, may not be false unless it is regarded to be fictitious or completely subjective. Apostolicity is certainly not the product of historicization or legend formation, but rather a conceptual vehicle, based on a historical notion but then used as a simplified yet valid tool that belongs to the oldest layer of the Christian vocabulary, by which the structure of revelation and its transmission are evoked. The strongest textual proof appears in the sentence "Whoever welcomes me, welcomes the one who sent me." It is repeated verbatim in the Synoptic triple tradition (Mt 10:40; Mk 9:37; Lk 9:48), but it is also found equivalently in the Johannine chain of sending of the disciples by the Son, who had been sent by the Father (see Jn 20:21), and by whom, when risen, the Spirit is transmitted from the Father (see Jn 15:6, 16:7). In none of these statements is the word "apostolos" found.[22] This leads to the

20. Paul's insistent arguing about being fully entitled to be called an "apostle of Jesus Christ" (see 1 Cor 9:1–2, 12:12, 15:9; Gal 1:1, 1:9, 2:8) is just as significant as the fact that in the pastoral letters no reference is made to any other apostle than Paul.

21. In twentieth-century German literature the subject of apostolicity is typically handled as a *mere theologoumenon* (product of "theologizing"—that is, a theological construct based on simplified historical memories combined with theological concepts); see Isidor Frank, *Der Sinn der Kanonbildung* [The Meaning of the Formation of the Canon] (Freiburg, Vienna, and Basel: Herder, 1971).

22. The words δέχεται τὸν ἀποστείλαντά με in Mt 10:40 and Lk 9:48 represent a so-called minor agreement against Mk 9:37 (οὐκ ἐμὲ δέχεται ἀλλὰ τὸν ἀποστείλαντά με), although the texts, in both vocabulary and meaning, testify to a triple agreement. In fact, this triplet of Synoptic text is also in close resemblance to Jn 13:20 and inevitably leads to the conclusion that this fourfold statement on the authority of the apostolic witness reflects oral tradition, antedating all written sources. The idea of God sending the Son and the Son sending the disciples resulting in a fully authentic communication between the Father and the believers (those who *listen* to the apostolic missionaries) is *pre*supposed, not only logically, but also temporally by the concept of apostolicity as it appears in the gospel texts and Paul's authentic letters.

conclusion that apostolicity, as *the main criterion of Christian authenticity, predates all other formal criteria* that may be considered as forerunners or antecedents to a New Testament canon.

The Marcionite Crisis

As we have indicated, present-day research about the origins of the Christian canon is deeply connected with attempts to evaluate the historical role of Marcion. The exact dating of Marcion's activities remain disputed, yet his first arrival to Rome, followed by a major donation by him to the Church of Rome and, consequently, some temporary success with the Roman congregation but subsequent expulsion in 144 A.D., are admittedly historical events; they are recognized even by those who accuse Tertullian's *Contra Marcionem* of providing a biased "negative press," which denigrated Marcion's image for the following 1,800 years.[23] Since no authentic text survived from Marcion, we can only reconstruct his doctrinal positions secondhand (mainly from adversaries). Marcion's success was probably due not only to money and organizational skills, but to his understanding of how to advocate authoritative texts to spread his ideas and combat his opponents. Marcion's rejection of the Jewish scriptures was undoubtedly an expression of his anti-Judaism, while his proposal of a "two-part" canon, consisting of the *Evangelion*, resembling the Lukan Gospel, and a ten-letter collection of Pauline epistles came from his "exclusive Paulinism"—that is, admitting only Paul's witness to be authentically that of a true apostle of Jesus Christ. However, the claim that he was committed to a rigorous methodology for reconstructing Paul's *authentic* teaching is dubious: von Harnack's effort to reconstruct Marcion's image as a "faithful champion" of the scriptural text in fidelity to the Bible alone (namely Paul) with the exclusion of all other apostolic authorities (and texts) as if he were an early forerunner of Luther with a program of *sola scriptura* is nothing but an anachronistic image. Marcion as an early genius of a textual critic is a projection of modern church historians. Of course, one must also accept that Tertullian's portrait of Mar-

---

23. A more optimistic portrait is found in BeDuhm, *First New Testament*, which contains the reconstruction of Marcion's *Gospel*, followed by a similarly reconstructed version of Marcion's Pauline letters, his *Apostolikon*.

cion as an arch-heretic is a caricature.[24] During Marcion's time there was no clearly defined scriptural canon that he could have rejected; however, Marcion certainly rebelled against the norm ("the canon") of tradition represented by the churches of Asia and their bishops, such as Polycarp in Smyrna and Pope Anicetus in Rome.

Marcion's exclusive Paulinism described earlier was probably based on a misunderstanding of the expressions "my gospel" (Rom 2:16, 16:25) and "the gospel preached by me" (Gal 1:11). He might have thought that Paul's Gospel meant a text (maybe a form of the Lukan Gospel) rather than the Pauline message of salvation. Furthermore, Marcion's belief that Luke was a close companion of Paul is founded on historical facts, but it applies only to Paul's last years of life and ministry, and it was not at this time that Luke wrote his gospel. Marcion's assumption that Paul rejected the Mosaic Law in its entirety is exaggerated, and, of course, the claim that Paul was the only apostle who faithfully followed Jesus' teaching about the Law is completely off target.

Martin Hengel and others have convincingly pointed out that one of Marcion's biases was his anti-Judaism. Although by no means excusable, it must be understood in its historical context. Around 135–40 A.D., after two Jewish revolts that caused an immense number of Roman casualties, Marcion's sense for public relations must have helped him perceive that Christianity's Jewish heritage became a liability. Some researchers believe that a rapidly growing anti-Jewish sentiment characterizes the early second century, and this is the reason that, in some of the apostolic fathers, like Ignatius of Antioch and Polycarp of Smyrna, references to Old Testament texts barely exist. It is certain that both Marcion's early success in Rome and the strong anti-Marcionite position that Justin, Tertullian, and Origen took can be well explained from the absurdity of Marcion's rejection of the Old Testament, as it appeared in the early second century. In any case, Marcion's anti-Judaism is an important argument showing that Marcion falsified Paul in his *Apostolikon* and distorted the gospel tradition in his *Euaggelion*.

24. But in every single work he writes, Tertullian reduces his opponents to caricatures before he demolishes them; this approach was part of his methodology.

Papias, Justin Martyr, and the Diatessaron

Papias and Marcion were contemporaries, but only one is easily dated; around 120 A.D., both were known in Asia Minor: Marcion came originally from Pontus, a northern province of Asia Minor, included in the address of 1 Peter (1 Pt 1:2), while Papias was the bishop of Hierapolis, one of the churches in Colossians (4:13). As Papias's fragments preserved by Eusebius reveal, Papias knew at least two of the earliest gospels, Matthew and Mark. Papias also transmitted a tradition from "an ancient presbyter,"[25] according to which Matthew was originally written in Hebrew, and, for that reason, it had to be translated to Greek, but, due to the variety of translations, doubts were raised about the reliability of the Greek text. He defends Mark's Gospel, stating that its text was based on the oral preaching of the Apostle Peter, whom Mark accompanied as his *hermeneutes* (translator or interpreter). While Papias's witness was frequently studied and quoted, it is often forgotten that, according to Eusebius, Papias claimed to transmit information he received from a man of the previous Christian generation who had been exposed to the oral preaching of the first disciples of Jesus. This reference by Papias to an older source shows that the information he transmits antedates Marcion and cannot be dismissed as Papias's invention. Equally important is the point Eusebius (who read the entire text of Papias, not only the fragments he preserved) makes about Papias's personal conviction of preferring oral tradition to written sources. Papias's mistrust of written gospels must not be exaggerated—his comments on Matthew and Mark show that he also cherished such written sources—but Papias certainly mirrors a problem that originated several years before Marcion: in the first decades of the second century the rising plurality of gospel narratives raised doubts about their authenticity and reliability. If we regard Marcion in the context of Papias's fragments (with his reference to an unnamed elder), his image, created by von Harnack and developed by von Campenhausen (depicting him as the genius who invented the canon),[26] is hard to uphold. Marcion fits into an era in which the written

---

25. This word, meaning "a veteran Christian" or "a veteran missionary" of the early church, one generation prior to Papias, is probably best translated by Bo Reicke; see Reicke, *The Roots of the Synoptic Gospels* (Philadelphia: Fortress, 1986), 150, 155–56.

26. Von Campenhausen, *Formation of the Christian Bible*.

deposits of the apostolic tradition are controverted so that Marcion simply represents a single extreme position, as he was trying to eliminate the heritage of the Old Testament and the authority of Peter and the twelve. Justin Martyr, a somewhat younger contemporary of Marcion, was a well-informed and well-respected member of the Christian community in Rome.[27] He might have even met Marcion personally in Rome; it is certain that he wrote a treatise against Marcion that is unfortunately no longer extant. Justin's position and way of speaking about the early gospels reflect the same basic set of problems for which Marcion attempted to find a remedy. Yet Justin Martyr clearly clings to a set of traditional tenets that Marcion rejected on behalf of his brand of Paulinism.

Justin provides the oldest Christian source of information about the use of Old and New Testament scriptures during the celebration of the Eucharist in the first half of the second century. He tells us that, at Eucharistic celebrations, readings from both the prophets and the reminiscences or memoirs of the apostles (ἀπομνημονεύματα τῶν ἀποστόλων) habitually took place.[28] There is no doubt that he tells here that in such assemblies both the Old Testament and some written sources about Jesus' words and deeds, attributed to an apostolic provenance, were being read, a custom that clearly antedates Marcion's arrival in Rome.

At this point, it may not be necessary to enter into the question of what Justin exactly meant when using the word "gospels" in the plural (εὐαγγέλια) for the first time.[29] The word in a plural form refers to *books, not a message*; it is most probable that Justin knew the Gospels of Matthew, Mark, and Luke in their present canonical form as separate literary works. As some modern authors opine, he might be alluding to a gospel harmony or a collection of excerpts from the Synoptics. All we can say is that Justin tends to fuse the quotations he cites, a tendency that might reflect the same traditional practice by which, for some time in the early second century, the church linked both oral and written sources without adhering to specific textual sources. Yet at Justin's time, the regular reading of written sources at the Eucharistic celebration shows that the

---

27. See Farmer and Farkasfalvy, *Formation of the New Testament Canon*, 141–43.

28. Justin Martyr, *First Apology* 67.3.

29. Justin Martyr, *Dialogue with Trypho* 103.9. This first *extant* usage may not indicate an absolute first occurrence.

content of the apostolic memory has been transposed into literary composition to aid the church's acts of remembrance when proclaiming the one Gospel of Jesus Christ.[30]

We know about a prominent disciple of Justin, named Tatian, of Syriac origin, who left Rome around 160 A.D., immediately after his teacher's martyrdom, and soon thereafter began to spread his solution to the problem of the multiplicity of the gospels with which, in the previous decades, Papias, Marcion, and probably Justin himself had been wrestling. He combined the *four gospels*, Matthew, Mark, Luke, and John, each an account of Jesus's words and deeds, into one single narration. Tatian's composition became known as the *Diatessaron* (literally meaning "through the four"—that is, one narrative created from four), and had an unusual success in Tatian's native Syria, where it was in official use for several centuries. It was only at the insistence of the Roman Church that in the fifth century the *Diatessaron* lost its official status as the gospel used by the Syriac Church. Due to imperial pressure, the *Diatessaron* was forced out of ecclesial practices so successfully that today we possess it only in those fragments that are quoted in St. Ephrem's homilies on the gospels.[31]

In short, the problem of the plurality of the gospels was known in the church at large in the first centuries, beginning with such important figures as Papias, Marcion, and Justin Martyr.[32] It is noteworthy that nobody but Marcion felt entitled to reduce the number of the gospels to one, nor did anyone else eliminate the plurality of the apostles for the sake of establishing a radical *literary oneness* of the gospel by claiming that only one apostolic figure was reliable and acceptable.

The picture I have depicted of the crisis triggered by "the plurality of the gospels" in the second century is far from complete. Rather, the opposite is true. Recent historical and archeological research has shown

30. Combining the references to the "Memoirs of the Apostles" and the use of a plural for "gospels" in the sense of written works, we can hardly avoid the conclusion that Justin speaks of the Synoptic Gospels as separate books rather than of a gospel harmony.

31. Ephrem de Nisibe, *Commentaire de l'Évangile concordant ou Diatessaron*, trans. from Syriac and Armenian with introduction, trans., ed. Louis Leloir, Sources chrétiennes 121 (Paris: Cerf, 1966).

32. See Helmut Merkel, *Die Pluralität der Evangelien als theologisches und exegetisches Problem in der alten Kirche* [The Multiplicity of the Gospels as a Theological and Exegetical Problem in the Ancient Church] (Frankfurt: Peter Lang, 1978).

that later in the second century a growing number of "gospels" began to circulate among Christians, a trend that lasted several centuries. Nonetheless, in spite of much contemporary excitement about the history of the apocryphal gospels, the size and importance of this movement must not be overstated. Although in the last several decades many such gospels were reconstructed from papyrus finds and forgotten literary sources, published, and studied, no canonical gospel has been proven to be earlier than the four canonical gospels. Only the Gospel of Peter and, according to some reconstructions, the earliest form of the Gospel of Thomas could be dated to the first half of the second century.[33] Yet, there is no doubt that in the second half of the same century the use of a four-gospel canon surfaced and coexisted side by side with the beginnings of popular gospel writing, creating unease among Christians who saw in the multiple renditions of Jesus' words and deeds a threat to orthodoxy. The idea of a *Diatessaron* as a single unified narration suggests that, besides Marcion, there were other attempts to try to solve this problem by reducing the multiplicity of parallel, but potentially conflicting, narrative sources on Jesus. How the fourfold gospel canon established itself and remained dominant up to today needs a closer examination, even if our sources cannot assure full certainties about the details of this process.

Polycarp's Trip to Rome and the Fourfold Gospel Canon

The canonical crisis that escalated in the second century was resolved at the end of the century in the adoption of a closed four-gospel canon and the finalization of the Pauline corpus. That much is evident and well known from the works of Irenaeus and Tertullian, but there is no scholarly consensus about exact dates, the details of the process, or the value of its outcome. Essential therefore, would be the reconstruction of the process that brought about the four-gospel canon as it stands in an explicit way in Irenaeus's *Adversus Haereses*, dated to about 185 A.D. The basic events can be narrated with a high degree of probability, and they are of capital importance for understanding the formation of the Christian Bible and its canon.

33. Hill, *Who Chose the Gospels?*

A central fact is the historic voyage undertaken by Polycarp, the bishop of Smyrna, to meet Pope Anicetus of Rome. Shortly after his return home, Polycarp was executed. The historical context is full of indicators that Polycarp's journey was surrounded by circumstances that highly influenced the birth of the four-gospel canon.

In the years 150–53 (and for a few years beyond), five important Christian personalities sojourned in Rome. Some of the time they lived in the city probably overlapped; moreover, it is known that while in Rome, they dealt with similar issues of what did or did not constitute authentic Christian teaching; at least some of them could have met each other personally and publicly. When Polycarp came from Asia Minor to meet Anicetus in Rome, Marcion was, in all probability, still living in Rome, and Valentinus, a famous Christian leader, had just moved to Rome from Alexandria, promoting the spread of what was later called the "Valentinian" brand of Gnosticism. Valentinus must have arrived somewhat earlier and was accompanied by several disciples; in Rome he began a ministry of preaching and teaching.[34] The fifth influential Christian was Justin Martyr, who, before his martyrdom (usually dated to 155–60 under Marcus Aurelius), ran a philosophical school in Rome. Even a sixth person of importance might have been there: Irenaeus, who claims to have known Polycarp and who, at the time of Polycarp's arrival, was a young deacon of the church of Lyons, a community of migrants to Gaul from Asia Minor. Irenaeus probably made a trip to Rome, if for no other reason than to see Polycarp at his arrival. He was accompanied by others from his homeland and was a leader of enormous prestige among Christians across the empire.

Of these personalities, Valentinus was allegedly of the highest intellectual ability and education; he represented the latest trends in Christian thinking, which we still tend to call "Gnosticism."[35] Gnosticism originally appeared in Alexandria presented by a person named Basilides and was diametrically opposed to Marcionism, as it tended to accept

34. Valentinus's arrival in Rome is set by Irenaeus (*Adversus Haereses* III.4.3) under the pontificate of Hyginus. He adds that Valentinus "remained" (= lived in Rome) during the time of Anicetus. All this would indicate that his Roman sojourn overlapped with that of Marcion.

35. According to Tertullian in *Adversus Valentinianos* IV, "Valentinus had expected to become a bishop, because he was an able man both in genius and eloquence. Being indignant, however, that another [Anicetus] obtained the dignity by reason of a claim which confessorship had given him, he broke with the church of the true faith."

a wide variety of versions and interpretations of the gospel. The Valentinians were also open to accepting a multitude of "gospels" (like "the Gospel of Truth," about which Irenaeus makes indignant comments) and had a particular interest in John's Gospel (mostly in its prologue). Two of Valentinus's disciples, Heracleon and Ptolemy (the latter accompanied his master to Rome), wrote the first known commentaries to John's Gospel, a fact that must have been widely known and disputed in Rome, since the main reason for Polycarp's trip and meeting with Pope Anicetus was closely linked with his agenda to vindicate the apostolic authority of the Johannine tradition. The confluence of these five or six personalities in Rome must be seen in the context of the specific purpose Polycarp had for making his trip. He came to straighten out questions stemming from conflicting apostolic traditions.[36] In Asia Minor, the so-called Quartodeciman discipline of Lenten observance with a corresponding calendar for Easter claimed its legitimacy with reference to the Apostle John, who, according to Asian tradition, had lived to an old age in Ephesus and left behind a rich local tradition. Experts widely recognize that the conflicting chronologies of the Last Supper in John and the Synoptics can be best understood as reflecting diverse liturgical customs in the early second century,[37] based on the Johannine tradition of Asia and the Synoptic tradition (with claims of Petrine and Pauline tradition) in Rome. At the time of Polycarp's trip, this diversity in understanding the apostolic tradition threatened to disrupt the unity of the church. Unfortunately, on both sides, that of Polycarp, representing the Christians of Asia Minor, and that of Anicetus, carrying a Christian self-understanding of even wider dimensions,[38] nonnegotiable principles

36. Justin Martyr knew John's Gospel but appears to be reticent about using it in his works. The Roman Church might have been ambivalent for some time about this gospel; yet, as Eusebius and Irenaeus testify, Polycarp's mission was about the validity of a purported Johannine tradition and the Fourth Gospel's Quartodeciman implications.

37. This tradition essentially followed the Jewish calendar, celebrating the Passover on the fourteenth day of Nissan rather than on a Sunday. We observe that in the Gospel of John, Jesus dies on the afternoon before the night of the Passover on which the Passover meal was to be eaten ["Then they brought Jesus from Caiaphas to the *praetorium*. It was morning. And they themselves did not enter the *praetorium*, in order not to be defiled so that they could eat the Passover"; Jn 18:28], while in the Synoptics, Jesus eats the Passover meal with his disciples the night before he dies; Mt 26:17; Mk 14:14; Lk 22:11, 22:13, 22:15.

38. Anicetus was of Syrian origin and nationality and thus represented both the Petrine *and* the Pauline traditions, which are linked with the Synoptic Gospels.

were at stake on both sides: the apostolic authenticity of their respective church communities.

Eusebius of Caesarea narrates that Polycarp's personal presence in Rome helped bring back many "heretics" (Marcionites and Valentinians) to Anicetus's fold. This is hardly just a hagiographic comment. Polycarp's immense authority was based, as in his Letter to Florinus,[39] Irenaeus testifies, on his reputation of being a living link with apostolic times: allegedly, in his youth Polycarp conversed with the Apostle John, and as a young bishop he was the recipient of a letter from Ignatius of Antioch on his journey to martyrdom in Rome. These facts were still a matter of living memory. The presumably eighty-four-year-old bishop (he died as a martyr in 155, aged 86) stood out among his Christian contemporaries, who, due to abiding presence, were feeling closer and more intimately connected to the living witness of Christ's apostles. He was a symbol of an aging church in search of authenticity, a visible, personal link to the first apostles' communities, but now disturbed and disoriented by growing heretical movements, losing members and showing signs of fragmentation because of divisions in their ranks. Polycarp's mission to gain support for the Quartodeciman tradition, at least in the way he planned it, had come to fail. For at their meeting, the two churchmen, Anicetus and Polycarp, declared that they could not leave their own apostolic traditions. Anicetus remained devoted to the traditions of the glorious martyrs Peter and Paul, portrayed as the Roman Church's founders and enshrined in the Synoptic Gospels and his letters, while Polycarp adhered to his traditions coming from the "Disciple of the Lord resting on the Lord's breast" (Irenaeus, *Adversus Haereses* III.1.1). Each side's position was impossible to assail or to abandon. Polycarp's name and fame were well known in Rome, and his link to the Apostle John could not have been called into doubt. The Valentinian presence only amplified the value of the Johannine tradition on which the Roman Church might not have yet taken an official stance. The meeting between Polycarp and Anicetus ended in a standoff, yet on amicable terms. Anicetus and Polycarp celebrated a shared Eucharist, and thus the unity of the church was preserved.

This story needed to be told in full context for understanding what followed. Shortly after his return to Asia, Polycarp was burned at the

---

39. *Historia Ecclesiastica* IV.14; see also *Adversus Haereses* III.3.4.

stake in Smyrna.[40] While the Quartodeciman dispute went on for half a century, at a much earlier date, before 185 A.D.—that is, less than thirty years after Polycarp's trip—Irenaeus's *Adversus Haereses*' third volume shows that a pact of unity had been formulated about the four apostolic gospels of the church with clear and undisputable reception of John's Gospel added to those of Matthew, Mark, and Luke as the Fourth Gospel. This text by Irenaeus is the oldest canonical statement about the four gospels. It is of capital significance for the rest of the church's history. It reads:

Thus *Matthew, among the Jews* in their own language, published the scripture of the *gospel* while *Peter and Paul*, in *Rome, evangelized* and founded the Church.

Then after their departure, *Mark*, a disciple and interpreter of Peter, he too *transmitted* to us in *writing* those things which had been *proclaimed* by *Peter*.

And then *Lukas*, the follower of *Paul*, the *gospel* which was *preached* by him [Paul] he has included in a *book*.

Afterwards *John*, the disciple of the Lord, who had reclined on his chest, he too *published* the *gospel* while staying in *Ephesus of Asia*.

I am not the first to surmise that this passage, found in the first chapter of the third book of the *Adversus Haereses*, is not a composition by Irenaeus,[41] but copied from an earlier document, possibly from the church archives of Rome. It represents a remarkably successful result of Polycarp's journey obtained in Rome by providing a joint statement about a *fourfold apostolic gospel canon*. This conclusion is strongly supported by both the discontinuities of its literary context in Irenaeus's work and many literary features of the passage itself.

In Irenaeus's text, there are important discontinuities with both the passage that precedes it (Preface of the Third Book) and the one that follows. The preface speaks about Irenaeus's intention to go beyond the scope of his first two books and demonstrate "from the scriptures" the falsehood of the heretical teachings that he had described. Irenaeus then begins to speak about what he calls the "apostolic gospels." Here he first speaks in generic terms about the apostles who would become ready to

40. Polycarp's martyrdom was described by eyewitnesses; *The Acts of the Christian Martyrs* edited with introduction and notes by H. A. Musurillo (Oxford: Clarendon, 1972).

41. See T. C. Skeat, "Irenaeus and the Four-Gospel Canon," *Novum Testamentum* 34, no. 2 (1992): 194–99.

begin transmitting Jesus' message only when receiving "power over the gospel" at large. Irenaeus insists that the apostles did not start their (oral) ministry without first being granted a supernatural understanding of the gospel message. Irenaeus clearly initiates here a theology of inspiration by stating that the apostles' collective preparation to their ministry took place at Pentecost to announce all they learned from Jesus' words and deeds and that only after their oral preaching began did the gospel they announced become enshrined in written compositions. At this point Irenaeus's line of thought is interrupted by the passage we quoted earlier about the four gospels. After that, he continues by coming back to the theological topic about the *scriptures as revelation of the triune God, channeled into writing*, very much in the way we generally find this topic in other early church fathers and in *Dei Verbum*. This is what he writes:

> These have all declared to us that there is one God, Creator of heaven and earth, announced by *the law and the prophets*; and one *Christ the Son of God*. If anyone do not agree to these truths, he despises the *companions of the Lord*; nay, more, he despises *Christ Himself the Lord; yea, he despises the Father* also, and stands self-condemned, resisting and opposing his own salvation, as is the case with all heretics. (*Adversus Haereses* III.2)

This passage, reproducing second-century language about a tripartite witness to revelation, shows that Irenaeus pursues a traditional position that is both anti-Marcionite and anti-Valentinian in defense of the "the gospels of the apostles" (*Adversus Haereses* III.4.9). The latter expression closely follows Justin's term "Memoir of the Apostles;" although his wording is more fortuitous than Justin's formula because the Hellenistic concept of memoirs was much too generic, and, by making no reference to the event of Pentecost, Justin also omitted specifications concerning who those apostles were. Irenaeus's text provides more information: he eventually uses the term "apostles" in a collective sense. From extant fragments of Irenaeus's Greek text, we know that his *evangelia apostolorum* stands for "τὰ εὐαγγελία τῶν ἀποστόλων," with definite articles, thus pointing to the heart of the Marcionite controversy: Irenaeus speaks of "the gospels" in the plural and "*the* Apostles," with a definite article, as the twelve *presented in Acts*. He makes this clear not only by referring to the scene of Pentecost (Acts 2:1–13), but to the story about Matthias replacing Judas (Acts 1:16–26). Thus "the Apostles" represent here the leaders of the first community built around the twelve exactly in the way they were presented in the book of Acts.

Now we can see even more clearly why the four sentences, quoted earlier from *Adversus Haereses* III.1.1, stand out for their exceptional importance. Suddenly, in four sentences, Irenaeus goes into specifics to tell how this message of "the Apostles" has been turned into written gospels. A further sign of discontinuity is in the vocabulary: the four sentences that follow do not contain the word "apostle," but refer to *eleven special words: six personal names, three geographic regions, and two languages.* The six persons are *Matthew, Peter, Mark, Paul, Luke, and John*; the three geographic designations come in reference to local churches: "among the Jews" (meaning *Palestine*), then *Rome* and *Ephesus.* These ten proper names, which do not appear again anywhere else in Irenaeus's five-volume book, obviously constitute an interruption that needs an explanation.

I think an additional indicator is just one word: the pronoun ἡμῖν (for us), inserted into the sentence about Mark's Gospel, nails the argument. This word is, in my opinion, "a smoking gun"—providing conclusive evidence. Here Irenaeus says that, after Peter's "departure" (that is, his death),[42] the preaching he did in Rome was written down *"for us."* *This set of words could not have been originally written by Irenaeus* because he never speaks about the Roman community as "us." He belonged to the church of Lyons and not of Rome. But, of course, Mark was said to have served Peter's ministry in Rome, both in its oral transmission and by writing it down. So the word ἡμῖν, firmly embedded in the text,[43] is an indicator of the Roman provenance of the whole paragraph of four sentences, which in a uniformly worded style constitute a textual block to state in a laconic style the apostolic origins of the four gospels. This para-

---

42. Peter's exit or *exodus* does not mean a physical departure but his death. This has been a bone of contention among scholars because it impacts the dating of Mark's Gospel; see Ellis, *Making of the New Testament Documents*, 360–63, supporting Adolph von Harnack. But Ellis overlooks that the word ἔξοδος (translated in the Latin text as *excessus*) is in the *Adversus Haereses* a hapax legomenon, but here, as I argue, occurs in a sentence that Irenaeus quotes from a source; therefore it must not be interpreted by comparing it to Irenaeus's general usage of the word θάνατος for "death." Ellis does not appreciate that here the use of the word ἔξοδος evokes 2 Pt 1:15, referring to Peter's death so that, in *Adversus Haereses* III.1.1, we may be dealing with a reference to 2 Peter.

43. The extant Latin text of the *Adversus Haereses* has *nobis* with no variant; an independent Greek fragment is also known to be in agreement with its reading of ἡμῖν. In the structure of his book, Irenaeus needs exactly at this point, before he scans the four gospels for refuting the Gnostic teachings exposed in books I and II, to state their apostolic authenticity and authority.

graph of four sentences, testifying in specific terms to the apostolic origin of four gospels, was ready-made before Irenaeus, who then inserted it
into his text. This passage must have been first written *sometime around
the middle of the second century in Rome* and was preserved verbatim until Irenaeus inserted it into his book-by-book apologetic presentation of
the four "apostolic gospels."

This reconstruction of the meeting between Polycarp and Anicetus
also ultimately tells us how the centerpiece of the New Testament canon
was born: it was not the result of an emergent development but rather
the fruit of a responsible decision of two church leaders, each representing the apostolic tradition of their communities, which all believed was
based upon and committed to embracing all authentic apostolic traditions. Their decision took place in fidelity to their apostolic origins as
well as to their commitment to fight both Marcion and Valentinus, of
whom the first was pressing for a single-gospel canon and the second
was ready to embrace a virtually unlimited number of gospels with questionable origins and pedigrees. When the four apostolic gospels were
accepted by both the Church of Rome and the local churches of Asia
Minor, a most important decision took place that decided the future of
Christianity by determining the New Testament canon for the rest of
the church's history.

II ✦ THE CHRISTIAN BIBLE
AT THE END OF THE
SECOND CENTURY

―――――・◆・――――

The Four-Gospel Canon Stabilized

Anicetus and Polycarp agreed in Rome that only apostolic gospel books can be accepted as authentic and authoritative. This principle was not new, and even Marcion agreed to the same principle, except for him Paul was the only true apostle. The four sentences, which Irenaeus quotes, probably come verbatim from a verbal or written agreement. The word *nobis* in Irenaeus's text is best explained if these four sentences were part of a written statement or letter preserved in the archives of the Roman Church. Of course, the information about Matthew and Mark agrees with the tradition found in the fragments of Papias. Assuming that Irenaeus depends on Papias regarding Matthew and Mark contradicts the evidence we presented earlier. Irenaeus uses a Roman source. Concerning Luke, we have no text earlier than the one transmitted by Irenaeus, but the secondary sources on Marcion constitute evidence that the Lukan *euaggelion*, Luke's first volume, was considered at Marcion's time "Pauline Gospel" or even "Paul's Gospel."[1] In any case, neither the tra-

---

1. See a recent reconstruction of Marcion's Evangelion and Apostolikon, available in English: BeDuhn, *First New Testament*. The author uses Tertullian and Epiphanius selectively as historically reliable sources on Marcion, yet he thinks that the attachment of Luke's name to the text Marcion published as *Euaggelion* was posterior to the anonymous origins of the text. He is contradicting the conclusions Martin Hengel reached in his research on the gospel titles without taking issue with Hengel's findings or even mentioning his name.

dition about an Aramaic Matthew and the Petrine authority of Mark's Gospel (both recorded by Papias) nor the Pauline pedigree of this Lukan or pre-Lukan text could have been Irenaeus's invention. Papias and Marcion antedate Irenaeus by several decades, and so do the texts by Justin Martyr.[2] At a critical moment of the church's life, Anicetus and Polycarp did not allow their apostolic traditions to clash, but agreed to link their respective traditions to create a united anti-Marcionite and anti-Valentinian stance.

It is useful to look at the way Bruce M. Metzger reached his view of dating the four-gospel canon to as early as the middle of the second century. When he undertook the study of the history of the New Testament canon, he opted for a careful, piece-by-piece method of examination to see which ancient gospels were used in different periods of the second century.[3] It is worth looking at some of his conclusions. About the *Diatessaron*, composed in Syria around 170 A.D., Metzger concludes that it "supplies proof that all four gospels were regarded as authoritative, otherwise it is unlikely that Tatian would have dared to combine them into one gospel account" (115). About Clement of Alexandria, who died around 190 A.D., he states, "That he accepted the fourfold canon of the Gospels is shown by a passage from his lost *Hypotyposes*" (132). Also in the East, Origen, who was active in the first half of the third century, first in Egypt and then in Palestine (Caesarea), "regarded the canon of the four gospels as closed" (141). With respect to the West, Metzger quotes Irenaeus of Lyons as representing the position of the Church of Rome (*Adversus Haereses* III.11.8) and writes that for Irenaeus, "the (fourfold) Gospel Canon is closed and its text is holy" (155). For Carthage in Roman Africa, Metzger examines the writings of Tertullian, who converted to Christianity in 195 A.D., although later, in 205, he attached himself to the Montanist movement. Metzger concludes that Tertullian's *New Testament* "is not per-

2. Irenaeus wrote around 185, while Marcion produced his scriptures around 130 or earlier, and Papias must be dated to 120 (and the "ancient presbyter," his source, to about 100). Justin Martyr died around 160 A.D. His references to the narrative of the annunciation (*First Apology*, no. 100) reflect knowledge of Luke's text. The *Protoevangelium of James* reflects similar acquaintance with Lk 1–2; recent scholarship dates this book to 160–70 A.D., much earlier than the *Adversus Haereses* by Irenaeus. Briefly, the Synoptic Gospels' unanimous attribution to their respective authors goes back to the first decades of the second century.

3. Bruce M. Metzger, *The Canon of the New Testament: Its Origin, Development, and Significance* (Oxford: Clarendon 1987).

ceptibly different" in these last two periods of his life. For Tertullian, the "four gospels are the *Instrumentum evangelicum,* and its authors are either 'apostles or companions and disciples of the apostles.'" (159) Thus, while in principle working with a paradigm of accretion and emergence that would allow a step-by-step formation of the gospel canon and a variance in final results, Metzger found that, indeed, consensus about the four-canonical gospel appeared within fifty years over a wide geographic spread of the whole Roman Empire, of which he had examined five samples: Rome, Syria, Egypt, Gaul, and Roman Africa.

Metzger's result might constitute the strongest evidence—clearly and inductively obtained without prefabrication—that the formation of the four-gospel canon happened in a sudden and point-wise way, likely to suggest one decision resulting in a virtual unanimity of the major churches as they embraced an identical position. The four-gospel canon is best understood as the result of a conscious agreement, reached by the Christian communities of Rome and Asia Minor through Polycarp and Anicetus and representing a common principle of apostolicity that they realized they should hold jointly and came to verify for no more or less than four gospels: those of Matthew, Mark, Luke, and John.

It is not negligible that in Irenaeus's text all four canonical gospels are attributed to an "apostolic" provenance, not in a global way but with exact references to both identifiable literary authors and specifically named apostles (one of the twelve or Paul) through whom each of the gospels obtained its apostolic origin. "Apostolic origin" of a canonical gospel means both a general qualification and a concrete, historically specified fact. The way the apostolicity of these four gospels is expressed in Irenaeus's four-sentence passage is a far cry from the contemporary majority opinion, claiming that the canonical gospels were anonymous compositions and obtained their status either by a slow emergence or a battle between bishops and heretics.[4]

---

4. In contradiction to *Dei Verbum,* this position is consistently adopted in the *New Jerome Biblical Commentary* of 1991, while the previous edition of 1981 (the *Jerome Biblical Commentary*) still spoke about "unanimous" traditions supporting the apostolic authorship of the four authors designated in the gospel titles. *Dei Verbum* quotes verbatim the Instruction *Sancta Mater Ecclesia,* published in 1964, which specifically states the authorship of the canonical gospels, closely following Irenaeus text: "For what the Apostles preached in fulfillment of the commission of Christ, afterwards they themselves and apostolic men, under the inspiration of the divine Spirit, handed on

Yet, the authorship of the four gospels is the strongest of all biblical traditions in the church's early history. With no exception, all ancient gospel manuscripts follow the same tradition and the same language as they speak not of four gospels but about *one Gospel according to four presentations*: those of Matthew, Mark, John, and Luke. The theological meaning of this usage implies a refusal to speak of four works of various individual origins, gathered eventually in one collection by possibly fictitious or uncertain attributions to various authors, as if gathered together in a slow secondary process. In the gospel titles, the church preserved an anti-Marcionite position and used an early second-century language to maintain both Paul's claim in Galatians that there was only one gospel (2:9) and the plurality of exactly four compositions, coming from four specific apostolic sources and four authors, named specifically, in whose texts the one Gospel of Jesus was deposited to be passed down and preserved for the rest of history.[5]

The Apostolic Letters

In the first decades of the second century, the scattered mentioning of the apostles as decisive authorities in matters of faith may appear to be either very generic or ambiguous. As it is known from New Testament documents, an apostle of Jesus Christ might speak in the name of Christ or in his own name. Paul might say, "I received from the Lord what I also handed on to you" (1 Cor 11:23) or "I have no commandment from the Lord, but I give my opinion as one who by the Lord's mercy is trustworthy" (1 Cor 7:25). However, in the formula "Prophets and Apostles" used by the earliest patristic sources, it is clear that there are basically two classes of divinely chosen and inspired transmitters of revelation; in this nomenclature, any writer ("hagiographer") of the Old Testament belongs to "the Prophets," while "the Apostles" are either witnesses of what they saw and heard from the earthly Jesus and functioned as his "ambassadors" (2 Cor 5:20)—that is, authorized delegates or as close associates to such persons.

to us in writing: the foundation of faith, namely, the fourfold Gospel, according to Matthew, Mark, Luke and John."

5. See Hengel, *The Four Gospels and the One Gospel of Jesus Christ*, trans. John Bowden (Harrisburg, Pa.: Trinity Press International, 2000).

The transition from inspired preaching and teaching to writing is usually attributed to the Apostle Paul, who turned to letter writing as a means of multiplying his personal presence in the churches that he had founded. If we recall Luke's rendition of the so-called Council of the Apostles, issuing a short letter to be circulated in all churches about their decision concerning the Gentiles' freedom from Mosaic Law (Acts 15:23–29) or, from much earlier, the Epistle of Jeremiah included in the Septuagint, the instrument of an apostolic letter may not appear to be a great innovation except for the way in which Paul personally used it. The comparatively rich literary output of the Apostle Paul, the early efforts to collect his epistles (testified to by 2 Pt 3:15), and the length of some of his letters (Romans, 1 Corinthians) show that the Pauline letters were not a routine feature of the early church's missionary practice. Certainly not everyone was doing it, as most Christian preachers would not have been able to do it in the way and to the extent Paul did.

There is every reason to suppose that Paul himself kept copies of his letters and that the local churches he addressed kept his letters and eventually shared them with other communities. We have, therefore, good reason to assume that it took some time, but only a short period, for the Pauline letters to become known as a special treasury of records from the earliest period of the church's life; this realization was quickly followed by the letters' accelerated spread and increased interest in reading and copying them, leading to their proliferation among church communities.

Furthermore, there is sufficient reason to assume that an early collection of ten letters destined to seven local churches (Romans, 1–2 Corinthians, 1–2 Thessalonians, Galatians, Philippians, Ephesians, Colossians, and a tenth letter sent to an individual, Philemon), had an anti-Marcionite origin and began circulating in an increasing number of communities.[6] At the same time, it seems that Marcion's claim that Paul was the only legitimate and authentic apostle was the cause of another, equally ancient or possibly earlier, edition of the Pauline letters. But it appears that Marcion has neither rediscovered Paul's faded memory nor invented the *Apostolikon*, the (Marcionite) edition of the ten letters. How the first Pauline collection of letters came about remains unclear, yet it has given rise to

6. See Clabeaux, *Lost Edition of the Letters of Paul.*

diverse theories, mixing facts with speculation.[7] The debate is far from being closed. It is rightly pointed out that the curious survival of the Letter to Philemon, a literary piece different in content, style, and addressee from the rest of the letters, but certainly authentic, needs an explanation. Any theory about the origin of the first collections must include a narrative explaining how Philemon made it into them. The fact that four of the ten letters (Ephesians, Colossians, Philippians, and Philemon) attest that the writer is in prison perplexes many researchers, yet there is no consensus that they all come from the same imprisonment or location. Paul is known to have been in prison for an extended time in Ephesus, Caesarea, and Rome. The three pastoral letters (Ti, 1–2 Tm), which were not part of the first, possible pre-Marcionite or Marcionite collection, allege that they were written at the end of Paul's life during his Roman imprisonment.

Unfortunately, the research about the collection of the Pauline letters is being done mostly in isolation from the canonization of other apostolic letters.[8] It is in this connection that we should bring up that curious snapshot, taken by Paul in Galatians 2:9 around the year 50 A.D., of what appears to be a leadership team in the apostolic church. They are called the church's "pillars" and identified by three names, "James," "Peter," and "John." Paul most probably means here that these three men were considered in Jerusalem to be the leaders of the church and that, when "recognizing the grace given to me (Paul)," they established a pact of fellowship with him.[9] One cannot avoid the impression that Paul refers to himself also by assuming—or at least bidding for—his own installation as the fourth pillar. For the second-century readers of the Pauline letters, Galatians 2:9 suggests that at that time, apostolic times, there were four pillars on which the edifice of the church was to be built. On the one hand, the informa-

---

7. Harry Y. Gamble summarizes them in four groups: (1) the "snowball theories," claiming a process of accretion; (2) a first period of disuse of the Pauline letters, followed by the "discovery" and "renaissance" of Paul; (3) the theory of an individual collector or editor; and (4) a "Pauline School" of Paul's disciples who gathered his legacy; see Gamble, *The New Testament Canon: Its Making and Meaning*, 2nd ed. (Eugene, Ore.: Wipf and Stock, 2002).

8. See the reference to "Jude, a servant of Jesus Christ and brother of James"; Jude 1:1.

9. "When James and Cephas and John, who were acknowledged pillars, recognized the grace that had been given to me, they gave to me and Barnabas the right hand of fellowship, agreeing that we should go to the Gentiles and they to the circumcised"; Gal 2:8–9. One must realize that, for historical accuracy, Paul includes Barnabas in the handshakes, but he claims recognition by the apostolic pillars only to himself, for, as he says, it was offered due to "the grace given to me" (in the singular). Thus, at no point can we cannot talk of five pillars, only four.

tion about the three pillars in the letter is doubtless factual: Paul named the three most important persons in the Jerusalem Church. On the other hand, one can see a subtext here: Paul counts himself among these apostolic pillars as of equal rank and importance. Therefore, to a second-century reader, it would not have appeared coincidental that the four names reflect the fourfold provenance of the apostolic letters in the canon.[10] Finally— and this appears to be a bit unusual—pretty much the same picture emerges from the Acts of the Apostles, telling us that besides the two sons of Zebedee (of whom James was martyred in 44 A.D., well before Galatians was written), the leadership of the apostolic church encompassed these same pillars. Acts is mostly about Peter and Paul, a little bit about John, and to a larger extent also about James, the brother of the Lord, while no other apostolic profile stands out with significance. Thus, even if we remain fascinated with the question of why, in Acts, Paul never appears to be a writer, we must recognize that the authors of the other canonical apostolic letters coincide with the men named pillars in Galatians and Paul, who are the only apostolic figures whose remembrance appears with some individual features in the narratives of Acts.[11]

In short, the process by which the New Testament canon came about is no happenstance, as if it had followed an unpredictable evolutionary path with a chancy outcome, but was a conscious process of canonizing two collections of apostolic books. These books were four apostolic gospels, a collection of Pauline letters, letters by the "three (other) pillars" of the church, James, Peter, and John, combined with the second volume of Luke's Gospel, the *Acts of the Apostles* (a second-century title) and added to the book of Revelation, a prophetic writing that opens with seven letters to "seven churches" (see Rv 1:4, 1:11) and is attributed to the "seer John," whom ancient tradition identified with the Apostle John, the author of the Fourth Gospel and of three epistles.[12]

---

10. This has been noticed by many people. Most recently, David Trobisch built much of his theory about a second-century, final redaction of the entire New Testament on this insight: Trobisch, *Endredaktion des Neuen Testaments*, 91–92.

11. A supportive argument for this observation comes from the manner in which the first verse of Jude's letter introduces its author as "the brother of James."

12. The oldest source naming the Apostle John to be the author of the book of Revelation is Justin Martyr (*Dialogue with Trypho*, no. 81). Two important second-century movements in the church, *Chiliasm* (also called *Millenarism*) and *Montanism*, appealing to the apostolic authority of this writing through the same identification of its author, indicate that Justin expressed earlier

The New Testament Canon as a Whole

There are two important issues at stake. One concerns the prehistory of the canon; the other is about the actual construction and closure of a twenty-seven-book set that constitutes the New Testament.

The first issue is a process of reflection and maturation by which the concept of apostolicity became crystallized as an external criterion for the authenticity of Christian doctrine. This process is rooted in Jesus' own life and teaching. At the origins of the process we find the twelve whose historicity cannot be seriously challenged. The ways "the twelve" are dealt with in the Synoptics and John, in references by Paul and Acts, and in the exalted image of the twelve foundation stones and gates of the heavenly Jerusalem signifying the "Twelve apostles of the Lamb" in the book of Revelation (21:14) would imply many issues for which most details are disputed. Most importantly, the etymology of the word *apostolos*, with its Hebrew/Aramaic background, is not fully resolved; neither is its varying meaning in the Synoptics nor Paul's insistence that he is an apostle just as Peter and the rest were. We find an unexplained absence of the term *apostolos* in the Johannine writings about the twelve (who are mentioned repeatedly) and a lack of reference to the "apostles" in some early sources like the Epistle to the Hebrews. Yet, apostolicity as a theological concept becomes important in the early second century. In fact, the question of Christian authenticity among various Christian groups dealing with orthodoxy versus heresy is often orchestrated in terms of apostolicity. Apostolicity is a key concept in Irenaeus and even more in Origen, whose biblical vocabulary dominates theological discussions of the following millennium. The time between the assumed compositional date of the first gospels (the last two or three decades of the first century) and the reception of the four-gospel canon (in the second half of the second century) is well under one hundred years. The first gospel was written, at the latest, during the outbreak of the Jewish war around 70 A.D., and, in our reconstruction, a historic agreement about the four apostolic gospels was reached *point-wise* at the meeting of Anicetus and

---

tradition. The unanimous dating of the book of Revelation to the last decades of the first century leaves little chance for explaining this tradition in any better way than by accepting that the designation of the author is as old as the book itself.

Polycarp around 153–55. But even those who doubt such a reconstruction must admit that, before the end of the second century, *apostolic provenance* became the main criterion of orthodoxy for any doctrine or New Testament book.

From around the year 200 A.D., there are extant fragments of papyrus codices that originally contained all four canonical gospels. There are also some fragments of other codices from about the same time that included full collections of Pauline letters. Textual criticism has demonstrated that the separation of Luke's second volume from the first (assuming they had originally circulated together) and the second volume being named "Acts of the Apostles" and copied into a common codex with the letters of Peter, Jude, and James happened around the turn of the second and third centuries.

How the canonization and reception of the book of Revelation took place and then met new obstacles is a complex question confused by disputes because it took place in various regional disputes against Milenarists and Montanists. This book was received by some with enthusiasm and has met with reluctant reception by others. Yet early, it was known as a work of the Apostle John, so that, at first (before suspicion about the Milenarists and Montanism began to spread), it entered the canon because of its apostolicity. How the pastoral letters, Hebrews, and 2 Peter and 3 John were included or excluded in various records on the canon cannot be followed closely because of lack of sufficient sources and a few side issues, such as pseudepigraphy and shifting vocabularies on canon and inspiration. Much depends also on how we define the closure of the canon. Yet, in all these processes, the decisive term was "apostolicity," about which the church obtained much clarity and consensus by the end of the second century.

The Old Testament in the Christian Canon

Much can be said about the similarities and dissimilarities of the canonization of the two testaments in Christianity. There were obvious structural similarities from antiquity: the Law (the Pentateuch) was compared to the gospel (the four-gospel canon). There is also parallelism between revelation and inspiration in the Old and New Testaments, suggesting that, with regard to these concepts, the New Testament was imitating the Old. Beginning with Matthew's Gospel, there appear parallelisms between Moses and Jesus, the prophets and the apostles, the nonprophetic hagiographers as companions to the prophets, and those apostolic men portrayed as companions of the apostles (Mark and Luke). Yet the previous examples often point to parallelisms between persons who are unequal. Moses is a prophet, but Jesus is the Son of God, the incarnate Word, God become Flesh (Jn1:13–14) and the fullness of revelation (see Col 1:19, 2:9).[13] These theological differences greatly reduce the parallelisms and underline the oneness of the Revealer, Jesus Christ, the only Mediator between God and man in the two testaments (Ti 2:5, Heb 8:6, 9:15, 12:24). The ultimate Christian concept of divine revelation results in the outline of "prophets—Christ—apostles," which then modifies the theological discourse about inspiration by introducing two sets of transmitters (prophets and apostles) with Jesus in the center, pointing to the risen Christ's transhistorical, exalted, and glorious presence that penetrates all books.[14]

On other levels, the process of canonization remains still unexplored and can be easily misunderstood. The thesis that Christianity took over the sacred books of Judaism is a misleading half-truth. Nascent Christianity could not have been born without the concept of Jesus fulfilling the scriptures and, therefore, leading all who believed in him to a reassessment of the revelation and inspiration of the Old Testament with a full meaning of both to attain in Christ. This new validation of the Old Testament implies much more than just taking over from Judaism a set of books as inspired by the Holy Spirit. The process of adopting the scriptures of old also means inserting the church into the continuity of Israel's salvation history. The first century of Christian history is therefore full of deep theological—rather than just ethnic or cultural—disputes with signs of *longing for unity* with Judaism but also with profound awareness that a painful process of separation between the two subsequent communities of salvation, Israel and the church, was impos-

---

13. The first part of the Sermon on the Mount, repeating the phrase "I say to you" (see Mt 5:18, 5:22, 5:26, 5:28, 5:32, 5:34, 5:39, 5:44), to illustrate a *contrast* built upon *parallelism* between Moses and Jesus.

14. See chapter 1 on Revelation.

sible to stop. Under the banner of Paul's Jewish *and* Christian identity, the church kept adhering to the Pauline verse: "Whatever was written previously was written for our instruction" (Rom 15:4), while Judaism claimed a similarly *exclusive* ownership of most of the same writings. The two positions appeared mutually exclusive for centuries, yet in the light of a more ecumenical ecclesiology as well as the way in which the study of Hebrew scriptures both united and separated Judaism and Christianity, we may be able today to begin to see in our shared scripture a paradox rather than a contradiction.[15] This is certainly more in harmony with Paul's expanded thoughts about the salvation of Israel in Romans 9–10, which presents a picture, both broad and nuanced, that cannot be reduced to the single verse of Romans 15:4. Here again the fullness of the context is indispensable for a correct understanding of the truth of the Bible:

Theirs is the adoption as sons; theirs the divine glory, the covenants, the receiving of the law, the temple worship and the promises. Theirs are the patriarchs, and from them is traced the human ancestry of Christ, who is God over all. (Rom 9:4–5)

Paul speaks about Israel's election as "a mystery" (Rom 11:24) that cannot be reduced to an either/or choice between the church's election and the universality of God's salvation plan as opposed to the election of the patriarchs or Moses or David. All that we said earlier about a Christocentric understanding of the two testaments leads to upholding the thesis that the inspired scriptures are the gift of the Holy Spirit, who continues to move hearts and inspire minds to reach and believe the fullness of the scripture's meaning. Hence we come to another Pauline text pointing out the Old Testament's fullness of meaning obtained only in Christ:

For to this day the same veil remains when the old covenant is read. It has not been removed, because only in Christ is it taken away. Even to this day when Moses is read, a veil covers their hearts. But whenever anyone turns to the Lord, the veil is taken away.

15. The PBC published a document on "The Jewish People and Its Scriptures in the Christian Bible" in 2002 that tried to establish a new basis for a scriptural dialogue between Catholics and Jews. See my book review, Farkasfalvy, "The Pontifical Biblical Commission's Document on Jews and Christians and their Scriptures: Attempt of an Evaluation," with critical remarks, in *Communio* 29 (2002): 735–37.

Now the Lord is the Spirit, and where the Spirit of the Lord is, there is freedom. And we, who with unveiled faces all reflect the Lord's glory, are being transformed into his likeness with ever-increasing glory, which comes from the Lord, who is the Spirit. (2 Cor 3:14–18)

This text, difficult as it appears, is important for explaining the relationship of the covenants. Paul speaks of the "old" covenant links to the Spirit and Christ. He does not say that the person of Christ and the Holy Spirit are identical, but he identifies their mode of existence in the glory of the Father, with whom the Lord and his Spirit form one single divine Essence. These relationships are veiled as long as one reads the scriptures without faith in Christ. Yet, once the gospel is appropriated with a response of faith, the full dimension of divine revelation becomes manifest as gloriously "constituted in the Spirit of sanctification."[16]

Paul is unambiguous about two claims. On the one hand, he received the gospel directly from God the Father who revealed to him Christ as his Son (Gal 1:16). On the other hand, Paul also says that this same Christ had been foreannounced through Moses and the prophets. Yet Paul explains further that the full meaning of Jesus' sonship remains veiled unless an illumination similar to the one he (Paul) received from the Spirit of the risen Christ happens according to the "good pleasure" of the Father (see Gal 1:15). Such illumination leads to faith and revelation of Christ as the center and the ultimate meaning of the scriptures.

It is ironic how Marcion's effort to eliminate the Old Testament by invoking the Letter to the Galatians stands in contradiction with the foundation of Paul's theology apparent in the opening chapter of Galatians. In his exclusive Paulinism, Marcion contradicted Paul's central intuition about Israel and introduced a self-contradiction in his own system. In spite of the sympathies one finds for Marcion in modern scholars, it seems that, for both Catholics and Protestants alike, there remains no other option than to reconstruct Paul's message in continuity with Jesus' self-understanding and reestablish our authentic relationship to the Old Testament as inspired scriptures.

---

16. To point out Paul's trinitarian thought unifying Christology and the theology of scripture, we need to quote the whole passage: "The gospel of *God*, which he promised beforehand through his prophets in the holy scriptures, the gospel concerning his *Son*, who was descended from David according to the flesh and was declared [or: constituted] to be Son of God with power according to the *Spirit* of sanctification by resurrection from the dead, Jesus Christ our Lord" (Rom 1:1–4).

12 ✠ CHRIST

THE ULTIMATE MEANING OF THE
CHRISTIAN BIBLE

Theological Integration of the Old Testament
in the Christian Bible

The logical last movement of this book may appear to be a very traditional one: revelation—inspiration—canon—[leading to] hermeneutics. Is this like a symphony in the classical tradition, with four sequentially linked movements? This theological understanding of the scriptures developed through historically linked experiences, yet with some temporal delay between individual phases, since, in general, reflexive thought always comes after the events become a memory of the past, and thus a delay between phases can be expected. Our previous chapters demanded both a sense of history for reconstructing the past and a rational assessment of the implications of what our faith says about God's self-giving through the incarnate Word within the flow of history. According to the Christian faith, human history is finite, reaching from creation to the *Eschata* or, equivalently, to the second coming and the resurrection of the body by which history ends. Within this flow, God gives his Son, the incarnate Word, so that fallen human creatures may return to him and become his children by participating in his nature through the Holy Spirit. This implies, among other things, sacramental tools, which, for carrying out God's salvation plan, the church dispenses and God's effective and life-giving presence sanctions for the sake of extending his words and deeds. We are speaking not only about the incarnate Word as enshrined in written tools of verbal communication. Justin Martyr spoke of reading at the Eucharistic Assembly from "the Prophets and the Apostles," both witnessing to the Logos; Irenaeus and Tertullian would say that these were inspired by the same Spirit; modern theologian may say, in the style of Karl Rahner, that these are writings used by God's hand as constitutive elements for building the church, a house built on a rock of divine revelation. While the metaphors are many, the truth of the matter is one: the scriptures provide the incarnate Word's permanent presence as speech in written form. They guarantee that God's word, which addressed Israel and its apostolic heirs, would echo throughout the rest of time as human word. The ongoing presence of the Holy Spirit in the church assures that the word is accompanied by God's efficacious force so that it may resonate throughout history and reach every generation "not in word only, but also in power and in the Holy Spirit and with full conviction" (1 Thes 1:5).

The history of the canon of the Jewish scriptures is a specialized field of study that this book is neither trying to explore nor cover in detail. We are speaking here specifically about the Christian Bible, whose canon began forming before the closure of the Jewish canon so that the last decades of the first century witnessed contemporaneous developments of the two testaments, Old and New. The historical development of the Jewish canon and that of the Christian Old Testament partly overlap. The Jewish canon reached its final, closed form at a time that it had to take into account the existence and the claims of the Christian church on the books of Judaism as part of its own heritage. The final Jewish canon ended up more restricted than the Septuagint, which essentially coincided with the Old Testament of Christianity until the Reformation. This fact is well known but rarely undergoes theological scrutiny.

Years before the First Jewish War, nascent Christianity realized its universal mission to all, Jews and Gentiles, and carried out its internal disputes about the Mosaic Law. With regard to the Jewish writings, already taken into Christian possession as scriptures, the church understood itself as facing a fait accompli for two reasons. First, since Jesus embraced the scriptures of the Jews, Christians had no other choice. Second, since the popular base of the apostolic church soon became a Greek-speaking and empire-wide community consisting mostly of Gentiles, the use of the Septuagint soon became general practice for the church. Not even the Pauline left wing wanted to dispute the divine provenance and authority of the Hebrew scriptures. Moreover, as the majority of the New Testament documents show, the Septuagint penetrated Christian parlance, giving the linguistic basis to most missionary activities. This is the way Paul himself uses the Septuagint. Throughout Galatians, Paul argues from these scriptures (Gal 3:8, 3:22, 4:30), and the same position is expressed with similar clarity in Romans:

But now the righteousness of God has been manifested apart from the law, though testified to by the Law and the Prophets. (Rom 3:21)

This sentence is particularly important, because in it Paul clearly distinguishes between two roles of the scriptures: their authority to regulate conduct and their role of witnessing. The first Paul denies, while on the second he insists that righteousness is not the fruit of the observance of the Mosaic Law, but that the testimony of the scriptures ("the Law and the Prophets") remains essential for the apostolic proclamation. Thus, in practical terms, the early church quickly made a canonical decision by adopting in its multilingual and multicultural community the use of the Septuagint, the Old Testament translated into Greek, a collection of books wider than what was typically in use in the Jewish synagogues in Palestine. In this way Jewish scriptures were adopted to regulate Christian conduct and, most importantly, to help define the religious identity of Gentile converts to Christianity as they began to be read, quoted, and disseminated as *their* holy scriptures.

As we mentioned, the nascent church's scriptures coincided only materially with the Septuagint. The early church's relationship to the Septuagint granted Gentile converts much greater freedom than Gentiles converting to Judaism enjoyed. Christians took into possession the Septuagint as their "Old Testament," but their exegesis served their faith in Christ. They remained rather distanced from literalism, although they never forgot the primacy of the Hebrew text, and routinely handled the Septuagint as a translation. One can best see the two sides of this coin exemplified in the Gospel of Matthew. By following the Septuagint's Jewish background with conviction, the evangelist Matthew regularly follows it, yet manifests a great deal of freedom in helping himself to the Hebrew text and its several variant readings, deviating from both the Septuagint and from what eventually became the official Hebrew (Masoretic) text. Whenever exploiting the scriptures, Matthew shows much freedom in reading the scriptures with a messianic faith. The so-called formula quotations in the Gospel of Matthew are clear examples of an attitude of searching the scriptures, which the Hebrew word *Midrash* also suggests, in an effort to reach out to a variety of Mosaic and prophetic text to uncover references to the gospel—that is, to Jesus' words and deeds and mostly his passion and resurrection. Matthew is often misread by exegetes who say that he is manipulating the scriptures to prove a literal fulfillment of the scriptural texts; rather, the contrary is true. According to Matthew, the scriptures are never fulfilled in the way one expects them to come to fulfillment. Jesus is David's offspring, but from a virgin who is married to Joseph, a descendant of David, yet he is conceived not from Joseph but by the Holy Spirit and is, therefore, not a physical Davidic offspring (Mt 1:18). From such a fulfillment the baffling question results: "Whose son is the Messiah?" This question is being raised in each of the four gospels (Mt 22:45; Mk 12:37; Lk 20:44; Jn 7:42) without providing a full explanation in Jesus' own words. According to Matthew 2:15, at Jesus' return from Egypt, Hosea's prophecy (Hos 11:1) was fulfilled: "Out of Egypt I called my son." The understanding of Jesus as Son of God is the backbone of Matthew's Gospel.[1] In this gospel, the insertion of the fulfillment formulas represents a particular mindset and invitation of the reader to a midrashic exploitation of the scriptures, proposing a rather particular approach to inquiring about Jesus' identity. Thus Matthew's use of the scriptures testifies to his use of an established Jewish mode of exegesis rather than to a desperate attempt by the apostolic church to invent exegetical tools for harmonizing Jesus' credentials and life story with curiously selected scriptural passages. There is little doubt that the Matthean author adheres to his "scriptures,"[2] which he abundantly quotes, yet, throughout

---

1. The concept of Jesus as Son of God runs through the whole composition from the temptation (4:3, 3:6, 3:9) the baptism (3:17), the walking on the sea (14:33), Peter's confession (16:16–17), the transfiguration (17:5), and the oath before the Sanhedrin (26:63–64) to the final scene of the risen Lord's manifestation in full power, followed by the universal sending (28:18–20).

2. Four times Mt refers generally to the scriptures (21:42, 22:29, 26:54, 26:56); in the last quotation he speaks of the "scriptures of the prophets."

his gospel he remains faithful to a settled vision of faith, accepting Jesus as Son of God and the Messiah in whom the scriptures came to fulfillment.

Thus the Jewish Bible, when becoming Old Testament, appears as an essential and constitutive element of the Christian church's self-understanding, looking at both Jesus and itself in the light of Jesus' resurrection. Luke's text best expresses this insight as an event that constituted the Christian faith. In the following verses, we can almost touch the seam that both separates and fuses the two testaments:

He said to them, "These are my words that I spoke to you while I was still with you, that *everything written about me in the Law of Moses and in the prophets and psalms* must be fulfilled." Then he opened their minds to understand the *scriptures.*

And he said to them, "Thus it is written that the *Messiah would suffer and rise from the dead on the third day and that repentance, for the forgiveness of sins, would be preached in his name to all the nations,* beginning from Jerusalem. (Lk 24:44–47)

The first three lines refer to the totality of the Jewish scriptures. The phrase "everything written about me" is not to be read restrictively, as if limiting the Jewish writings only to those that specifically prove themselves to be messianic. Rather, this phrase simply implies that, in fact, "everything was written about me."[3] The next three lines are a résumé of the apostolic kerygma, which consists of three elements: (1) passion and resurrection; (2) the *euaggelion* of repentance resulting in forgiveness; and (3) a universal mission of preaching to all nations,[4] proclaimed by the use of the prophetic scriptures and by apostolic preaching.

The Canonicity of the Jewish Scriptures in Christianity

The adoption of the scriptures, therefore, happened as a constitutive act at the church's own birth for expressing and propagating its original belief in Christ and referencing its beginnings to that of the people of God

3. The Greek text in its compact structure is more explicit than an English translation can ever be, because it puts the tripartite listing of all scriptures immediately before, rather than after, the words "about me."

4. It might be important to point out that, in the light of this interpretation, the concluding passage of the "universal mission" at the end of Matthew's Gospel (28:20) is virtually identical with the last three lines in this Lukan passage.

as children of God and a nation created at the Exodus. Concretely, for the apostolic church, consisting of Jews and Gentiles, this happens when the apostolic missionaries adopt the *Septuagint as Jewish scriptures in translation*—that is, originally Hebrew scriptures but offered for use to the Gentiles in the Hellenistic world into which Jesus has sent his apostles with the power and enlightenment of the Holy Spirit, descending at Pentecost. This constitutive act implied declining literalism in the sense of refusing a restrictive adherence to an original text. Quite the contrary is being implied: freedom to explore the meaning of the text through searching the inspired text by past efforts made by previous Hellenistic readers who tried to render them in translations and with variants and translations that should be read as various interpretive approximations. The acceptance of the Septuagint is not equivalent to believing in the historicity of the miraculous story of the seventy translators, as narrated in the Letter of Aristeas, no matter how much credibility that letter obtained throughout antiquity, including with many church fathers.[5]

As the church achieved its separation from Judaism, differences between the church's use of the Greek Bible and the Hebrew canon (established in the second century in more restrictive terms) became increasingly evident. Some sort of a triangular relationship came about, since, besides Jews and Christians disputing Greek quotations from the Septuagint, the church fathers themselves became divided over the so-called deuterocanonical books—that is, the books of the Septuagint missing from the Jewish canon. Origen's immense authority in biblical matters in both the East and the West had a double effect. On the one hand, he quoted all books of the Septuagint, but, on the other hand, he was inclined to grant only a second-rank status to the deuterocanonical books. The Vulgate, which became the official Bible of Latin Christianity, also had an ambiguous impact. St. Jerome forcefully promoted the priority

---

5. The use of the LXX was connected with knowledge and/or credence in the authenticity of its legendary origins reported in the pseudepigraphic Letter of Aristeas, well known and reproduced in "constant repetition in Jewish and Christian circles." The church, however, never declared the historical authenticity of the legend (about seventy or seventy-two interpreters producing an identical translation); it was read and repeated by all who used the LXX as the Greek text of the Old Testaments. See Brown, Fitzmyer, and Murphy, *New Jerome Biblical Commentary*, 1091–92. A remarkably positive view about the Septuagint is expressed by R. Glenn Wooden, "The Role of the 'Septuagint' in the Formation of the Biblical Canon," in Evans and Tov, *Exploring the Origins of the Bible*, 129–46.

of the Hebrew text as he insisted on the importance of translating the Old Testament from Hebrew, referring to it as *Hebraica Veritas*; nonetheless, the Vulgate ended up containing the deuterocanonical books, which Jerome also, in the footsteps of Origen, abundantly quoted.

The history of the Old Testament canon remains a fascinating and worthwhile task. A caveat must be kept in mind: while the patristic church remained aware of the New Testament's frequent use of the Septuagint, it also knew that, being a translation, its value derived from *the original texts*. At the same time, the early church globally embraced the Septuagint as an apostolically sanctioned tool of access to the Hebrew scriptures.

The last steps in the history of the Christian canon, including its deuterocanonical determinations, reflect various ecclesial uses with liturgical and exegetical practices. The restrictions imposed on the Hebrew canon after the two Jewish wars barely affected Christian communities, which used the Greek texts of books, which had no known Hebrew edition. In general, the church fathers typically considered the Hebrew text to be original and the Septuagint an inspired translation. Origen and Jerome were exceptions among them: the majority of the church fathers (and the local churches) were monolingual, reading their Bible either in Greek or Latin and interpreting the Old Testament from the perspective of New Testament texts.[6] Only in rare exceptions did Christians consult Jewish rabbis about variant readings or the precise meaning of individual Hebrew words. In matters of etymology, Christian exegetes followed Origen and Jerome, whose reputations as experts in the Hebrew text were rarely challenged. Between the time of Marcion and the Reformation—roughly fourteen hundred years—disputes about the canon of scriptures never disrupted Christian unity. This shows either the solidity of the boundaries of apostolicity as understood at the end of the second century or simply the lack of exegetical importance attributed to the deuterocanonical books.

A major change occurred when the Protestant reformers introduced a new outlook that claimed to explain how the church fell away from its original purity and the standards of the apostolic church. The quarrels of the reformers were not merely ideological, but attacked concrete is-

---

6. The discovery of the Dead Sea Scrolls brought about a sudden growth in data for the Hebrew text's relationship to the LXX; see Emmanuel Tov, "The Relation between the Textual Witnesses," in *Textual Criticism of the Hebrew Bible* (Minneapolis: Fortress, 1992), 135–51.

sues. Typically, we can point to the sixteenth-century controversies over prayers and masses offered for the deceased—one of the major scandals for the Lutheran reforms—and the counter-arguments of Catholic apologists who quoted 2 Maccabees 12:44–46, which praises Judas Maccabaeus for making a monetary donation to the Temple for expiatory sacrifices to be offered for fallen soldiers.[7] Of course, an easy reply was denying the canonicity of this text. In retrospect, it was clear that the rejection of the deuterocanonical books by the reformers was due to the unrelenting interconfessional disputes following the Reformation and then the Council of Trent, which reedited the documents of the Council of Florence. Trent published an official and compulsory list of the canonical books, sequenced according to the Septuagint's table of contents via the Vulgate. The latter had an interesting effect on the Western church by following the Septuagint in many ways as well as by insisting on the secondary character of those Greek texts for which a Hebrew original existed. Yet, in its true historical context, the Council of Trent did not act as a referee between various patristic trends and practices but intended to contradict the Protestant reformers' dreams of returning to the very beginning of Christian history to decide which books the apostolic church has considered (or must have considered) to be inspired. Disputes about the canon between Catholics and Protestants have quieted down but have not fully died out in the past hundred years. Such disputes became ultimately stuck in a theological vacuum on both sides, created by an ongoing weakening of the theology of inspiration.

The Council of Trent defined the Catholic Church's adherence to a full canon as including all deuterocanonical books. The way Catholic apologetics dealt with this issue gave the impression that the matter was mainly historical and that Catholics claimed that the Council fathers at Trent had a superior knowledge of which books the apostolic church had thought belonged to the canon.

---

7. "He then took up a collection among all his soldiers, amounting to two thousand silver drachmas, which he sent to Jerusalem to provide for an expiatory sacrifice. In doing this he acted in a very excellent and noble way, inasmuch as he had the resurrection of the dead in view; for if he were not expecting the fallen to rise again, it would have been useless and foolish to pray for them in death. But if he did this with a view to the splendid reward that awaits those who had gone to rest in godliness, it was a holy and pious thought. Thus he made atonement for the dead that they might be freed from this sin"; 2 Mc 12:43–46.

The truth is that the Council fathers only reflected on what tradition held to be inspired books. Since more than a hundred years earlier, at the Council of Florence, Eastern and Western Christians had easily agreed on the canon and made a binding resolution, the Council fathers of Trent had no other choice than to repeat the same canonical list. Their historical knowledge was neither superior nor inferior to that of the reformers, and they had no tools to research the history of the Old Testament canon scientifically. They simply codified that which they knew was theologically binding. To use a modern expression coined by Pope Benedict XVI, the reformers interpreted what they knew about the history of the canon with an "exegesis of discontinuity," using their independent judgment while Trent applied its awareness of continuity between Jesus, the apostolic church, the church fathers, and the medieval church. Thus, they basically reembraced the Septuagint's canon as the depository of God's inspired word.

A theological discussion could be resumed, but more probably, as seems to be today's trend, the contestation of the deuterocanonical books initiated by the reformers may sink into further oblivion, allowing interconfessional confrontations about the canon decline. Today we can meet Catholics and Protestants more and more frequently who are genuinely surprised when they discover differences in the tables of contents of their respective Bibles.

The *Rule of Faith* and Its Anti-Marcionite Significance

When the Protestant reformers wanted to reestablish the Old Testament in its purity, Trent intended to save its integrity, but there have been, and there still are, further theological questions that cannot be solved by mere good will. While it is correct to say that, for the ancient church, no ecumenical council was needed to define the biblical canon, we might also state that long before the church was in the position to convoke an ecumenical council, the two testaments became a burning problem. Marcion was the first to take a radical step by rejecting the Jewish scriptures and experiment with a de-Judaized Christianity. This meant getting rid of texts like the creation stories of Genesis (Gn 1–3), the Ten Commandments, declarations of a strict monotheism, and laws regulating marriage, sexual unions, and procreation. Unfortunately, we do not have enough documentation to explain exactly why and how, at that historic moment in 144 A.D., Marcion's attempt to infiltrate the Church of Rome first succeeded and then failed, or why, at previous confrontations with Polycarp of Smyrna and the churches of Asia Minor, he was rejected. But the anti-Marcionite positions of Justin, Irenaeus, and Tertullian sufficiently prove that Marcion not only rejected the Jewish scriptures and the authenticity of revelation in Judaism, but rejected *the God of the Old Testament*, of whom he spoke as the creator of evil. Rejecting the Old Testament's monotheism, Marcion embraced a radical dualism. When rejecting the Christian doctrine of creation and universal salvation history, Marcion happened to be in alliance with Gnostic teachers, experimenting with those philosophical currents that prepared the spread of Manichaeism. The rejection of Marcion must have been greatly facilitated by the early church's reliance on the first chapters of Genesis combined with efforts to gather available philosophical support for monotheism. The aseity of God, the universality of the Logos, and the rejection of all Gnostic interpretations of the Johannine prologue penetrated much of the writings of the early apologetes, seeking to vindicate monotheism and a Logos theology, which was especially important for Justin Martyr.[8] Theophilus of Antioch and later Irenaeus and Tertullian fought, in explicit terms and with no compromise, for the full retention of the Old Testament.

In this context we can appreciate the role of the so-called the *Regula Fidei* (*Rule of Faith*), which represented the Christian faith as believing in *one* God as creator of *one* mankind and initiator of *one* single salvation history; this concept was repeatedly promulgated throughout the second century, forming a firewall against Marcionism.[9] This rule goes beyond demonstrating the Christians' canonical adherence to Genesis or the Pentateuch for its role as an indispensable instrument for reminding Christians of their commitment to monotheism even if, within Jewish-Christian controversies,[10] the Jewish interlocutors would raise

---

8. Jason D. BeDuhn recognizes Justin Martyr's deep commitment on behalf of the Jewish scriptures; see BeDuhn, *First New Testament*, 13.

9. See Everett Ferguson, *The Rule of Faith: A Guide* (Eugene, Ore.: Cascade, 2015).

10. Most importantly, see Justin Martyr's *Dialogue with Trypho*, nos. 40 and 46.

doubts about it. The *Regula Fidei* was tripartite, projecting a trinitarian theological outline, which Nicaea and later creedal formulas mirrored. In Christian theological discourse, the *Rule of Faith* was like an outline for disputes between Christians and Jews, sorting out their differences about the Christian view of the Christological fullness of the scriptures in a two-testament scheme vs. a single-testament Mosaic understanding of revelation and a rejection of Christ as absurd or irrelevant. Besides being used in anti-Jewish efforts, the *Rule of Faith* was also useful for arguments against pagan and syncretistic systems. The rule's first part, with its insistence on the one God and Creator, embraced the foundational beliefs of the patriarchs and Moses as read in the Pentateuch, while its second part made assertions about the incarnation, passion, and resurrection following a Christological understanding of the scriptures. In all its references to the unity and universality of salvation through Christ (also to the apostolic kerygma and the church), the *Rule of Faith* expressed the oneness of God, revelation, salvation, and mankind's eschatological goal.

For the early church fathers, the *Regula Fidei* was an ancient tool, used as a "rule of thumb" for deciding about a teaching's apostolic orthodoxy or for discerning between correct and incorrect theological thinking. There were ultimately three tools: (1) the *Rule of Faith*; (2) creeds (including liturgical formulas used at baptismal rites); and (3) the norm of the prophetic and apostolic scriptures. Of these, the *Rule of Faith* was shortest and most flexible, easy to remember and quote from memory while providing a summary of the essential elements of Christian doctrine.

We find here also linkage connecting the Greek word κανών, the Latin *Regula*, and the modern expression of scriptural canon. In the case of the *Regula Fidei* we face traditional usage pointing to a doctrinal norm of orthodoxy, while the term of scriptural canon points to a set of books with a similar intent of emphasizing their normative role. Of course, the latter came about with some delay and could not have been formulated before the church took clear and firm possession of the books that were to be assessed as a depository of divine revelation that formed Israel and then God's eschatological convocation in the church of Jesus Christ.

Irenaeus and the *Canon of Muratori*

The *Canon of Muratori* is, according to a large number of scholars who studied it, the oldest list of books constituting the New Testament. Its dating to the very end of the second century was the traditional opinion until it began to be disputed, with the debate not likely to terminate soon.[11] Its dating remains disputed due to disagreements about the identity of the second-century author Hermas and his relationship to alleged brother Pius, the bishop of Rome, both named in the document. The text refers to Pius, brother to Hermas, as a bishop in Rome "most recently" (*nuperrime*). Since Pope Pius I is securely datable to about 146–55, this ancient list cannot be more recent than 200 A.D. However, there are still positions, held in current scholarship, supporting different conclusions. They are as follows:

1. The text is an incomplete transcription of a Latin text, incompetently translated from Greek, and impossible to date (this opinion is nothing but a default position, occasionally expressed in debates).

2. The text is a fourth-century product made to look like a second-century canon.[12] Since the document is loaded with many philological problems and grammatical mistakes, its route of transmission cannot be easily established, but some authors claim that the views it contains do not fit the second century.

3. The text is a genuine scriptural canon in the sense of a list of books, summarizing views on this matter around 200 A.D.[13]

---

11. For the text itself and an up-do date report on the present state of the research, see Eckhard J. Schnabel, "The Muratorian Fragment: The State of Research," *Journal of Evangelical Theological Studies* 57, no. 2 (2014): 231–64.

12. See Albert C. Sundberg Jr., "Canon Muratori: A Fourth-Century List," *Harvard Theological Review* 66 (1973): 1–41; Sundberg, "More on Redating the Muratorian Fragment," *Studia Patristica* (Louvain: Peeters, 1989), 19:359–65.

13. Soon after the document was found in the eighteenth century, this became the traditional view, accepted by leading scholars (von Harnack, Lightfoot, Lietzmann, Lagrange) and is still found in most lexicons and introductions. Sundberg, in his essay quoted earlier, challenged it, but it seems that the following responses are supported by the majority of scholars: Everett Ferguson, "Canon Muratori: Date and Provenance," in *Studia Patristica: Eighth International Congress on Patristic Studies, Oxford, Sept. 3–8, 1979*, ed. Elizabeth A. Livingstone (Oxford and New York: Pergamon, 1982), 677–83; see Hill, *Who Chose the Gospels?*, 95–99; 112–221.

It seems that the opinions about the *Canon of Muratori* depend on the researcher's *Vorverständniss*—that is, a concept formed in advance, about the status of the New Testament canon at the end of the second century. The data on the provenance and peculiar literary features of the *Canon of Muratori* can be fitted into several scenarios, although a late second century would leave the least amount of unsolved issues. However, in my opinion, there is no absolute need for convincing the skeptics or disappointing the enthusiasts. Irenaeus's *Adversus Haereses* alone offers a rather clear answer about the status of the canon in the church at the end of the second century. Books III–V of *Adversus Haereses* are based on what the church at Irenaeus's time (around 185 A.D.) acknowledged as *apostolic* writings (therefore inspired and, in this sense, canonical).[14] These writings are the four gospels, Acts, all Pauline letters (except possibly Philemon), the First Epistle of Peter, that of James, two of John, and the book of Revelation. Irenaeus gives no hint as to what he thinks about Hebrews, Philemon, 3 John, or Jude; maybe he has a reason for not quoting some of these. He holds in high esteem some additional texts; among them is the *Shepherd of Hermas* to which he once refers as "scripture" (IV.22.2). However, in his usage, "scripture" (*graphe*) is not a decisive term.[15] In any case, the texts to which he attributes apostolic authority constitute a well-developed New Testament canon, although not achieved with final clarity. But certainty and clarity about the principle that canonical status in the New Testament come from apostolicity, as well as the conviction that apostolicity is a theological concept and that such a status comes by tradition, not by historical research, turn Irenaeus into a solid source about the church's testimony to the canon of the New Testament in his time. My conclusion is, therefore, that, regardless of the controversies about the actual background of the *Canon of Muratori*, there is nothing anachronistic about dating it to around 200 A.D. The list that the *Canon of Muratori* contains could be just as well extracted from the writings of Irenaeus's *Adversus Haereses*. In some sense, the

---

14. "In his *Adversus Haereses* he [Irenaeus] quotes 1,075 passages from almost all the books of the New Testament: 626 from the Gospels, 54 from Acts, 280 from the Pauline Epistles (but not from Philemon), 15 from the Catholic Epistles (but not 2 Peter, 3 John or Jude) and 29 from the Book of Revelation"; Metzger, *Canon of the New Testament*, 153. Metzger refers also to "echoes" from 1 Pt, 2 Tm, and Heb.

15. Farkasfalvy, "Theology of Scripture in Saint Irenaeus," *Revue bénédictine* 78 (1968): 319–33.

authenticity of the document of Muratori is independent of the question of how early the church was able to provide for a list of inspired (in second-century terminology, "prophetic and apostolic") books. The answer: Irenaeus's writings show that the Old Testament books were available and used as provided in the Septuagint; in addition, the church possessed as apostolic writings four apostolic gospels, a set of apostolic letters by Peter, Paul, John, and James (with Jude), Acts (a book written as a sequel of the Third Gospel) and the book of Revelation. Irenaeus tells us in around 185 A.D. that these books formed those scriptures, from which he was—in agreement with the Church of Rome and the rest of the apostolic churches in communion with it—pursuing his arguments against all heresies in a work that claimed to provide proofs from "all the scriptures."[16]

16. In doing an electronic search into the English translation of Irenaeus's *Adversus Haereses*, I found 108 references to "the scriptures" in this general sense.

CONCLUSION

THE INSPIRED TRUTH OF THE
HOLY SCRIPTURES

———————

The conclusions I draw from this study mostly concern the two topics Pope Benedict XVI assigned to be studied after the Synod of Bishops in 2008. The first concerns biblical inspiration, while the second is about the truth in the Bible.

Biblical Inspiration

Dei Verbum has effectively put an end to the neo-Scholastic theology of inspiration that reigned in Catholic theology for more than a century. This happened because it was proven irrelevant for biblical scholarship and was unfit to become part of the new vision about revelation that *Dei Verbum* initiated. *Dei Verbum*, however, did not fully develop its own agenda. From the traditional theology of inspiration, it preserved the basic idea of a double authorship, just as theologians continued to refer to this concept in both professional and popular writings: God is the author of the scriptures, but the human authors are also authors, and, of course, while human beings are fully engaged as "real authors," God uses them as his instruments of communication. Although Rahner was actively engaged in preparing *Dei Verbum*, his influence on the document is only moderately discernible. There may be a few reasons that explain this. It seems that, after publishing his book on inspiration, Rahner became disengaged from this topic. Two reasons easily come to mind. On the one hand, even for German-speaking readers, Rahner's book on inspiration was quite difficult to comprehend and to further discuss; on the other hand, Rahner, who previously (1950) suffered "collateral damage" from the publication of *Humani Generis*, was now (1958) probably also discouraged by the lukewarm reception of his book. A few more reasons could be added on a more speculative basis. First, because of its difficult style even for native German speakers, Rahner's book did not appeal to an international readership.[1] In its effort to demolish the neo-Thomistic inspiration theory, Rahner incessantly bombarded Augustinus Bea's widely used textbook of 1935 on inspiration. Meanwhile Bea, Rahner's fellow Jesuit, saw his star continue to rise to a remarkable career. After being one of Pius XII's closest collaborators and his personal adviser and confessor, under John XXIII and throughout Vatican II he advanced to become a major church leader and later cardinal; from staunch conservative, he evolved to become a chief ecumenist. He and his academic record were beyond reach to any successful attack by Council theologians. Anyway, during the Council, the neo-Thomistic synthesis was not directly criticized, but only ignored, while after the Council it underwent sudden death due to continued neglect rather than scathing criticism.

However, this traditional textbook theology of inspiration fell into oblivion for two specific reasons. First, while making general statements about a unanimous tradition backing it, its basic assumptions were based on incomplete or misunderstood patristic documentation. Second, its faulty methodology of using St. Thomas's theory on prophecy (and an awkward Aristotelian psychology applied to prophecy), in combination with an unclarified concept of authorship, could not withstand contrary evidence accumulating in the postconciliar years. There was possibly a third reason: the apologetic mindset still reigning over Fundamental Theology in the 1950s operating with a theology of revelation was replaced by a brand-new approach in *Dei Verbum*. A fourth reason possi-

---

1. An English translation was published relatively soon in 1961, but then it needed to be republished with corrections in 1964. Still, on account of its aprioristic methodology and light bibliography, it remained very difficult to penetrate.

bly came from exaggerated claims on the role of the literary genres combined with God's literary authorship and the succeeding entanglements with Bultmann's *Formgeschichte*. The insistence of the encyclicals *Divino Afflante* and *Humani Generis* on the literal meaning's primacy as the real sense of the biblical texts, a dubious heritage from Fr. Bea's reign over Catholic biblical studies, pushed the mood of Catholic exegetes from elated enthusiasm to fear of another new antimodernist crisis. Again, the problems of inerrancy began to gather like dark clouds on a bright sky, when the death of Pius XII (October 9, 1958) led to the election of the arch-conservative John XXIII.

This study claims that disentangling these problems should have begun by a clarification of the issue of God's authorship of the Bible. The meaning of the thesis *Deus Auctor Scripturae*, formulated as early as the third century, was correctly represented by the Council of Trent and Vatican I and by later magisterial documents, but it became misinterpreted by Bea's article of 1943, which then obtained undeserved approval in theological literature.[2] Neither Trent nor Vatican I has defined that God was the *literary auctor* of scripture. The papal encyclicals on inspiration made no attempt to further specify the meaning of that thesis, either. Because of Bea's prestige, most readers of his essays and textbook were inclined to believe that he had indeed delivered conclusive proof for *literary* divine authorship, so that this thesis was widely taught and believed in as the near unanimous teaching of the church fathers and of the last two ecumenical councils. Bea's ambiguous patristic dossier was never checked. Although in 1965 Alonso Schökel has shown that, in patristic literature, literary authorship has never been the main paradigm for inspiration, at the end he, too, for reasons not entirely clear, expressed his preference to embrace Bea's position. He proposed that the traditional term *auctor* applied to God meant something more than a mere *Urheber* (originator) but failed to explain what this "more" would entail.

In *Dei Verbum* the use of *auctor* carries a fingerprint of Karl Rahner: *verus auctor* for the human author is followed by *Inspirator et Auctor* for God. Fifty years later, however, when the PBC's document about inspi-

---

2. Bea's essay was quoted and argued against but not refuted by Karl Rahner in 1958; debated but then upheld by Alonso Schökel in 1965. It kept on being quoted in both the *Jerome Biblical Commentary* in 1980 and the *New Jerome Biblical Commentary* in 1990.

ration was published, it dealt with the concept of divine authorship as equivalent to divine provenance, ignoring whether this expression had ever meant anything more specific. This is like the proverbial approach of cutting the knot of Gordius rather than disentangling it. Logically, in this document, written in modern Italian, the term *autore* would lead to the conclusion that it means literary authorship, but its drafters did not seem be aware of such an implication; it was not even discussed in the sessions.

In *Dei Verbum*, however, the concept of divine revelation is correctly defined and leads to a correct understanding of the divine authorship of the Bible. In the same way that the words and deeds of revelation come from the living God, in the inspired books his active presence also accompanies the signs of self-disclosure he posits. Thus, due to a divine initiative and intervention, mediated by human messengers and writers (in traditional language: prophets, apostles, and hagiographers), an uninterrupted divine presence is achieved in his speaking through the written attestation of his words and deeds. Thus, embedded into the same history of revelation, the biblical texts represent a written extension of the divine speech; they produce continuous presence in the form of a permanently accessible deposit of God's uninterrupted self-disclosure. This divine authorship is analogous to the authorship of the human writers but fully transcends it. The human author *writes*, redacts, or edits at a given point of history, while the one and same divine author *speaks* through the scriptural texts, in an overarching continuity, as the one and only author whose voice and presence assure the Bible's unity and cause it both to *come about* and to *remain* God's word. The human formation of a biblical book terminates when the book is physically finished, but, since the book is meant to be inserted into a two-testament canon, it is elevated to the role of the prophets and apostles as it is being read at the liturgical assemblies of the church. For that purpose, the divine author accompanies by divine charism the book's process of coming about until the book reaches its final destination in the canon of the church. The divine author continues to actively author the inspired word and keeps on offering through it a live channel of communication with listeners and readers. Obviously, we are not speaking of mere parallelism between a principal and a secondary author in a scheme of dual authorship. For, although God is like a human author, he is even more unlike it. God speaks through the inspired text while he also has direct spiritual access to the reader, whom he in fact also inspires to penetrate the meaning of his word in the text. Furthermore, the human author, no matter how prophetic he might be, is boxed into the context of his time and a concrete frame of history, while God, the divine author, knows—he alone knows—the whole context of salvation history that he initiated and keeps directing to reach its targets both individually and collectively in the readers up to the end of the ages.

The concept of the divine author that we may distill in this way is in continuity with that of the divine revealer, but this theological meaning cannot be derived from the dictionary meaning of *auctor* in any language. God as author of the scriptures is God who reveals and provides for a verbal expression of his revelation and provides, in the way and to the extent he wants to, its written transmission. We might say that, while the document *Dei Verbum* is not in agreement with the neo-Scholastic concept of revelation, it demands, as theological schools did in the past, a conceptualization of inspiration that largely remains a task for the future.

We may throw some additional light on the matter by approaching it from what we know about the patristic interpretation of the Bible. Revelation is God's word *happening in human history* but addressing human beings at different junctures of *their personal history*. Christian revelation envisages a history that has a beginning, a peak, and a final fulfillment. Accordingly, it addresses people for the sake of bringing them to the goal of history by carrying them to its peak and fulfillment. The peak is Christ, who, however, also lived in a concrete human lifespan, with its peak at his passion and its fulfillment at the inception of his risen life, when he began to draw to himself all human beings (see Jn 12:32). Each human being lives within his time frame of life and with that portion of the light of revelation he is granted. For everyone God's Logos is "the true light that enlightens everyone coming into the world" (Jn 1:9).

The Logos came at the peak of revelation as the incarnate Word, Jesus Christ. His words and deeds became written word, the fourfold gospel; his prehistory consists of "the Law and the Prophets," and his self-extension into ongoing history happened through the apostolic church with its preaching and scriptural treasury. As a set of written words constitute the scriptures, the church plays the role of identifying them and transmitting them as revealed word in the middle of a world that further evolves while the church seeks to navigate over the waves and storms of history, preparing the world for encountering the risen Lord at his return to pronounce his last words of judgment and mercy.

The Truth in the Bible

The traditional treatises of biblical inspiration stated the argument for inerrancy correctly: since the Bible is God's word, it does not contain error. Yet in their actual way of discussing inerrancy, the neo-Scholastic textbooks were seriously handicapped by working with a mistaken concept of mostly (at times merely) cognitive revelation in terms of propositional or categorical truths (*adaequatio rei et intellectus*).[3] But the "*res*" (the realm of the reality) of revelation that words signify is divine reality, or simply God whom the finite intellect cannot adequately reflect. Here we encounter the topic *Dei Verbum* did not deal with: the epistemology of religious knowledge and the possibility of revelation. In the preconciliar years, these matters of philosophical presuppositions gained relatively little attention, as they were minimally involved in the renewal of the theology of revelation. Since replacing "inerrancy" with "truth" at the Council turned out to be little more than a cosmetic measure, a conservative minority inserted in the text its amendment of "without error" so that, from then on, the dispute about *veritates salutares* (and its replacement in the text) became the main stumbling block. Yet, in fifty years, no matter how many times various authorities attempted to remove (or overcome or bypass) this obstacle, none of the many official and semiofficial efforts (by Pope Paul VI, the Theological Commission of the Council, the finalized text of *Dei Verbum*, *Verbum Domini*, by Pope Benedict XVI, and finally the PBC document published under Pope Francis), the same ambiguities resurfaced in some way, either by new formulations of hazy ideas ("truths for the sake of salvation") or the special characteristics of biblical truth—all these expressions feeding the suspicion that some biblical texts are not errorless.

---

3. This means "conformity of the mind with reality (or 'the thing')." This is used by Aquinas as the definition of truth in his *Questiones Disputatae de Veritate*; he attributes it to St. Anselm and to the Arab Jewish philosopher Isaac Israeli.

My study led me to the conclusion that it was the classical scheme of a double *literary* authorship that has allowed theologians working with inspiration to engage in such confusing mind games when dealing with the Truth of the Bible. For as long as God is considered the literary author of the biblical text, all human deficiencies will be attributed in some sense to God—a position that contradicts longstanding theological tradition—and thus the Truth in the Bible will be an ambiguous concept. Appealing to literary genres, as was encouraged by *Divino Afflante*, has brought only some temporary relief because of the dangerous implication that the literary genre could be attributed to the divine author. The only way I saw and proposed to follow out of this trap was the affirmation of God's role as that of the living God speaking *once and always* (initially and permanently) in the course of a historical salvation plan, thus assuring inerrant truth in an imperfect text as the context for divine condescendence and pedagogy. But for that each of the following three considerations must be engaged and used as auxiliaries:

1. The incarnational analogy of inspiration;
2. The divine condescendence that accompanies revelation; and
3. Divine pedagogy extended to the human person both *to whom and through whom* God speaks.

The first consideration implies that the truth communicated in revelation necessarily includes anthropomorphisms because, ultimately, the history of revelation is about "God becoming *anthropos.*"[4] It implies that God wants us to see him, hear him, commune with him on the level of our human experiences, and thus he speaks to us in ways human beings communicate: by reasoning, by showing joy and anger, by being irritable and pleased, by being remunerating and vindictive, magnanimous and judgmental, endowed with justice and mercy.

The second consideration is an expansion of the first. The neo-Scholastic theory of inspiration considered it well taken care of by the instrumentality of the human author. Yet, in the patristic tradition God is the one who is said to be condescending not only to the human author as

---

4. Note how the Nicene Creed (*et homo factus est*) and the Johannine prologue (*Verbum caro factum est*) complete each other. In both texts the English translation must be "has become" (from *fieri*) and not "has been made" (from *facere*).

his instrument but to all those he addresses by his inspired word. Moreover, his condescension is personal: "the Power of the Most High" came over Mary and "the Holy Spirit overshadowed" her as the Word became flesh; therefore, the Logos should be expected to do the same when approaching a human being to address him in thought forms and words adjusted to our level of preparedness within our cultural context and concrete setting of salvation history. The understanding of revelation as a historical process with divine condescendence refers not only to bridging the metaphysical chasm between God and man but to God's adjustments to the various historical and cultural contexts (including those of religious history). This is definitely one of the new aspects in the teaching of *Dei Verbum*, which unfortunately did not become extended to the theology of inspiration. If God speaks in a manner of condescension, the biblical word must be conceived as something fitting into human history, not only in terms of its literary genre, but also according to its adaptation to the various stages of man's development and of his learning to understand himself and his experiences, to explore the realm of the sacred, come to terms with his own spiritual existence, and advance in his dialogue with God. If God is not the literary author of the biblical text, then all its limitations flow, on the one hand, from man's limitation who receives his word, yet, on the other hand, from God's gracious willingness to meet the human being on his own terms. The human author should neither be expected to receive and transmit God's word in ways and terms he cannot understand nor to think of the divine author as "missing his target" by approaching the human author and speaking to him above his head.

Condescendence does not mean speaking to man on his level so that he would remain on that level. It implies divine pedagogy—that is, a divine art of education by which man, who is exposed to God's word—in fact, we talk about the human community: the people of God whom he addresses—is elevated gradually, learning step by step in a course of gradual ascendancy, the thoughts of God through the learning process called "the divine *Oikonomia*."

The Truth in the Bible ultimately means Christ, who cannot be seen as a propositional truth of rationally sound observations and reasoning, but is by his divine and human constitution the Truth about God and

Man, God's internal trinitarian life made manifest so as to constitute the truth of man's relationship to himself, his neighbor, and God, which facilitates his journey to God from sin to salvation, while mirroring the journey through which God's people wander in history in pursuit of the revealed truth.

From the beginning, I proposed on these pages to formulate a theology of inspiration integrated into the concept of revelation proposed by *Dei Verbum*. I was most importantly helped by the fact that this very closely reflects what early church fathers, mostly Irenaeus and Origen, had first proposed and others, like Ambrose, Augustine, and the Cappadocians, further developed. Their theology of inspiration has not been sufficiently explored in monographic studies, as their interpretation of the scriptures was also waiting for centuries for resuscitation. Admittedly, however, we are today still far from having reached the point where the riches of patristic exegesis and the immense advancements achieved by modern historical-critical studies of the Bible could be integrated into one single vision of a theological exegesis that would grant each method its due and allow us to harvest more abundantly its fruits.

A Theology of Revelation and Inspiration

The integration of canonical studies into a theology of revelation and inspiration is rarely voiced as a *desideratum* for the sake of completing the study of revelation and inspiration. But about this, modern biblical theology cannot relent. One main reason is canonical exegesis. It has by now been promoted in various Christian circles for a considerable time. Brevard Childs's initiative, first echoed in evangelical circles, soon began to receive endorsements from others.[5] While Childs aimed at restoring and fortifying the theological interpretation of the Bible, my purpose has been only to point out that any theology of inspiration that supports such hermeneutics must assume that the perspective of the divine author, in which he inspires the human authors, must be thought of as canonical. For God, and he alone, has a comprehensive perspective of

---

5. Brevard S. Childs, *Introduction to the Old Testament as Scripture* (London: SCM, 1979); Childs, *The New Testament as Canon* (Philadelphia: Fortress, 1984); Childs, *Biblical Theology of the Old and New Testaments* (Augsburg: Fortress, 1993).

the whole history of salvation that transcends the human authors' limitations in space, time, and culture. If the biblical text's full meaning is that which the Holy Spirit intends us to appropriate, then that must be nothing short of the full canonical meaning—a meaning obtained by the totality of salvation history that alone can manifest the canonical context. In Christian theological perspective, just as revelation starts off before inspiration, the process of inspiration transmitting God's word into written medium is incomplete until the canon reaches both materially and formally its completion—that is, until the books of both testaments reach their fully written form and are recognized as scripture by the community of salvation, ultimately the church of the New Testament. In a theological sense of the word, "biblical canon" means the canon of the two testaments, read and interpreted in and by the church for believers gathered from all nations. Revelation becomes accessible in its full dimension only when its focus, the event of Christ, not only comes about but becomes recognized and deposited in stabilized texts in the church.

This argument is not supposed to be overplayed so that it would be understood in an exaggerated sense. The biblical canon as the product of a historical process can be observed as incrementally becoming manifest, developing and reaching closure in the history of God's people. Yet, regardless of how we explain the details of this process, it is clear that for the people of Israel, first the Pentateuch reached a level of visibility and wide reception and was only afterward followed by the canonization of the collection of prophetic and sapiential books. In the sense we speak here of a Christian canon for a Christian Bible, completeness is *essentially* reached when the four-gospel canon is achieved, and, at the same time, the principle of apostolic normativity is applied to the church's literary heritage in that the Pauline, Petrine, and Johannine writings and letters by James and his brother Jude become accepted, although the borderline of this New Testament canon might remain clouded by some obscurity due to the incarnate nature of the church, spread out in time and divided by geography, culture, and theological disputes.

One may say with sufficient security that, by the end of the second century, the church at large (the "catholic church" as opposed to Marcionites, Montanists, Ebionites, various Gnostic groups, or the Syriac church with its single-minded attachment to the *Diatessaron*) is essentially in possession of a canon, as the *Canon of Muratori* and the list of the Old Testament books by Melito of Sardis attest.[6] The church needed and obtained further clarifications about outstanding details as the Canon of Eusebius (265–340, in his *Hist. eccl.* III.25.1–7), the *Easter Letter of Saint Athanasius* (367), and other documents show.[7] The finalization of the canon is usually ascribed by Catholics to the Council of Trent, which indeed listed a canon of seventy-two books, including all deuterocanonical books of the Old Testament. But Trent only repeated a list that the *Council of Florence* (1431–49) had issued, first in *The Decree for the Armenians*, then in its decree of union with the Greeks. It is remarkable that the Protestant Reformation proposed no changes for the New Testament canon. All that happened to the canon in the sixteenth century was a weakening of the status of the deuterocanonical books of the Old Testament, although, in response, Catholics closed their ranks in support of their extended Old Testament canon. What we said here about the canon might prompt controversies, but I hope for the opposite. As it happened in the past century, one would expect that the Christian canon of the Bible would be strengthened further, or that, at least, disputes would significantly decrease in intensity.

6. Eusebius, *Historia Ecclesiastica*, Sources chrétiennes IV.26.13. Melito reproduced the Hebrew canon, not the Septuagint, yet calls it "the Old Bible" or "the Bible of the Old Testament," a nomenclature that implies not only the concept of a Bible of the New Testament, but all the particular features of the apostolic scriptures using as a rule the Greek text of the LXX as an Old Testament.

7. Cf. Metzger, *Canon of the New Testament*. Catholic textbooks prefer to quote the decisions of a local Synod of Hippo (393) and of Carthage (397) and an even earlier Synod of Rome from 382 under Pope Damasus I. These list the Old Testament according to the Septuagint but with Latin titles. Retrojecting the sixteenth-century disputes about the deuterocanonical books to the fourth century falsifies the perspective. On such canonical issues East and West never parted, mostly because the deuterocanonical books were peacefully used in the Eastern churches just as well.

Bibliography

Achtemeier, Paul J. *Inspiration and Authority: Nature and Function of Christian Scripture.* Expanded ed. Peabody, Mass.: Hendrickson, 1999.

Aland, Kurt, and Barbara Aland. *Der Text des Neuen Testaments: Einführung in die wissenschaftlichen Ausgaben sowie in Theorie und Praxis der modernen Textkritik.* Stuttgart: Deutsche Bibelgesellschaft, 1982.

Allert, Craig D. *A High View of Scripture: The Authority of the Bible and the Formation of the New Testament Canon.* Grand Rapids: Baker 2007.

Alonso Schökel, Luis. *La Parabla Inspirada.* Barcelona: Herder, 1966. Translated by Francis Martin, OCSO, as *The Inspired Word: Scripture in the Light of Language and Literature.* London and Rome: Burns and Oates and Herder: 1967.

Atkinson, Joseph C. "The Interpenetration of Inspiration and Inerrancy." In Hahn, *For the Sake of Our Salvation,* 6:191–222. 2010.

Balás, David. "Marcion Revisited." In *Texts and Testaments,* edited by W. Eugene March, 95–108. San Antonio: Trinity University Press, 1980.

Bartholomew, Craig G., and Heath A. Thomas, eds. *A Manifesto for Theological Interpretation.* Grand Rapids: Baker, 2016.

Bea, Augustinus Cardinal. *De Scripturae Sacrae inspiratione.* Rome: Pontificio Istituto Biblico, 1935.

———. "*Deus Auctor Sacrae Scripturae*: Herkunft und Bedeutung der Formel." *Angelicum* (1943): 16–31.

———. *Vatican II and the Truth of Sacred Scripture.* In Hahn, *For the Sake of Our Salvation,* 6:377–82. 2010.

BeDuhn, Jason D. *The First New Testament: Marcion's Scriptural Canon.* Salem, Ore.: Polebridge, 2013.

Benedict XVI [Joseph Ratzinger]. *Jesus of Nazareth.* New York, Doubleday: 2006.

Benoit, Pierre. *Aspects of Biblical Inspiration.* Translated by Jerome Murphy-O'Connor and S. K. Ashe. Chicago: Priory, 1965.

———. *Inspiration and the Bible.* Translated by Jerome Murphy-O'Connor and M. Keverne. London and New York: Sheed and Ward, 1965.

Bodard, C. "La Bible: L'expression d'une expérience religieuse chez S. Bernard." In *Saint Bernard théologien: Analecta S. Ordinis Cisterciensis* 9, no. 1 (1954): 24–45.

Bouyer, Louis. "Où en est le movement biblique?" *Bible et vie chrétienne* 13 (1956): 7–21.

Bernard of Clairvaux. *In laudibus Virginis Matris*. In *Sancti Bernardi Opera Omnia*, edited by Jean Leclercq and Henri Rochais. Rome: Editiones Cistercienses, 1966.

Brooks, Roger, and John J. Collins, eds. *Hebrew Bible or Old Testament? Studying the Bible in Judaism and Christianity*. Notre Dame: University of Indiana Press, 1990.

Brown, Raymond E. "The History and Development of the *Sensus Plenior.*" *Catholic Biblical Quarterly* 15, no. 2 (1953): 141–62.

———. "The *Sensus Plenior* in the Last Ten Years." *Catholic Biblical Quarterly* 25, no. 3 (1963): 262–85.

———. *The Critical Meaning of the Bible*. New York and Ramsey, N.J.: Paulist Press, 1981.

———. *Biblical Exegesis and Church Doctrine*. New York and Mahwah, N.J.: Paulist Press, 1985.

———. "The Canon of the Old Testament." In *The New Jerome Biblical Commentary*, edited by Raymond E. Brown, Joseph A. Fitzmyer, and Roland E. Murphy, 1037–43. Englewood Cliffs: Prentice Hall, 1990.

———. *An Introduction to the New Testament*. New York: Doubleday, 1997.

Brown, Raymond E., Joseph A. Fitzmyer, and Roland E. Murphy. *The Jerome Biblical Commentary*. New York, London, and Sidney: Prentice Hall, 1968.

———. *The New Jerome Biblical Commentary*. Englewood Cliffs: Prentice Hall, 1990.

Casarella, Peter. Introduction. In *Scripture in the Tradition*, by Henri de Lubac, xi–xxii. New York: Crossroad, 2000.

Charlier, Celestin. *La lecture chrétienne de la Bible*. Maredsous: Editions de Maredsous, 1947. English translation: *The Christian Approach to the Bible*. London: Sands, 1961.

Childs, Brevard S. *Introduction to the Old Testament as Scripture*. London: SCM, 1979.

———. *The New Testament as Canon*. Philadelphia: Fortress, 1984.

———. *Biblical Theology of the Old and New Testaments*. Augsburg: Fortress, 1993.

Clabeaux, John J. *A Lost Edition of the Letters of Paul: A Reassessment of the Text of the Pauline Corpus Attested by Marcion*. Catholic Biblical Quarterly 21. Washington, D.C.: Catholic Biblical Association of America, 1989.

Collins, Raymond F. "Inspiration." In *The New Jerome Biblical Commentary*, edited by Raymond E. Brown, Joseph A. Fitzmyer, and Roland E. Murphy, 1023–33. Englewood Cliffs: Prentice Hall, 1990.

Congar, Yves. "Inspiration des écritures canoniques et apostolicité de l'Église" [Inspiration of the Canonical Scriptures and the Apostolicity of the Church]. *Revue des sciences philosophiques et théologiques* 45 (1961): 32–42.

———. *Tradition and the Life of the Church*. London: Burns and Oates, 1964.

———. *La Tradition et les traditions: Essai historique*. Paris: Fayard, 1963. Originally published in 1960. Translated into English as *Tradition and Traditions: The Biblical, Historical, and Theological Evidence for Catholic Teaching on Tradition*. San Diego, Calif.: Basilica Press; Needham Heights, Mass.: Simon and Schuster, 1966.

Crehan, J. H. "*Verbum Dei Incarnatum* and *Verbum Dei Scriptum* in the Fathers." In Hahn, *For the Sake of Our Salvation*, 6:345–8. 2010.

De la Potterie, Ignace. "Reading Holy Scripture 'in the Spirit': Is the Patristic Way of Reading the Bible Still Possible Today?" *Communio* 13, no. 4 (1986): 3–4.

———. "'Interpretation of the Holy Scripture in the Spirit in Which It Was Written' (*Dei Verbum* 12c)." In *Vatican II: Assessment and Perspectives Twenty-Five Years After (1962–1987)*, edited by René Latourelle, 1:220–66. New York: Paulist Press, 1988.

———. "The Spiritual Sense of Scripture." *Communio* 23, no. 4 (1996): 738–56.

De Lubac, Henri. "Bernard, Grégoire, Origène." in *Exégèse médiévale*. Vol. 1, part 2. Paris: Aubier, 1962.

———. *Histoire et Esprit: L'intelligence de l'écriture d'après Origène*. Paris: Aubier, 1950. Translated into English by Anne Englund Nash with Juvenal Merriell as *History and Spirit: The Understanding of Scripture According to Origen*. San Francisco: Ignatius Press, 2007.

Dempster, Stephen G. "Torah, Torah, Torah: The Emergence of the Tripartite Canon." In *Exploring the Origins of the Bible: Canon Formation in Historical, Literary, and Theological Perspective*, edited by Craig A. Evans and Emmanuel Tov, 87–128. Grand Rapids: Baker, 2008.

Ellis, E. Earle. *The Making of the New Testament Documents*. Atlanta: Society of Biblical Literature, 1999.

Enns, Peter. *Inspiration and Incarnation: Evangelicals and the Problem of the Old Testament*. Grand Rapids: Baker, 2005.

Epp, Jay Eldon. "The Codex and Literacy in Early Christianity and at Oxyrinchus: Issues Raised by Harry B. Gamble's *Book and Readers in the Early Church*." In *Perspectives on New Testament Textual Criticism: Collected Essays 1962–2004*, edited by Jay Eldon Epp, 521–50. Atlanta: Society of Biblical Literature, 2005.

Esposito, Thomas, OCist, and Stephen Gregg, OCist. *Ispirazione e Verità della Sacra Scrittura*. Rome: Libreria Editrice Vaticana, 2014. Revised by Fearghus O'Ferghail in Pontifical Biblical Commission, *The Inspiration and Truth of Sacred Scripture:*

The Word That Comes from God and Speaks of God for the Salvation of the World. Collegeville, Minn.: Liturgical Press: 2014.

Evans, Craig A. *Jesus and His World: The Archaeological Evidence.* Louisville, Ky.: Westminster John Knox Press, 2012.

Evans, Craig A., and Emmanuel Tov, eds. *Exploring the Origins of the Bible: Canon Formation in Historical, Literary, and Theological Perspective.* Grand Rapids: Baker, 2008.

Farkasfalvy, Denis M. *L'inspiration de l'Écriture sainte dans la théologie de saint Bernard.* Studia Anselmiana 53. Rome: Herder, 1964.

———. "Theology of Scripture in St. Irenaeus." *Revue bénédictine* 78, nos. 3–4 (1968): 319–33.

———. "'Prophets and Apostles': The Conjunction of the Two Terms before Irenaeus." In *Texts and Testaments: Critical Essays on the Bible and the Early Fathers,* edited by W. E. March, 109–34. San Antonio: Trinity University Press, 1980.

———. "The Pontifical Biblical Commission's Document on Jews and Christians and their Scriptures: Attempt of an Evaluation." *Communio* 29 (2002): 716–37.

———. "The Eucharistic Provenance of the New Testament Texts." In *Rediscovering the Eucharist: Ecumenical Conversations,* edited by Roch A. Kereszty, 27–51. New York: Paulist Press 2003.

———. "The Apostolic Gospels in the Early Church: The Concept of Canon and the Formation of the Four-Gospel Canon." In *Canon and Biblical Interpretation,* edited by Craig C. Bartholomew, Scott Hahn, Robin Perry, Christopher Seitz, and Al Wolters, 7:111–22. Grand Rapids: Zondervan, 2006.

———. "Biblical Foundations for a Theology of Inspiration." *Nova et Vetera* 4, no. 4 (2006): 719–46.

———. "How to Renew the Theology of Inspiration?" *Nova et Vetera* 4 (2006): 307–13.

———. "The Dogmatic Constitution on Divine Revelation, *Dei Verbum*: Inspiration and Interpretation." In Lamb and Levering, *Vatican II: Renewal within Tradition.* 2008.

———. "Inspiration and Interpretation." In Lamb and Levering, *Vatican II: Renewal within Tradition,* 77–100. 2008.

———. *Inspiration and Interpretation: A Theological Introduction to Sacred Scripture.* Washington, D.C.: The Catholic University of America Press, 2010.

———. "Inspiration and Incarnation." In *"Verbum Domini" and the Complementarity of Exegesis and Theology,* edited by Scott Carl, 3–11. Grand Rapids and Oxford: Eerdmans 2014.

Farmer, William R., and Denis M. Farkasfalvy. *The Formation of the New Testament Canon: An Ecumenical Approach.* New York: Paulist Press, 1983.

Fastiggi, Robert. "Communal or Social Inspiration: A Catholic Critique." In Hahn, *For the Sake of Our Salvation*, 6:247–64. 2010.

Ferguson, Everett. "Canon Muratori, Date and Provenance." In *Studia Patristica: Eighth International Congress on Patristic Studies*, edited by Elizabeth A. Livingstone: 677–83. Oxford and New York: Pergamon, 1982.

———. *The Rule of Faith: A Guide*. Eugene, Ore.: Cascade, 2015.

Fitzmyer, Joseph. *The Biblical Commission's Document "The Interpretation of the Bible in the Church." Subsidia biblica 18*. Rome: Pontifical Biblical Institute, 1995.

Frank, Isidor. *Der Sinn der Kanonbildung* [The Meaning of the Formation of the Canon]. Freiburg, Vienna, and Basel: Herder: 1971.

Gabel, Helmut. *Inspirationsverständnis im Wandel: Theologische Neuorientierung im Umfeld des Zweiten Vaikanischen Konzils* [Understanding the Changing Concept of Inspiration: New Theological Orientations in the Area Surrounding the Second Vatican Council]. Mainz: Matthias Grünewald Verlag, 1991.

Gamble, Harry Y. *The New Testament Canon: Its Making and Meaning*. Philadelphia: Fortress, 1985.

———. *Books and Readers in the Early Church: A History of Early Christian Texts*. New Haven, Conn.: Yale University Press, 1995.

Geiselman, Joseph. *Schrift und Tradition*. Freiburg im Bresgau: Herder, 1959.

Gignilliat, Mark S. *A Brief History of Old Testament Criticism: From Benedict Spinoza to Brevard Childs*. Grand Rapids: Zondervan, 2012.

Gohee, Michael W., and Michael D. Williams. "Doctrine of Scripture and Theological Interpretation." In *A Manifesto for Theological Interpretation*, edited by Craig G. Bartholomew and Heath A. Thomas, 48–71. Grand Rapids: Baker, 2016.

Grisez, Germain. "Inspiration and Inspiration of Scripture." In Hahn, *For the Sake of Our Salvation*, 6:181–90. 2010.

Hahn, Scott W., ed. *For the Sake of Our Salvation*. Vol. 6, *Letter and Spirit*. Steubenville, Ohio: St. Paul Center for Biblical Theology, 2010.

Hanson, Anthony, and Richard Hanson. *A Reasonable Belief: A Survey of the Christian Faith*. Oxford: Oxford University Press, 1980.

Harrison, Brian W. "The Truth and Salvific Purpose of Sacred Scripture according to *Dei Verbum*. Article 11." *Living Tradition* 59 (1995).

———. "Restricted Inerrancy and the 'Hermeneutic of Discontinuity.'" In Hahn, *For the Sake of Our Salvation*, 6:240–42. 2010.

Heath, Thomas A., Jeremy Evans, and Paul Copan, eds. *Holy War in the Bible: Christian Morality and an Old Testament Problem*. Downers Grove, Ill.: IVP Academic, 2013.

Hengel, Martin. *Studies in the Gospel of Mark*. Translated by John Bowden. London: SCM Press, 1985.

————. *The Four Gospels and the One Gospel of Jesus Christ.* Translated by John Bowden. Harrisburg, Pa.: Trinity Press International, 2000.

Hill, C. E. *Who Chose the Gospels? Probing the Great Gospel Conspiracy.* Oxford: Oxford University Press, 2010.

Höpfl, Heinrich, Benno Gut, Adalbertus Metzinger, and Louis Leloir. *Introductio Generalis in Sacram Scripturam.* Naples and Rome: Polyglottis Vaticanis, 1950.

Kittel, Gerhard, ed. *Theological Dictionary of the New Testament.* Vol. 1. Grand Rapids: Eerdmans, 1967.

Lamb, Matthew L., and Matthew Levering, eds. *Vatican II: Renewal within Tradition.* Oxford and New York: Oxford University Press, 2008.

Lampe, G. W. H. *A Greek Patristic Lexicon.* Oxford: Clarendon, 1961.

Latourelle, René, SJ. *La théologie de la révélation.* Paris: Desclée de Bouwer, 1963.

————. *Theology of Revelation.* Cork, Ireland: Mercier, 1968.

Laurentin, René. *Enjeu du Concile: Bilan de la Première Session.* Paris: Seuil, 1963.

————. *Comment réconcilier l'exégèse et la foi.* Paris: O.E.I.L. 1984.

Leclercq, Jean. *L'amour des lettres et le désir de Dieu: Initiation aux auteurs monastiques du Moyen Âge.* Paris: Cerf, 1957.

————. "Les sermon sur les Cantiques ont-ils été prononcés?" In *Recueil d'études sur saint Bernard et ses écrits.* Rome: Edizioni Storia e Letteratura, 1962.

Leclercq, Jean, and Henri Rochais, eds. *Sancti Bernardi Opera Omnia,* VI.1. Rome: Editiones Cistercienses, 1970.

Lentini, Anselmo. *Te Decet Hymnus: L'Innario della Liturgia Horarum.* Vatican City: Typis Polyglottis Vaticanis, 1984.

Levering, Matthew. *Participatory Biblical Exegesis: A Theology of Biblical Interpretation.* Notre Dame, Ind.: University of Notre Dame Press, 2008.

————. "The Inspiration of Scripture: A *Status Quaestionis.*" In Hahn, *For the Sake of Our Salvation,* 6:281–314. 2010.

————. *Engaging the Doctrine of Revelation: The Meditation of the Gospel through Church and Scripture.* Grand Rapids: Baker, 2014.

Loretz, Oswald. *Das Ende der Inspirationstheologie: Chancen eines Neubeginns.* Vols. 1 and 2. Stuttgart: Katholisches Bibelwerk, 1974–76.

Martens, Peter W. *Origen and Scripture: The Contours of the Exegetical Life.* Oxford: Oxford University Press: 2012.

Martin, Francis. "Literary Theory, Philosophy of History and Exegesis." *Thomist* 52 (1988): 575–604.

————. *Sacred Scripture: The Disclosure of the Word.* Naples, Fla.: Sapientia Press of Ave Maria University, 2006.

————. "The Transmission of Revelation." In Lamb and Levering, *Vatican II: Renewal within Tradition,* 6:55–76. 2008.

Martin, Francis, and Sean McEvenue. "Truth Told in the Bible: Biblical Poetics and the Question of Truth." In *The International Bible Commentary*, edited by William R. Farmer, 116–30. Collegeville, Minn.: Liturgical Press, 1998.

McDonald, Lee Martin. *The Biblical Canon: Its Origin, Transmission, and Authority.* Grand Rapids: Baker, 2007.

———. *Formation of the Bible: The Story of the Church's Canon.* Peabody, Mass.: Hendrickson, 2012.

Meade, David G. *Pseudonimity and Canon: An Investigation into the Relationship of Authorship and Authority in Jewish and Earliest Christian Tradition.* Grand Rapids: Eerdmans, 1986.

Merkel, Helmut. *Die Pluralität der Evangelien als theologisches und exegetisches Problem in der alten Kirche* [The Multiplicity of the Gospels as a Theological and Exegetical Problem in the Ancient Church]. Frankfurt: Peter Lang, 1978.

Metzger, Bruce M. *The Canon of the New Testament: Its Origin, Development, and Significance.* Oxford: Clarendon, 1987.

Mohrmann, Christine. "Observations sur la langue et le style de saint Bernard." In *Opera Omnia*, ed. J. Leclercq, C. H. Talbot, and H. M. Rochais, 2:ix–xxiii. Rome: Editiones Cistercienses, 1958.

Morrow, Jeffrey L. "The Modernist Crisis and the Shifting of Catholic Views on Biblical Inspiration." In Hahn, *For the Sake of Our Salvation*, 6:265–80. 2010.

Mouroux, J. "Sur les critères de l'expérience spirituelle d'après les sermons sur le Cantique des Cantiques." *Analecta S. Ordinis Cisterciensis* 9, no. 1 (1954): 253–67.

Murphy, Roland E., OCarm. "The Old Testament/*Tanah*: Canon and Interpretation." In *Hebrew Bible or Old Testament? Studying the Bible in Judaism and Christianity*, edited by Roger Brooks and John J. Collins, 1–8. Notre Dame, Ind.: Notre Dame University Press, 1990.

Musurillo, H. A., ed. *The Acts of the Christian Martyrs.* Oxford: Clarendon, 1972.

Neusner, Jacob. *Christian Faith and the Bible of Judaism: The Judaic Encounter with Scripture.* Grand Rapids: Eerdmans, 1989.

Niditch, Susan. *Oral World and Written Word: Ancient Israelite Literature.* Louisville, Ky.: Westminster John Knox Press, 1996.

Origen. *Commentary on John.* Edited by Cécile Blanc. Sources chrétiennes 120. Paris: Cerf, 1966. English translation from *The Early Christian Writings*, by Alexander Roberts and James Donaldson. http://www.earlychristianwritings.com/text/origen-john1.html.

Osiek, Carolyn. *What Are They Saying about the Social Setting of the New Testament?* New York and Ramsey, N.J.: Paulist Press, 1984.

Pitre, Brant. "The Mystery of God's Word: Inspiration, Inerrancy and the Interpretation of Scripture." In Hahn, *For the Sake of Our Salvation*, 6:47–66. 2010.

Pontifical Biblical Commission. *The Inspiration and Truth of Sacred Scripture.* Translated by Thomas Esposito, OCist, and Stephen Gregg, OCist. Reviewed by Fearghus O'Fearghail. Collegeville, Minn.: Liturgical Press, 2014.

Rahner, Hugo. "Das Menschenbild des Origenes." *Eranos Jahrbuch* 15, no. 47 (1949): 197–248.

Rahner, Karl. *Über die Schriftinspiration* [Inspiration in the Bible]. Freiburg im Breisgau: Herder, 1958.

———. *Inspiration in the Bible.* Translated by C. H. Henkey. New York: Herder and Herder, 1961.

Rahner, Karl, Cornelius Ernst, and Kevin Smyth, eds. *Sacramentum Mundi.* Vol. 5. New York: Herder, 1969.

Ramage, Matthew. *Dark Passages of the Bible: Engaging Scripture with Benedict XVI and St. Thomas Aquinas.* Washington, D.C.: The Catholic University of America Press, 2015.

Ratzinger, Joseph. "Origin and Background." In *Commentary on the Documents of Vatican II,* edited by H. Vorgrimler, 3: 155–56. New York: Herder and Herder, 1969.

———, ed. *Schriftauslegung im Widerstreit* [Exegesis in Dispute]. Freiburg, Vienna, and Basel: Herder, 1989.

Reicke, Bo. *The Roots of the Synoptic Gospels.* Philadelphia: Fortress, 1986.

Robinson, Robert B. *Roman Catholic Exegesis since Divino Afflante Spiritu.* Atlanta: Society of Biblical Literature, 1988.

Romeo, Antonio. "The Encyclical *Divino Afflante Spiritu* and the *Opiniones Novae.*" *Divinitas* 4 (1966): 378–456.

Schnabel, Eckhard J. "The Muratorian Fragment: The State of Research." *Journal of Evangelical Theological Studies* 57, no. 2 (2014): 231–64.

Seitz, R. Christopher, *The Goodly Fellowship of the Prophets: The Achievement of Association in Canon Formation.* Grand Rapids: Baker, 2009.

Seitz, Christopher R., and Kent Harold Richards, eds. *The Bible as Christian Scripture: The Work of Brevard S. Childs.* Atlanta: Society of Biblical Literature, 2013.

Skeat, T. C. "Irenaeus and the Four-Gospel Canon." *Novum Testamentum* 34, no. 2 (1992): 194–99.

Smith, Richard F. "Inspiration and Inerrancy." In *Jerome Biblical Commentary,* edited by Raymond R. Brown, Roland E. Murphy, and Joseph Fitzmyer. New York, London, and Sidney: Prentice Hall, 1968.

Sundberg, Albert C., Jr. "Canon Muratori: A Fourth-Century List." *Harvard Theological Review* 66 (1973): 1–41.

———. "More on Redating the Muratorian Fragment." *Studia Patristica* 19:359–65. Louvain: Peeters, 1989.

Theron, Daniel J. *Evidence of Tradition.* Grand Rapids: Baker, 1957.

Tov, Emmanuel. "The Relation between the Textual Witnesses." In *Textual Criticism of the Hebrew Bible*, 135–51. Minneapolis: Fortress, 1992.

Trobisch, David. *Die Endredaktion des Neuen Testaments: Eine Untersuchung zur Entstehung der christlichen Bibel* [The Final Redaction of the New Testament: An Essay on the Formation of the Christian Bible]. Freiburg, Switzerland: Universitätsverlag; Göttingen: Vandenhoeck and Ruprecht, 1996.

Tromp, Sebastian, SJ. *De Sacrae Scripturae inspiratione*. Rome: Pontifical Gregorian University, 1932.

Tyson, Joseph B. *Marcion and Luke-Acts: A Defining Struggle*. Columbia: University of South Carolina Press, 2006.

Vanni, Ugo. *Lectura del Apocalipsis*. Navarra: Verbo Divino, 2005.

Vawter, Bruce. *Biblical Inspiration*. Philadelphia: Westminster, 1972.

Von Balthasar, Hans Urs. *Origenes: Geist und Feuer: Ein Aufbau aus seinen Schriften*. Salzburg and Leipzig: O. Müller, 1938.

————. *Thomas von Aquin: Besondere Gnadengaben und die zwei Wege des menschlichen Lebens; Kommentar zur Summa Theologica II–II, 171–82* [Thomas Aquinas: Special Charisms and the Two Ways of Human Life; Commentary on the *Summa Theologica*, 171–82]. Vol. 23, *Die Deutsche Thomas-Ausgabe* [The German Thomas Edition]. Edited by H. M. Christmann. Vienna: Pustet, 1958.

Von Campenhausen, Hans. *Die Entstehung der christlichen Bibel*. Tübingen: Mohr, 1968. Translated as *The Formation of the Christian Bible*. Philadelphia: Fortress, 1972.

Von Harnack, Adolf. *Marcion: Das Evangelium vom fremden Gott; Eine Monographie zur Geschichte und Grundlegung der katholischen Kirche*. Leipzig: J. C. Heinrichs, 1924.

Waldstein, Michael. "*Analogia Verbi*: The Truth of Scripture in Rudolph Bultmann and Raymond Brown." In Hahn, *For the Sake of Our Salvation*, 6:93–140. 2010.

Watson, Francis. *The Fourfold Gospel: A Theological Reading of the New Testament Portraits of Jesus*. Grand Rapids: Baker, 2016.

Westermann, Claus. *Genesis 1–11: A Continental Commentary*. Translated by John J. Scullion, Minneapolis: Fortress, 1994.

Wilder, Terry L. *Pseudonymity, The New Testament, and Deception: An Inquiry into Intention and Reception*. Lanham, Md.: University Press of America, 2004.

Williams, D. H. *Tradition, Scripture, and Interpretation: A Sourcebook of the Ancient Church*. Grand Rapids: Baker, 2006.

Zerafa, Peter Paul, OP. "The Limits of Biblical Inerrancy." In Hahn, *For the Sake of Our Salvation*, 6:359–76. 2010.

Zia, Mark. *Biblical Inspiration? WATSA (What Are They Saying About)*. New York and Mahwah, N.J.: Paulist Press, 2011.

Index

A Theology of the Christian Bible: Revelation—Inspiration—Canon was designed in Garamond and composed by Kachergis Book Design of Pittsboro, North Carolina. It was printed on 60-pound House Natural Smooth and bound by Sheridan Books of Chelsea, Michigan.